"Proof positive that success is possible while "Following the Golden Rule through Life." Gail Black's fascinating anecdotes and insights of being a woman and single mom managing a farm and Agri-tourism business while surviving small town politics and learning to trust the Master Planner is a journey of resilience, integrity, and faith. A delightful read!!"

—BETINA HENDERSON, Chief Master Sergeant (retired), former Command Post Functional Manager, Air Force Special Operations Command, United States Air Force

Asses and Angels in Business

Blending Business and Pleasure

GAIL L. BLACK

Gail L. Black

11-2020

iUniverse®

ASSES AND ANGELS IN BUSINESS
BLENDING BUSINESS AND PLEASURE

Photo Credit: Norman E. Taylor

iUniverse books may be ordered through booksellers or by contacting:

iUniverse
1663 Liberty Drive
Bloomington, IN 47403
www.iuniverse.com
1-800-Authors (1-800-288-4677)

ISBN: 978-1-6632-0500-1 (sc)
ISBN: 978-1-6632-0499-8 (e)

Library of Congress Control Number: 2020913319

Print information available on the last page.

iUniverse rev. date: 09/23/2020

Dedication

I DEDICATE THIS BOOK to my family who has been supportive and understanding during my hours, days, months, and years of creating this second book. Operating the Sugar Shack and the Fruit Farm is, and has always been, a family business. Andy, Larry, and Rob and their families have brainstormed, worked and been involved in fruit growing, maple syrup making, web design, and decision making all along the way. Even though they all labor with intensive pursuits of their own, they are available to lend a hand when I need help. The best parts, most successful areas, and the happiest times I remember about my life are centered on my family. Each son has given me three grandchildren and now those grandchildren are providing great grandchildren. Love to you all, always. Granny Grape aka Grandma Gail

Acknowledgements

THERE ARE MANY FOLKS who deserve to be acknowledged on this page. Writing a book is a cooperative effort and without these kind, wise, and patient helpers I could not succeed. First and extremely important is Norman E. Taylor. His understanding of motivations in business ventures, his opinions on which events are most important, the kindness and truthfulness in his feedback are all qualities that helped me with this book. As my significant other, he has provided the quiet solitude and efficient space for me to work, while also giving me time, love, support, and some great dinners.

The readers of my first book are also important because they have written, called, emailed, and visited while supplying me with encouragement and motivation to write this second book in the Asses and Angels series. I hope you find the pages filled with laughter, indignation, anger and lots of love.

Not least on my list of people to thank are my constant core of tea drinkers and "Let me read you this. What do you think?" friends. Linda Koenig Peg Beckman, Danielle DuBois, Carol Baumet, Sue Robbins, Karen Reidesel, Sherry Simons, Tina Henderson and the writers' group in Mayo Florida are the names of a few. There are more wise and helpful friends from afar who have provided early edits, comments on content, phone consults, visits and feedback even though they had heavy schedules and pressing problems of their own. Thank you to Bobbi Montgomery, MaryAnn Eidemiller, and Michelle Haden.

My family and extended family are always an inspiration and a reason to keep writing.

Names and places have been altered in some cases, removed in others, to protect privacy. Some instances have been removed completely, but early copies of manuscripts are still on file for future use in another book in this series. An endless supply of asses and angels will guarantee many more book writing opportunities.

Thank you for reading my books and there is always a tour waiting for you at the Sugar Shack. Mirror will be here with me as we wait for your visit.

PREFACE

MIRROR SCREAMED AT ME the moment I entered the Sugar Shack. "I still want the next book. Everyone else does too. I think you're procrastinating, becoming mentally lazy," Mirror accused.

I had been resting from the hectic summer schedule of growing, picking, processing, bottling, and labeling the fruit syrups I offered in my agritourism shop on my grape farm. Visits from grandchildren, the changing views of winter storms crashing ashore from Lake Erie, and warm cozy fires in my fireplace filled my days. I was resting and regrouping. The stress was off. Apparently, Mirror noticed.

Mirror continued to harangue me. "You think you've done your best, accomplished your life's goal, and now you just want to coast. That's not your style. I hear every conversation at your tasting counter now that I am finally living here in your gift shop. Your readers are curious about your business experiences. They want to know what has worked and what has not. They want to know what kind of challenges you encountered. They want to know how you think and what makes you succeed or fail in business as well as in your personal life."

As usual, the dictatorial advice irritated me. "I don't even know where to begin, Mirror. I don't have a clue about how to motivate myself to write another book. It takes a huge amount of time, commitment, and thought. I'll just add the writing to the bird-watching, bread-baking, and backbreaking snow removal," I said sarcastically.

Mirror ordered me around a lot. "Get your laptop. Get started. You know the words will flow. Remember your dad's advice: 'Once begun, half done; never begun, you missed the fun.'" Good old Mirror remembered everything my dad ever said.

"I have already written about my three marriages. One culminated in divorce over differing religious beliefs; another ended with suicide, which created my widowhood; and the last became a memory when annulment helped me avoid the fraudulent declarations of love intended to make me lose my farm. I have shared stories about personal relationships that involved unfaithfulness, more attempts to legally take what was mine, and just plain meanness. You are all I have left, Mirror; you and my love of work are my only constant companions. The Master Planner and my darling little cocker spaniel provide me with my only unconditional love."

Mirror reflected the pondering roll of my eyes, my finger pressed against my upper lip, and saw the glimmer of hope for more storytelling. "Just the other day, I heard a guy ask you how you found all those awful men you wrote about in your first memoir, *Asses and Angels.* His wife pointed her finger at you and demanded, 'Why didn't you leave at the first sign of trouble?' I think everyone would like to know those things. I think they would like to know what makes you so strong and how you bounce back from difficulty time and time again. Your readers want to know if your struggles are over or if the drama continues, smarty-pants."

Mirror was on a roll and kept going. "You're not done sharing. You're not finished exposing the asses and angels in your life. Your vulnerabilities have been opportunities to get stronger. You need to inspire others with your business struggles and successes. Get to work. Tell your readers more of the story of your Sugar Shack life. They will recognize and understand that you mix business with pleasure and the challenges that presents. For you, the unusual experiences and the people who show up at the Sugar Shack are a collection of opportunities to live life to its fullest. Whoever said 'never mix business and pleasure' didn't know you."

Mirror's advice, although dictatorial at times, is usually correct. After all, Mirror has been my constant counsel for over seventy years.

"Okay, Mirror. I'll write this second book about my experiences, situations, successes, and failures. I may have to repeat a few things from my first book for clarity in places, but my recall and files will serve as the basis for this second book. I hope the information will give insight, comfort, education, laughter, and tears to my readers."

I finally realize that my experiences were the building blocks upon which my current life stands. They were raw examples of love, deceit, greed, jealousy, kindness, control, power, and compassion, along with many other examples of people just being people. They were lessons that led me to my calling at the Sugar Shack, and those lessons became intertwined as I traveled the paths to business success interspersed with personal fulfillment. The Master Planner was in control, not me or my constant subconscious, my very insightful critic named Mirror.

I have altered some details in this book to protect innocent folks who stumbled down my long driveway. The events are my recollections of life before and during my years at Vinewood Acres Sugar Shack.

I believe that my life and experiences on the farm I call home are gifts from God and learning experiences with purpose. I am thankful every day.

Contents

Chapter One: Childhood

In an ongoing effort to give my mother some relief from an energetic, curious little girl, my father gave me an upbringing that made me as tough as overcooked liver. I loved to follow him around while he worked on our family mink farm. He raised thousands of animals for their hides, which were sold at auction in New York City. Highly skilled craftsmen transformed them into luxurious fur coats and garments.

Dad fed the animals once a day but redistributed any uneaten food every morning so that each animal had a snack before he filled their water cups with fresh water. Such time-consuming, constant care was essential to producing high-quality furs. I tagged along, and by the age of four, I was dragging a hose and filling those water cups while he spread out the feed leftover from the day before.

The food the mink ate contained cows, horses, roadkill deer, grains, and even vegetables we grew in the summer months and stored in a root cellar. We ate some of the cabbage, Swiss chard, carrots, beets, and potatoes ourselves, but most of it went into the mink feed. Our neighborhood was filled with dairy farms where cows, teams of horses, and other farm animals were common. When a farmer had a sick or injured animal, he would ask my dad to come get it for mink feed. Most of the time, Dad or Grandpa would be able to walk the animal back to our place.

I remember the day my grandpa led a horse into the yard. I ran out of the house and said, "Oh, Grampy, did you buy me a horsey?"

Dad decided that it was time for me to explore the reality of the mink business. He asked, "Gail, would you like to be my assistant? Now that you are four years old, I think you are old enough to help me."

I jumped up and down with excitement. I was so proud to be his assistant. I eagerly helped him gather a huge graniteware basin, a long butcher knife, and then his .22 rifle. We walked to where the horse was tied to a tree, and he said, "I see that you've grown some, so I know you can handle the horse. Here, you take this long rope and walk out in the field to that bucket of grain. Let the horse eat, and you walk to the end of the rope, but don't let go of it."

I followed the directions with proud steps and held tightly to the end of the rope. Sure enough, the horsey began to eat the grain, and I walked to the end of the rope, uncoiling it as I went, to about twenty feet away. Dad stepped up close to the horse, facing away from me. He was between the horse and me, so I couldn't really see, but I jumped when the rifle cracked and the horse fell dead.

Dad said, "Drop the rope and please bring me the basin and the knife. I'll lift the head, and you shove the basin underneath so we can catch the blood. It is good to put in the mink feed."

As I followed his instructions, he said, "I knew you were old enough to help me, and what a great helper you are." He slit the throat of the horse, and I held the basin in place.

"You look a little sad, young lady, but you have to know that the horse was old and very sick," he said quietly. "You saw Grampy walking him slowly home. The reason for that is that the horse could no longer run or walk fast. He couldn't pull a load of manure or a hay wagon anymore. His owner said he was not eating and was getting thinner by the day."

I remember that my eyes never left that horse. I felt a tear starting to trickle down my cheek. Dad saw it and said, "You are such a strong young lady and smart enough and old enough to understand this whole business. I paid the farmer for this horse, and therefore he had money to go out and buy a new, younger, healthy horse to do the work on his farm. You will help me butcher this animal and sell its hide. The meat will go in the freezer and become part of the mink feed. Eventually, the mink will be pelted, and their skins will be made into warm clothing. With the money I am paid for those hides, I will buy your clothes, pay for the load of coal for the furnace to heat our house, and buy the groceries and other things we need to live. Do you understand how all that works?" he asked.

I dried my tears and nodded my head. I remembered how I always got a new doll when we got paid for the mink hides.

We finished with the basin of blood, put it in buckets to go in the freezer, and washed up the knife and basin, and then it was time to butcher the horse. As I held tools and watched him work, Dad explained that this particular horse had arthritis in its hips, and he showed me the deformed parts of the joints. He said the horse had been in pain from the deformed joints and now suffered no more. That day, I learned this was a productive way for sick and injured animals' suffering to end and for them to be used instead of going to waste.

"But Daddy, I wanted a horsey to ride," I whined.

"I know, sweetheart, but now you know another fact

3

about life," he said gently. "All creatures, including us, will die someday. It is the way of the world. Death is sometimes a relief from suffering, and if the animals we buy could still live useful, productive, pain-free lives, we would not make them into mink feed. I know you want a horsey, and someday perhaps you'll have one. Right now, sit down on that stool and let me show you the lungs of this great animal. They are what enabled it to breathe, just like yours do for you."

I forgot about wanting a horse as Dad explained the veins and arteries, stomach, teeth, brain (which looked like a tangled ball of yarn), and intestines, which looked somewhat like the brain, only bigger and smelly. Butchering the horse was a complete education in animal anatomy, including how each part was important to the whole animal, what its function was, and as I continued to be his assistant, how and why certain parts of the animals failed.

I learned that it was natural, humane, and logical that the animal's death was quick and purposeful. I felt good knowing that the bones, hide, intestines, and parts we couldn't use were hauled to the reeking, rank rendering works, where such things were processed into soap, cosmetics, leather, or cat and dog food.

My entrepreneurial education had begun with farming and a "waste not, want not" mentality. Before I entered kindergarten, I had been introduced to the natural evolution of life and had developed a deep respect for the intelligence, perseverance, and work ethic of farmers. They just never quit.

Chapter Two: Farm Lessons

I SPENT ALL MY spare time with my friend at a nearby dairy farm. When I was six, she and I were playing in the barn, and her father shooed us out, saying, "Run along and play now. The bull has some work to do, and he is dangerous when he is working. You girls have to go outside to play."

I asked my friend, "What kind of work does your dad make the bull do?"

"I don't know," she answered. "Let's sneak up in the haymow and peek down through the cracks in the floor, and we'll find out."

Through those cracks we saw the bull at work as he serviced a cow. "That looks like what the mink do in March," I said. "When they do that, they are making babies."

We weren't impressed, so we didn't stay to watch anymore and went about our business. It was just part of a normal day on a farm. From time to time, we saw dogs, cats, rabbits, and other animals doing the same things, and it was just part of nature. No judgments and no sex education classes were necessary to teach the facts of life. We experienced the natural process of learning by observation.

I had daily chores at the mink farm, and my friend had daily responsibilities on her family dairy farm. When I visited, we often found our way to the farm kitchen, where we were lured in by the aroma of bread baking and chocolate chip cookies cooling. A cookie in each hand and a basket over our arms, we headed off to the chicken coop to gather the eggs. We knew there were sixteen chickens, and so we had to find sixteen eggs, teaching us that a chicken lays only one egg a day.

If a chicken dinner was needed on Sunday, we had to catch a chicken and deliver it to the kitchen door, where a large block of wood served as a chopping block. Then we would find only fifteen eggs. One of us held the legs while the farmer's wife chopped off the head. We would jump out of the way while the chicken flapped and flopped around without its head until all the blood was dispersed on the grass and gravel driveway. We helped with the feather plucking. Then the chicken was singed by being held over burning newspapers, and the pinfeathers (fine, hairy feathers) were burned off.

We knew where our food came from and how it arrived in the kitchen. We helped with the process, and we ate well. We never questioned the source of our food, the maltreatment of farm animals, or the diet they ate. We took excellent care of the animals in our care because they were our survival, our dinner, our responsibility. We got what we earned.

We lived very much like the early pioneers and our country's forefathers. We learned to survive, to use what we had, and to depend on our ingenuity for anything we lacked. Children worked and played without the benefit of television, computers, or cell phones. The exercise we got and a diet high in homegrown veggies, fruits, eggs, milk, and meats kept us strong, lean, and healthy. What some refer to today as a work ethic was just a good upbringing, where we learned that the rewards of hard work meant a new doll or, in my case, a BB gun under the Christmas tree. We were reminded daily that "the devil finds work for idle hands," and good parents never let that happen. On long summer days when school was out, my dad found useful ways for me to spend my time.

Christmas brought that BB gun along with a large supply of ammunition and targets. Dad found time to teach me about gun safety, starting with a wooden toy gun. The most important rule was to never point the gun, real or not, toward another person or anything that was not the target. I became a master at hitting the bull's-eye on the paper targets propped up against a tree at the base of a hill. The hill was my backstop. It was my guarantee that a stray bullet would not do any damage, and that was part of the basic gun safety lessons.

The cherries began to ripen on our cherry tree as spring turned to summer. My mother and grandmother brought empty quart jars up from the cellar. They washed and sterilized them along with our big dark blue canner that held seven quarts at a time. There was supper-table talk about canning the cherries and worries about the birds taking most of the fruit. This was during World War II, and nobody had netting. They did have me, a BB gun, a wood and canvas lawn chair, and time on my hands.

I was stationed under the cherry tree just before full daylight when the birds arrived for their breakfast. It was my job to shoot as many birds as possible to protect the cherries we needed to can for the following winter. At first it was fun. Soon, at supper I would complain, "I don't want to kill birds tomorrow. I want to go play. I don't want to get up in the dark and sit out there all day long."

"Don't complain, child," my mother would say. "You seem to eat all the cherry pie and cobbler I can make, and you eat it all winter long. This is how you do your part. It's how you earn your keep. It will be only a few days until the cherries are ripe enough to pick, and then you can play."

"But I hate it. I'm so bored. I just sit there and pull the trigger, and the dead birds stink," I continued to whine.

"Young lady, you have an important job to do," my dad said, taking up the argument. "And if you don't do it, who will? Where will your mother get cherries to fill all those quart jars? What will you have for dessert next winter? You're not a quitter, and I know it. You're tough, and you'll see the job through. Now that's enough of this nonsense. Please pass the meat and potatoes."

The next day, one of the barn cats rubbed against my leg as I guarded the damned cherries. A light bulb of inspiration flashed on in my brain as I swiveled my head to the right, and sure enough, a pile of wire mink cages was stacked up only a few feet away. The cages were waiting for repairs, but sometimes there was only a tiny hole a mink could escape through, but surely not a cat. I put the BB gun down and scooted over to the pens. They were only about three feet long and one foot deep. I found a good one, shoved it up in the crotch of the cherry tree, and waited for that barn cat.

Soon that cat was yowling and pacing in the pen in the crotch of the cherry tree, and not a bird was in sight. The longer the cat was in the cage, the madder it got. It hissed and yowled and crashed against the wire pen, and the birds were terrified. I set the gun down and calmly went to the house. My lunch was waiting on a tray, and Dad was due to deliver it to me at the cherry tree.

"What in God's name are you doing in the house? Who is keeping the birds out of the cherries?" he yelled.

"Dad, I got it handled," I said as he grabbed me by the back of my shirt.

Carrying the tray in his other hand, he dragged me back to my post, not listening to a word I tried to say.

"Is that gun loaded? Did you leave a loaded gun propped up on your chair? What the hell is the matter with you?" he asked. Then he saw the cage and the cat and no birds. He stood silent for a minute. "I see the gun is not cocked. Good girl. Let's go in the house and eat. Looks like you got this under control."

I rotated the barn cats and the two house cats for a couple more days, and when the cherries were ready to be picked, nobody could get near those cats. Like me, they had learned quickly that guard duty was no fun.

Dad began pelting and harvesting the mink hides just before Thanksgiving, and since I was allowed to stay up past 7:00 p.m., he asked me to be his assistant in the skinning room. I had noticed there were fewer and fewer animals to feed and water each day. As I listened to the conversations at the dinner table, I knew Dad was killing them so we could pay our bills and get snowsuits for my sister and me.

It was an honor to help and receive attention for handing the dead animals to my father so he could cut and pull off the hides. Afterward, he would hand the carcass to me to put in a barrel. Those by-products would then be sold to dog food companies, cosmetic manufacturers, and shoe polish companies that used the mink fats and oils in their products. He passed the hides to Grampy, who put them on stretching boards. While we worked, we listened to our favorite programs, *The Lone Ranger*, *The Blue Hornet*, and *Sergeant Preston*, on the radio. I enjoyed the exchange of prideful banter between Hank, the hired man, Grampy, and my dad. They were enjoying the harvest after a successful growing season. They talked of fewer daily chores outdoors in the bitter winter cold and wind. The crop was of great quality. The fur was deep and thick.

Guard hairs had luster, shine, and good coverage, and many hides were too long for the stretching boards. The fur buyers would pay a premium for the year's crop.

Meanwhile, my older sister was spending time with my mother in the house, where she was learning to sew, cook, embroider, knit, and be a lady. I was learning about labor, pride in accomplishment, marketing the by-products that were usually wasted, and prices. Bonuses were promised to our hired men for a job well done. Dad said we were paying off debt and reinvesting some of the profit, and he explained free enterprise. Talk of competition with foreign-market buyers was explained as I listened to the conversations of the men. I was getting paid for my help with an increase in my allowance. I was hooked. I was productive. I was part of an industry that was independent of politics and control. I learned that furs were one of the highest exports our country enjoyed, helping our balance of trade. It was a lot for an eight-year-old to understand, but most of it stuck. What I learned surfaced years later when I needed those lessons.

While I helped the men with their work, my sister, mother, and grandmother were filling the house with delicious aromas as they baked fruitcakes from old family recipes. My sister, who wasn't too fond of me, was six years older than me and more interested in household activities. She hated farm work. We were not close.

While she was helping the womenfolk with Christmas preparations, I listened to stories about the men's youthful escapades and helped in the skinning room. Their stories always had a moral lesson. I thought those accounts were the most exciting things I had ever heard and tried to think of things I could do to one-up the tales being told. I thought housework and cooking were sissy activities.

Chapter Three: Fair Play

FAIR PLAY—THAT'S WHAT happened when my cousins came for their annual two-week visit at our mink farm during the summer I turned nine.

I had received a new bicycle for my birthday and learned to ride it on our cinder driveway. I skinned my knees many times. It was a full-sized, bright red girl's twenty-six-inch Schwinn. I was tiny for my age, so as I learned to ride, it was hard for me to hold the bike up, balance it, and push off while straddling it. With perseverance, I managed the skill. I kept it clean. I polished it. I loved my beautiful red bike.

Cousins Susan and Sally arrived. Susan was six months older and Sally was six months younger than me. Susan thought she was the boss of me. She was big and strong for her age. Her mother referred to me as "puny and undernourished." My mother never challenged the remarks, leaving me to believe they were true.

Susan waited until she and I were out of my mother's sight and then hissed, "Give me your shiny new bike, you puny, spoiled brat." She wrestled it out of my grip. She jumped on it and rode as hard as she could toward a very large sugar maple tree. At the last second, she jumped off and let it crash into the tree trunk. "Aw, pretty broken bike," she gloated.

The handlebars were bent. The front wheel no longer was aligned with the back wheel. The front fender was twisted off. I began to cry and ran to pick it up. She continued to laugh and laugh when I couldn't make the wheels turn and couldn't push it. With tears making dirty streaks on my dusty cheeks, I yelled, "You damn, dumb, mean, stupid city bastard, you!"

I had hardly finished the sentence when I felt the wrath of my mother's grip on the back of my neck. "You will not talk like that, young lady! In the house with you right now!" she screamed as she alternately pushed and dragged me into the kitchen, where she kept a bar of Fels-Naphtha soap.

I spit and gagged and fought and struggled to escape the grinding assault on my bottom teeth. "Maybe this will teach you a lesson," she yelled as she finished the bottom ones and started on the top teeth. "You will not use that language ever again. I don't care what happened—you will not call your cousin a nasty name. We do not use that kind of language in this house. Do you understand?" she demanded as she finished and as I struggled free, spitting in every direction. "Your cousins don't have a father living with them. He died, and you will not call them names. They are our guests here."

I knew right then that I had to get even on my own. It was already bad enough that her mother called me names, and my mother just stood there and did nothing about it except to tell my dad. His reaction was to tell me, "Gail, it is okay to be small. You are not a runt. Just remember, they keep hay in a barn and jewels in a jewel box. You are a precious jewel. You'll grow up someday."

Susan had learned her meanness from her mother. I didn't like her either. Susan thought she was old enough to hang around with my sister, who was a teenager. Her sister Sally was kind and polite.

The following day, we all went to the farm next door to play hide-and-seek with the neighborhood kids. I was "it" and had to count to one hundred. I had just started to count when Susan demanded, "Tell me where to hide. Tell me right now and don't come and find me, or you'll be sorry." She twisted my arm behind my back and bent one of my fingers the wrong way until I knelt and agreed to her terms.

A flash of inspiration hit me. "Okay, okay. I'll do it. Come right over here." I opened the silo door and found that it had recently been emptied of all the silage. She marched right into the awful remaining stench of rotting vegetation, which had started to ferment. I slammed the door shut and swiveled the wood and leather turnbuckle to lock it shut.

Soon all the other kids were yelling, "Home free," and someone else was it. Nobody missed Susan in the crowd of neighborhood children, and we all went on with other games. We'd each brought a bagged lunch and thermos bottle of cold milk, and the day passed quickly outside the silo.

Nine in the morning to four in the afternoon is a long time to yell and scream and pound on silo walls, trying to get someone's attention. The men were all in the fields working, and the cows were out to pasture. No one heard her. Just before the men came into the barn for the afternoon milking session, I finally went back and let her out. I knew she would be missed at the supper table.

She came out with her fists clenched, screaming every obscenity I had ever heard. "I'll tell your mother, you stupid runt. You're a little bitch. Goddamn you! I'll break your finger off next time."

I stared her down, firmly planted my feet wide apart, and

put my hands on my hips. I stuck out my jaw and said, "Go ahead, you big hay barn. You can tell my mother. You are nothing but a coward and a tattletale. But if you do tell, just remember that any punishment I get is worth every bit of it because you broke my bike on purpose. You just remember that, you big-headed hay barn. You'd better learn that they keep hay in a barn and jewels in a jewel box. Your big head is full of hay, and mine is like a jewel in a jewel box. That's why I'm small. You're a coward and a bully."

She left me completely alone after that.

CHAPTER FOUR: TOUGH LESSONS AT SCHOOL

SCHOOL WAS ALWAYS CHALLENGING, both academically and socially. Mrs. C was my teacher in first grade when I got tonsillitis. I missed six months of important basic math and reading lessons. She never visited me or sent any work home for me to complete. She was still incensed over my calling the school lunches pig slop in the early part of first grade. She passed me on to the second grade and relegated me to the "slow" group, treating me like I was stupid and couldn't learn. When I managed to pass to third grade, she moved up along with my class again. It was too much to bear. I hated school, the lunches, the teacher, and the whole show.

One day she was reading a story to the class, and I was listening when I felt sick. I raised my hand and asked to be excused. She lowered the book and in an exasperated voice said, "Now, Gail, you just sit in your seat, put your hand down, and be quiet."

I tried. I knew her wrath would come down upon me if I raised my hand again. Then my stomach growled, softly at first but then louder. I had a terrible cramp, and a little gas escaped. I tentatively raised my hand again. She glared at me, and I put it down. All of a sudden, the bile was rising in my throat. I waved my hand in the air with a fast and bold insistence.

Mrs. C slammed the book shut, stared me in the eye, and yelled, "Don't interrupt me again, ever!" She opened the book to continue. Lunch was erupting like a volcano. I jumped from my seat and raced down the aisle. She stomped to her left, blocking my path at the end of the aisle just as the stomach volcano erupted. The full force of it hit her in the chest, and stomach lava flowed all over the story she was reading and down the front of her dress.

She screamed and threw the book on the floor. She desperately jumped and did little dancing stomps, like she was running in place, in an effort to shake the vomit from her chest. In one swift movement, she grabbed me by the neck and thrust me toward the door. "To the principal's office, *now!*" she yelled. "You're nothing but trouble—stupid, worthless trouble."

Vomit dropped here and there as we raced toward the principal's office. The rest of the class sat in silent horror.

My mother was called as I waited in that office. She arrived, listened to the teacher's account of the incident, witnessed the sight and smell of vomit on her dress, and firmly but quietly announced, "I will not tolerate another minute of this woman as Gail's teacher. I want my daughter transferred to the other grade school as of right now."

Mrs. C pounded her fist on the desk and declared, "Good riddance. I never want to lay eyes on your little brat again."

The principal held up both hands and said, "Ladies, enough. I am offering to send Gail to our main campus tomorrow morning. She will finish the year in Mrs. B's class. Next year, she can continue in fourth grade here in this facility."

"Not good enough, sir. I don't want my daughter in the

same building with this sorry excuse for a teacher. Do you understand?" Mom asked as she pointed at Mrs. C.

No debate was necessary. Everyone present agreed that I would finish my elementary education in the other grade school twelve miles away.

Mrs. B welcomed me to her class with a kind smile, a pat on my shoulder, and an introduction to a kind little girl. The girl became my guide in the new environment and also a lifelong friend. All was well, and I was happy.

A week into my new class, Mrs. B called my mother. She said, "I think you need to take Gail to the eye doctor. I don't think she can see. I write words on the blackboard and ask her to read them, and she just stares at the board, shrugs her little shoulders, and then looks out the window. I don't think she knows there's anything there."

I soon had glasses. I was amazed at the signs along the highway as we drove home. I saw cows in the fields and apples on some trees. I was also really surprised at the words on the blackboard. I had thought Mrs. B was going to be like Mrs. C and was just trying to make me look stupid when she asked me to read stuff that wasn't there. My grades improved, and I loved school for the first time since kindergarten.

One morning a stranger appeared in the classroom instead of Mrs. B. This woman was just like old Mrs. C had been. She had mean eyes, and her hair was piled in a tight bun on top of her head. She looked like the Wicked Witch in *The Wizard of Oz*. I was immediately afraid of her. She glared at each of us as we entered the classroom. She stood with her arms crossed over her chest. She didn't say "good morning" or even smile. I was frantic to get out of there. I had to think of something fast; I had to get home. As soon as the bell rang, indicating the start of the school day, she began to speak. "I'm here today as your substitute teacher. I'm taking Mrs. B's place. I have rules, and all of you will follow them. There will be no exceptions, no talking or whispering, no shenanigans. You will sit in your seats and speak only when I ask you to. You will do as you're told when you're told. Do you all understand my rules?"

I raised my hand and asked to go to the restroom. She motioned for me to go and went right on yelling and declaring what the day would be like.

I ran to the bathroom and turned on the hot water faucet. When the water was really hot, I bent down and got a mouth full, held it, swished it around, and spit it out. Then I repeated the process again and again. Finally, when the water was really hot and so was my mouth, I took a mouthful and ran as fast as I could to the nurse's office. Just as I opened the door, I swallowed the water and said in a soft, sickly, whiny voice, "I don't feel good."

The nurse was on it fast. My reputation had preceded me, and I could see the fear in her eyes. She grabbed an empty wastebasket and thrust it into my hands at the same time that she thrust a thermometer into my mouth. She stood at attention, never taking her eyes off her watch or her hand off the thermometer, until the time was up. She pulled the thermometer out of my mouth, and sure enough, the hot water had worked. I had a temperature. She called my mom, who picked me up and took me home, where she put me to bed on the couch. She gave me books to read, crayons and a coloring book, dry crackers to eat, and even some ginger ale to sip. My plan was great. I was home. I didn't have to deal with Mrs. Substitute. This episode was just the beginning of such escapes.

The substitute-teacher fevers continued occasionally. Mom picked me up each time and finally took me to visit my pediatrician. No cause was found for the episodes of low-grade fevers, and they continued when I needed them to escape from educational challenges.

It was around this time that my older sister became ill while away at college. She was hospitalized and diagnosed with an incurable condition that changed our family forever.

Chapter Five: Truth and Consequences

MOM WAS VERY BUSY caring for my bedridden sister. She decided that I was getting more and more out of control, so she arranged for me to go to Sunday school with a neighboring family. It wasn't an option. I felt that she really wanted to get rid of me for a while on Sundays.

On Saturday night she would wash my hair and tie it up in little rag curls. I hated sleeping on the knots, but she insisted on curly hair, a taffeta dress, and white socks with lace on the top. Shiny black leather shoes completed the "little lady" look. This was my Sunday school outfit, and I wore those same clothes every Sunday morning.

One Sunday morning some of the other little girls asked, "Is that the only taffeta dress you own?" They snickered, and one whispered to her twin sister, "She lives out in the sticks somewhere on a farm. Look close, and you can see the mud on the bottom of her shoes." I was mortified, but Sunday school was mandatory.

My paternal grandmother was visiting from Florida. We didn't get along. Mom insisted that I have my hair curled, don my taffeta dress, and be presentable. Bad Grandma, as I called her, was having ladies in for afternoon tea.

I endured a lecture on behavior and table manners as I left my beloved flannel shirt, blue jeans, and farm boots in my room. When I was introduced, I curtsied and murmured "hello" as Bad Grandma glared from behind her dark glasses.

A severe, straight-backed, silver-haired old woman peered over her glasses. With a pinched set of thin, unsmiling lips, she said, "I believe you attend Sunday school with my darling little twin granddaughters, Marie and Mary. Do you know them? Do you like them? We almost brought them along this afternoon. Now wouldn't that have been fun?"

In a very polite, soft voice, as I looked down at my feet, I replied, "Yes, ma'am, I know the stuck-up, mean little city snobs. I don't like them, and I'm glad you left them home. They make fun of my clothes."

I had spoken politely and quietly just like I'd been told to do. I had told the truth, which was highly valued by my delightful good grandparents. The slap across the back of my head and being shoved toward the stairway leading to my room were a complete surprise as Bad Grandma yelled, "Send that incorrigible little brat to her room!"

Mom escorted me to my room and hung up my clothes as I flung them onto the floor. She said, "I can't believe you said that. You never learn. You don't even know what the word 'tact' means. I've tried and tried to teach you manners and to say the right things to be polite. Those things are what 'tact' is. They are socially acceptable behavior. You need to learn to say things in a way that doesn't hurt the feelings of others, no matter what you really think."

Before I climbed into my bed at two o'clock in the afternoon, as punishment for telling the truth, I said, "I will never, ever become a social liar."

Mom slammed the door, and I heard her stomp down the stairs and apologize to Bad Grandma's guests. I stayed in my bed until six o'clock, when supper was ready. I vowed that I would always say the truth just exactly as it seemed to be. That way, I would never have to try to remember the contents of a social lie. Sometimes the lessons you are supposed to learn lead to other lessons you really need.

The tension was extreme the next day, but when my maternal, good grandma came to visit, she saved my hide. She suggested that I should go out in the woods and gather wild currants for jelly making. She assured all the angry sourpusses that it was just punishment for my faux pas and would give me time to think about what I had done. Grampy, my good grandpa, winked at me. I knew in an instant that the berry picking was an intervention. It was a relief from the tension and discipline I was experiencing.

I was given a large white enamel pail with a red edge around the top. It had a heavy wire bale with a red wooden handle in the middle. Currants were tiny, and it would take all day to fill the big bucket. It was all I could do to carry it empty. I didn't know how I'd ever get it home when it was full. I remember hoping my Airedale puppy, Happy, would follow me.

As I trudged off in my jeans and barn boots, the pail over my arm, I looked back, and there stood Bad Grandma with her arms crossed over her chest and a mean smirk on her face. She called out, "That's what you get to do when you insist on wearing those awful clothes and can't behave properly."

Nobody knew that Grampy was waiting for me on the far side of the ravine. He had a tin picnic basket with a brown and yellow woven design painted on it. Inside were sandwiches, cookies, and a thermos full of ice cold milk. We wandered the day away, searching for the little stems of wild bright-red berries. It was a perfect day with my favorite grandfather, summer sunshine, and Happy tagging along. I knew Good Grandma had brought the picnic from her house. She must have been told how awful I was, but she loved me anyway.

Grampy and I found lots of wild blackberries as we roamed the woods, filling my bucket with the tiny wild red currants. Grampy commented, "You know, Gail, the city folks in my neighborhood would pay good money for a quart of these luscious blackberries when they get ripe. They can't get fresh wild berries like these shiny black gems."

He had my attention immediately. "Grampy, do you think that I could pick them and sell them?" I asked.

"You bet I do," he answered. "I'll even get the quart baskets and make you a carrying tray. You can bring them to our house and take them door to door."

When we walked home at the end of the afternoon, Grampy stopped at the creek with the picnic basket in one hand and the bucket of currants in the other. "Here you go, honey. Take these to your other grandmother and just smile when you hand them to her. Don't say a word." He and the picnic basket disappeared through the woods on an unseen, roundabout path to his car.

From then on, I was in the blackberry picking business. I picked and sold enough to buy a brand-new pair of barn boots. I was so proud. It was so much fun to earn money that was all my own, money that was separate from my allowance and the work in the mink yard. This money didn't have to go into my savings account at Daddy's bank. The valuable lessons about wild berry picking, supply and demand, packaging, sales and customer satisfaction, the shelf life of the berries, and the cost of the baskets when I paid my grandpa from my berry sales were lessons I never forgot. But most important, I learned that I could work at my own entrepreneurial business, make money, and use it any way I wanted to. A need to be self-sufficient was born in me as I knocked on doors in my good grandparents' neighborhood and sold my wild blackberries for fifty cents a quart. I also learned to look for opportunities everywhere, even outside the woods.

Chapter Six: Too Smart

TIME MARCHED ON FROM my childhood activities and episodes. I learned to roller-skate on the hardwood floors in our home. At school I heard there was a roller-skating rink, and my friends were going there on Sunday afternoons. I pointed out to my mother that I would be busy and involved in something other than troublemaking if she would take me there each week. She and I struck a deal: I joined 4-H, where I could learn to cook and sew, and she delivered me to the skating rink, where I used my own money to buy new precision skates and take skate-dancing lessons on those Sundays. I learned that if you work, get paid, and save some of your money, you can spend it on things you want. It was the budding of my entrepreneurial education.

School was a challenge. I hated the rules, confinement, and regimen of daily schedules. Junior high and eighth grade were tough. My test scores were awful. Mom made many trips to the principal's office because of my impulsive pranks. She met a new school superintendent at a PTA meeting. When they were introduced, he said, "I know your daughter Gail. Do you have other children in our school district? I never get to know the good ones."

That year New York State administered the very first statewide IQ tests. Like the New York State Regents exams, these standardized tests were timed and occurred on the same day and time across the state. They were given in the gymnasium to all junior and senior high school students.

We all marched into the gym, found our places, received a packet, and listened to instructions before the teacher blew her whistle and we could begin. We were told that we had exactly thirty minutes and that when the whistle blew the next time, that would be a five-minute warning, and then the test would be over and the packets collected. We were told to use the first answer we thought of for each question. The teacher said there were no wrong answers.

Simple, I thought. We all started frantically, and it seemed to me like only seconds before the warning whistle blew. It couldn't possibly be that twenty-five minutes had passed. The test was hard, and it took me a while. My grades were terrible, and I didn't want to fail. All of a sudden, I remembered that there was no penalty for wrong answers. I randomly marked the squares for the rest of the questions on the multiple-choice test. The whistle blew, and the booklets were collected.

"Boys and girls, you won't know how you did on this test until the state gets all the results tabulated," the teacher said as she dismissed us.

I forgot all about the test. At that point in my life, I was more worried about how I did with the boys at roller-skating and 4-H meetings than about that stupid state exam.

About a month passed, and when I got off the school bus one day, my mother was waiting. "What's gone wrong at school now?" she asked. "What kind of trouble are you in this time? I got a call from the principal today. Your dad and I have to meet with him and the guidance counselor tomorrow morning at nine o'clock. He said you have to be there too. What's this all about, young lady?"

"Mom, I don't have any idea. I didn't do anything wrong that I know about, and if I had, I would be the first to know. I couldn't find my flute at band practice yesterday, but that isn't a crime," I answered. I was instantly scared that somebody had set me up or that I hadn't turned in some assignment and I was going to fail eighth grade. Maybe I had spilled my milk in the cafeteria. I instantly checked my mouth to see if my bite block (retainer) was in there. It was, so I hadn't lost it again in the garbage, and the current boy vying for my attention hadn't taken it and put it on the teacher's desk. It didn't matter. I was in trouble again, and I didn't know why.

The next morning, we were all assembled around the conference table in the principal's office. He said, "I asked you to come here this morning to meet with the guidance department because your daughter is doing poorly scholastically. She barely passes, and she seems to think that is acceptable. We now have proof that it is not acceptable. We want to figure out what is wrong and why she isn't working up to capacity."

I wondered why there weren't any other kids in the room because there were a lot of them just like me, who didn't care, didn't want to be in school, and did just enough to squeak by with a D.

My parents were not happy. In fact, they were looking at me like they wanted to kill me right there in the principal's office.

"Let me be clear," the principal continued. "New York State required every school to administer intelligence quotient tests that came in sealed containers, were opened at the exact same time across the state, and then were collected thirty minutes later."

"Oh my gosh," I said as my hand flew up to my mouth at the memory of randomly filling in all the boxes for the questions I didn't have time to finish answering.

The principal held up his hand to silence me. "Your daughter achieved the highest score in our whole school district. Because of her score, we know that she could excel in her studies if we could just figure out what she wants to do with her life. We could then design a curriculum that interests her, and we think that she would then work up to her potential."

I was horrified. I had completed only about two-thirds of the questions and had just randomly marked the rest without even reading them. I had sabotaged myself, I thought.

The principal turned to me. "Dear," he said (now it was "dear" instead of "young lady" or "you incorrigible child"), "what do you want to do with your life? We realize, and so should you, that the sky is the limit. You can be or do anything you want to; there are no limits to the possibility of accomplishments you can achieve. We feel that you are bored with your class work and uninterested in the subjects, so we want to find out where your interests lie. What do you want to be when you finish school?"

Everybody swiveled their heads and stared at me. I was in the hot seat. They wanted answers, and they wanted them right now. I started to speak and then closed my mouth. I opened it again but hesitated. I was sure they would think I was crazy, but I knew what I wanted to be. Finally, I just spit it out. "I want to be a veterinarian."

"What? You want to be a what?" the guidance counselor asked.

"I want to be a veterinarian, a doctor for animals," I whispered.

"No, no, you can't be a vet. Only boys can be veterinarians. Girls can't do that. They don't belong in vet school."

"But you asked me what I wanted to be, and that's what I want to be," I said. "I already doctor the mink when they are sick. I take care of the ones that get hurt when they fight in their litters. I'm good at it, and I like it. I feed the tiny abandoned babies with an eye dropper and keep them on a heating pad, and I've saved their lives lots of times. Why can't I be a veterinarian?"

"Now listen," the principal said, "you cannot be a vet. If you have to have an answer as to why not, it is because it would embarrass the boys in the class. There are classes on anatomy and artificial insemination, and it would not be proper for a girl to be in the class. Which would be your second choice, a teacher or a nurse?" he inquired.

"If I can't be a veterinarian, I don't want to go to college. I don't want to be a teacher or a nurse. I hate those things!" I yelled.

"Young lady"—we were back to that instead of "dear" the minute I tried to speak the truth—"just exactly what would you like to be then?" the guidance counselor asked.

Everyone leaned forward and looked expectantly at me. My parents were staring at me with piercing anticipation.

I said, "Well, if I can't be a veterinarian, I guess I just want to get married and have babies."

There was instant pandemonium. Everyone was talking at once. My mother leaned over close to my ear and said, "I'll be forever grateful that you put it in that order."

Years passed with the conventional order of things disrupted, out of order with me. I married before my last year of high school with the blessings of my teachers and the principal, graduated high school, became a mother a year later, and then became a partner in my father's fur business. I lost my mother to breast cancer when I needed her strength and wisdom most and when I was much too young. At least we had time to become best friends and gain a mutual love and understanding of each other. At twenty-eight I divorced the man I had thought was perfect when I was fifteen, but who had grown in a different direction and who was not, I had discovered, the man I thought he was.

A very wise old woman had cautioned me that young people between fifteen and twenty-five grow and change in ways they never imagine. For me those ten years encompassed the birth of two children, the death of my mother, the overwhelming illness of my sister, the hospitalization of my dad, and the added responsibility and care associated with all that difficulty as well as overseeing six hired men and a fur farming operation.

My wonderful, handsome, sexy young husband, who had been perfect in my eyes, found seven other things more important than me. He said that I was number eight on his list of priorities. I ranked right after his church, his job, his golf game, his car, Sunday school teaching, the cat, and mowing the lawn. I came in just before our dog. He didn't include our children on the list.

I got a divorce. I moved back into my widowed father's home and worked odd jobs to pay for school clothes for my little boys. I acquired skills in customer service, sanitation, organization, supply and demand, and more as I worked as a cocktail waitress and dinner waitress.

If only I could have become a veterinarian. But then I would not have enjoyed my wonderful sons or the success of designing and owning my own business. God's plan is always best. My education and experiences were just beginning, and they would be much longer, much more expensive, and much more difficult than the total cost of a formal education to become a veterinarian.

I was beginning to recognize the work of the Master Planner as my life unfolded in diverse, unplanned directions.

CHAPTER SEVEN: POLITICAL LESSONS

IT'S ALWAYS IMPORTANT TO know background and facts in order to understand the reasons for crop failures and successes—why the weed spray failed or the fertilizer program didn't yield a bumper crop. It's crucial to identify the predators sneaking out from under the uprooted trees of life to destroy or hamper one's chosen destination or success. It's enlightening to realize that even though the weed spray and fertilizer programs are designed to clear the underbrush and weeds so crop fruition can be achieved, sometimes those efforts are undermined by species not identified. It is a lot like our path to eternal life. There is a program already in place that is designed to enable us to escape the misery and destruction of this worldly life, but there are predators and potholes to be overcome and avoided on our journey to the other side and eternal peace.

In business matters, those species are often known as politicians and economic development personnel with personal agendas and power-grabbing efforts intended to enhance their own egos and pocketbooks. Along the road to eternal life, there are lots of devil's advocates putting up roadblocks and detours to keep us from our salvation. Mirror advised over and over, "Follow the money trail, and be aware of jealous, fearful competitors and people who would benefit from your failure or who would feel the rush of power and control."

When time allowed, I looked back through old newspaper clippings and photo albums and watched old video clips. Mirror continued, "Do you remember the near demise and extinction of the mink farm when the town board sent a registered letter to your dad advising him that he was in violation of the Mink and Swine Ordinance? They allotted him six weeks to cease and desist, remove, and destroy the mink farming business he had operated for twenty-five years. Do you remember the disbelief, absurdity, and fear—the sheer stress—of that political action? You need to write about your memory of that fiasco so others can learn and heighten their awareness of the power that local elected officials believe they wield. You should share the nuggets of wisdom you gleaned from that experience."

I responded, "Mirror, I forgot that you hung in the living room of the old mink farm at that time. No wonder you can give such good advice. I still have some news clippings and paperwork from back then. I will never forget what happened and how it sculpted the future of our old family business, Moon Brook Fur Farms. That was over sixty years ago, but I remember it vividly. It was an early example of an elected official's unscrupulous use of power and control. The mentality of lies, cover-ups, and lack of accountability seems to continue in today's world too."

Chapter Eight: Taking Sides

===

My sister and I grew up in spite of our struggles through the muck and mire of swamp-filled underbrush, where quicksand bogs of illness and fields filled with sinkholes of disappointment tried to keep us from finding love and fulfillment. We climbed the hills of maturity, surmounted the rock piles of challenge, married, and brought home a baby girl and a baby boy to the mink farm. My parents became doting, proud grandparents. They finally enjoyed yearly vacations and decent vehicles to drive. The mink business thrived, and the sunshine of success illuminated the financial struggles of darker times in the 1950s.

Mirror reminded me that the illumination of those dark times was brief when I laid a folder of news clippings and letters on the kitchen table. The memory was vivid as I perused the material in that folder. I felt like I was nineteen years old again.

The mailman had delivered a registered letter from our local town board. My mother ripped it open and read it on her way back to the house from the mailbox, where she had signed for it. As she came in the front door, we heard her gasp in disbelief and say, "Call your father in here now. There must be a mistake. This just can't be happening. I can't believe it."

I ran to the mink yard to find Dad and convince him to come to the house. He took the letter she held out to him, read it solemnly, and said not a word. He just kept staring off into space.

I asked, "What's going on? What does the letter say? Let me see it."

He folded up the letter and put it in his pocket as he walked out the door.

Finally, Mother said, "The letter said that we have six weeks to get rid of the mink and close the business. It says that we are in violation of something called the Mink and Swine Ordinance. It says that they will fine us one thousand dollars a day for every day we continue after six weeks. It says the town board voted on the issue and it is nonnegotiable."

Dad fed the mink herd in record time. When he finished, he was red-faced and livid. It was only four o'clock in the afternoon, and he washed his hands in the kitchen sink and headed straight for the telephone. After one quick look in the phone book, he had an attorney on the line. As he read the letter to the attorney, Sis and I heard it for the first time.

We heard Dad yell, "What the hell do you mean I don't have a problem? I just read to you where it says, 'You are in violation of the Mink and Swine Ordinance. You are directed to appear at the next regularly scheduled town board meeting to answer these charges. You have six weeks to cease operation of Moon Brook Fur Farm, remove all equipment and buildings, and end your fur farming enterprise ...'" Then he yelled even louder, "I can't dispose of thousands of animals in six weeks' time and tear down the mink sheds. I can't find freezer storage for tons of meat, fish, and chicken by-parts. My God, what about the people who work here? What about my full-time hired man and the high school kids who work on weekends?"

We could hear only one side of the conversation as we listened intently. Mom was wringing her hands, and Sis, who was in remission from her life-altering dystonia, began to shake. We had never had any disagreements with the town officials that I could remember, except that Dad wanted to drag the road supervisor naked over the mud and ruts on our dirt road. However, he never made his desire known except at our own kitchen table. It was a hollow threat that served to dissipate his anger.

Now he was listening intently to the lawyer on the phone. "Okay, that's better," Dad said. "You don't see a problem because of the grandfather clause in the law."

Soon the conversation was over, and his shoulders relaxed as he put the receiver back on the cradle and came into the kitchen. He looked worried but not as stressed as he said, "The attorney says he will handle it, and he thinks there has been a misunderstanding. He'll represent me, and he says that we are grandfathered in, which means that because we have been here for twenty-five years, there is no way they can make us leave."

A few days later, there was a knock on the door, and when Dad opened it, the lawyer announced, "I'm here to tell you that I can't handle your case with the town board. I have too many clients on the other side of the issue." He turned and walked to his car and drove away while Dad stood there speechless.

News about our dilemma spread quickly in the farming community. Soon there were neighboring dairy farmers visiting daily, insisting that they would back us completely if the elected officials succeeded in their effort to throw us out.

Dad smelled a political rat immediately and told us that he was going to get a lawyer from another town because he felt the local ones had been threatened or bought off.

We noticed that in the last couple of years many new and expensive homes had begun to infiltrate our farming community. Two especially luxurious ones were located only a half mile down our rural road. Mom always baked cookies, visited the new neighbors, and welcomed them to our neighborhood. One of the new ladies had asked a lot of questions about the mink farm and mentioned that she was planting flowers around her home and had heard that mink manure was great fertilizer. Mom remembered her asking, "Would your husband sell me a few bushels of mink manure for my gardens?"

Mom assured her that she could just come get it if she brought her own containers. Dad even had the hired men shovel it into her baskets and then load them into the trunk of her Cadillac. We were shocked when we saw her name on the copy of the letter of complaint that the new out-of-town attorney had in his file.

The six weeks we had been given to disband our mink farming business began to race by. The new attorney assured Dad that we would win our case and wouldn't have to move out, but we also heard horror stories about cities expanding, wealthy people buying farmland, and farmers being displaced or forced out of business. It was a scary problem in the 1950s. The new lawyer said, "Of course, there is always a chance a judge could find for the town, but it's not likely."

Dad read between the lines and began his own creative defense and retaliatory strategy. First, he asked every neighbor who came by if they had any idea what had caused this action by the town board. Arnie, the nearest dairy farmer, suggested that the new city slickers who had built fancy homes in the midst of our tranquil farming neighborhood might be upset about the smell of mink manure spread on the fields surrounding their homes.

Dad was a firm believer that every action had a reaction, so we held another family brainstorming session and recalled the history of land sales in the last few years. We recalled various incidents. A factory owner, Mr. Smith, had traded my dad horseback riding lessons for me in exchange for all the mink manure we produced. He had then spread the manure on the fields surrounding the new homes. Because of increasing land values, taxes went up, and farmers went out of business, sold off their road frontage for development, and rented the remaining land to gentleman farmers like Mr. Smith, who used his horse stable and cropland rental expenses to supplement the profit from his factory. Farming was threatened, and farmland was being rapidly converted to housing developments across the country. The new developments had low tolerance for farm odors. We wondered if that was one reason.

"Larry, do you remember when you asked the town board to reimburse you for the wheel you broke on our car because of the ruts in the road? Maybe they're mad about that," Mom contributed.

My sister piped up and said, "Maybe they're still upset about the land where the one-room schoolhouse sat. Remember, it reverted back to you, building included, when the school district centralized."

"You know, I'd quicker think that they are getting some kind of payoff from the wealthy new neighbors or the promise of votes, or they are just so power-hungry and self-important that they have to throw their weight around somewhere, and we happen to be an easy target," Dad reasoned. He continued, "No matter what prompted this action to kick us and our business out of the community, I have a plan. If by some chance they win and we have to quit mink farming, I know what I'm going to do, and it will be a win-win situation for not only us but some others as well."

"Oh, Larry, what are you going to do now?" my mother warned. "Don't do something irrational or illegal just because you're mad."

Looking back to this stressful, troubled time, I remember that my family and our friends found the whole experience incredible. We could not comprehend that politicians were willing to lie, invent stories, and control neighborhoods, businesses, people's livelihood, and more. It was a time of a prospering economy in the 1950s. It was the beginning of long-overdue equality for minority races and women. Promise was in the air.

Dad's plan considered all those things. This plan was imbued with his genuine concern for investing his time and money in an environment free from political manipulation.

CHAPTER NINE: DESPERATE MEASURES

OUR FARMING COMMUNITY STOOD behind us in every way they could. We anticipated and planned for the town meeting, where the issue would be heard and explored in an open format. Farmers were worried about their own businesses and "right to farm" security. They visited often, and one day when they left, Mirror looked back at me and said, "Gail, your dad hasn't disclosed his plan to anyone. You need to get that out of him in case it might land him in jail."

"I know, Mirror, but how? How do I get him to tell?"

Mirror, who had observed and listened to all of us fret and worry, said, "He left a few minutes ago, dressed in his Sunday best. I heard him tell your mother that he wouldn't be long, and no matter which way the hearing went, he would be okay with the outcome. He also assured her that he would never invest another dollar in the local township with its apparent crooked leadership and politicians' personal agendas."

Soon Dad was back, a huge smile spreading like sunshine across his face where there previously had been an ominous, cloudy scowl. He assembled our little family and disclosed his plan.

"The town board is obviously interested only in the high-dollar tax return on land usage around here. I thought about this a lot, listened to all the neighbors and their ideas, and then realized that we had all brainstormed this crap right down to the same bottom line every time we talked. Money moves the world, elects self-serving people to office, gets folks put in jail and put out of business, and just plain screws with the lives of innocent people who don't recognize this. Well, I do see it. There are two things that would upset them terribly. One would be if they lost this fight, and we were able to continue in business. I'm fighting for that with a new lawyer. He's a bright man, and even though he assures me that I'm grandfathered in, he does raise the possibility that a judge could find in favor of the town. We all feel pretty sure that the politicians were influenced by the people with money. The hearing or a lawsuit will settle all that."

Dad was on a roll. "As insurance, in case the judge also falls in with that crooked ilk, I've implemented an alternative solution. I will take away their dream of a housing development, or some other tax-lucrative plan they may have. If they force us out, they'll never see another tax dollar from this land."

"Oh, Larry, what have you done?" my mother cried while wringing her hands. She looked haggard and drained. She was an extreme worrier and hadn't slept in weeks.

"I just had a meeting with the reverend from the Negro church downtown," Dad said. "I explained our dilemma. The reverend pointed out that it was a lot like what the Negroes are experiencing with integration. He said there are new laws assuring them equality, but politicians don't want to honor those laws. His people are not wanted wherever they try to go. They're discouraged, and laws are passed to make them fail in business whenever they try to move forward."

I heard Mirror softly whisper, "So that's why your dad just bought the forty-five-acre farm twenty-five miles away."

We thought his secret plan was to move the mink ranch to the new land he had acquired. He had planned to expand and build a dozen new 225-foot by 22-foot mink sheds, but now he would not give the township any benefit of increased property taxes, to say nothing of the new jobs that would occur in the construction phase, or the materials he would buy at the local lumber yards, or the permanent employment he would create.

Dad continued, "I told the good reverend about the registered letter, the attorney who quit, the neighbors who pledged their support to us, and the fact that the new attorney still thinks it's possible the town will win in a court of law. The reverend said he understood, so I explained my unusual plan."

The reverend asked, "So how can we help you? Why are you here explaining all this to me?"

"Because I think the prejudice and unfair dealings are the same in my situation as in yours," Dad told him. "If I lose my case, I want to offer you my home and buildings on a ten-acre parcel of land nearby, as a gift to your church. It actually has two homes and several buildings suitable for a recreation hall and cafeteria, complete with freezer and refrigeration capabilities. There's a two-story wooden barn for maintenance equipment. If I donate this property to your church, I'll avoid all the tax liabilities, and I won't have to sell or tear down the buildings, including four shed-type buildings that are approximately five hundred feet long and twenty-two feet wide and would make excellent shelters, pavilions, or a number of other things. There are ponds, woods, gardens, and open fields. It would take very little to convert it to a campground. You wouldn't have any tax liability because you are a not-for-profit organization. It's near your church. If I lose this case and have to close my business, it's a winning solution for both of us. The town's leadership appears to have decided we are all undesirable. This way, they'll lose the tax revenue. Your church would have acreage, buildings, and opportunities to worship as you wish."

Dad told us that the reverend jumped to his feet, stuck out his hand, and said, "What an ingenious idea. We'd be replacing one 'undesirable' with another, in their view, and costing the political crooks some tax income. I have to bring this before the church board, but I'm sure you have yourself an understanding. Thank you."

Mirror was reflecting the looks on all our faces and whispered to me, "Brilliant. What a brilliant plan. Now you need to leak it to the town board. It'll scare the shit out of them."

Mom asked, "What happens if we win and don't have to move?"

"I will never invest another dime in this town," Dad said. "They did this without consideration of our business or our employees, the taxes we pay, or the school kids we hire part-time. They offered us no mitigation. We've bought the forty-five acres to the west, and I'll build a state-of-the-art fur farm there. On top of that, we have a whole church full of new friends."

Chapter Ten: Justice

DAYS AND WEEKS OF worry and alternative planning passed slowly, and finally, the forced, legal dissolution of our mink farm would be aired before the community at a public hearing.

Neighbors prepared their speeches of support. Whole families planned to attend. Our farm neighbors enlisted every family member and friend from miles around to pack the town hall. They wanted to appear strong with large numbers to support our cause.

When we arrived, rows and rows of wooden folding chairs had been set up, and the antifarm folks had packed their side of the room also. The meeting commenced, and when the town supervisor asked if anyone wished to speak, our attorney rose and took the floor.

"Gentlemen of the town board, members of the press, and fellow interested citizens," he said, "I have only one initial question regarding the dissolution of Moon Brook Fur Farm. Do you have a copy of the Mink and Swine Ordinance you quoted in the papers you served on this businessman and the courts?"

I remember that the town supervisor directed the secretary

to retrieve the requested document from the town office. She left, and the meeting was temporarily paused. There was a lot of talking, speculating, and excitement to finally see the ordinance. We had asked to see it before, but there had always been an excuse for not producing it. The Freedom of Information Act had not become a law at that time.

A very heavyset latecomer arrived. She wobbled from side to side as she made her way toward an empty wooden folding chair. A boy about eight years old was sitting in the next row behind her. Just as she positioned herself above the little chair to sit down, he fired off his cap gun. This startled her as she was beginning her descent to the tiny chair, and she came down hard, splitting it into kindling wood as pieces flew everywhere.

When she was safely seated in a sturdier chair and had assured everyone she was not hurt, the crowd settled down. The crowd was then startled to see several black community members arrive. We heard murmurings and speculation about their interest, and lots of angry looks from the antifarm contingency were directed their way.

The secretary arrived back at the front table, where she whispered something to the town supervisor.

Our attorney was on it immediately. "Mr. Supervisor, I have another question. You don't have a Mink and Swine Ordinance, do you? This terrible, unreasonable, stressful situation was all smoke and mirrors. Am I correct? There is no document?"

The town board huddled with the secretary in private whispers and finally admitted there was no such document. The meeting was adjourned, and the antifarm folks slunk out of the hall.

Our supporters shook hands with all our family members and wished us well. The black church members thanked my dad and wished him well. It had been much ado about nothing. We were all fortunate.

Mirror couldn't wait to look me in the eye and ask, "Did you leak the plan to the town board?"

I smiled.

Mirror said, "Even if there was a Mink and Swine Ordinance, your dad's brilliant plan made it disappear forever."

I'll always wonder if Mirror was right. This political heavy-handedness was a precursor to difficulties in my future that I couldn't foresee. It was a valuable learning experience that made me certain that I could never pursue a political career of any kind. I still believed in telling the truth, the whole truth, and nothing but the truth. I promised myself I would not engage in social lying or tact or political spin in my future.

Chapter Eleven: Early Business Ventures

I REMEMBER HOW I learned about sales, political interference, prejudices, etiquette, and appearances in business.

During my mink farming career, which encompassed the first forty-two years of my life, I accidently discovered the three-sided heater when I picked up some newborn baby mink that had fallen through the bottom of their cage. I thought they were dead. I had no place to put them. My hands were covered with mink feed, and I was strapped into the feed cart. I had forgotten to bring an empty coffee can to carry the little dead babies, so I just dropped them in my bra between my breasts. It wasn't long before the cold, lifeless, apparently dead little hairless newborn mink, the size of my little finger, began to wiggle. At first I thought I was imagining it. I felt a tiny movement, and then all of them began to wiggle. As years went by, I warmed and revived hundreds of hairless, lifeless baby mink when they were actually suffering from hypothermia. I learned to mark where I found them, figured out a way to keep them separate for identity purposes, and was able to return them successfully to their rightful mothers. If, for some reason, I could not tell from where they had fallen, I learned that a female mother of a different color would accept and raise them. All that knowledge was important when pedigrees were recorded for each litter. It was also an education in record keeping that has served me well. As in most of nature, the animals' behavior mirrored human behavior.

I loved the mink business. The seeds of interest that my dad planted in the little girl I was at eight years old bloomed in unexpected ways. I couldn't get enough of the mink industry and examined other facets of the business.

Dad took me to New York City to see our furs sold at auction at the Hudson Bay Company Auction House. He introduced to me to the companies that tanned the hides and the furriers that created beautiful garments, and I discovered an industry that used imperfect hides referred to as cull pelts. Furriers created mink ballpoint pens, bow ties, hair ties, sweater collars, hats, key chains, earrings, and other novelties that were sold in stores in New York City. I had never seen them in stores in upstate New York.

With help from our contacts at Hudson Bay Company, I was able to find the individual furriers who created and manufactured the novelty items. I made arrangements to have a variety of items made from our own cull pelts and paid to have them shipped to me at manufacturing cost. While I was waiting for the delivery, I made lists of department stores and upscale clothing stores within one hundred miles. I was prepared and excited to drive from store to store, selling my unique mink fur novelties.

When America was great and individual retail businesses thrived, when most of what we bought had "Made in America" printed on the label, our economy was strong. We had raw goods, inventions, and creations. We added value to raw materials, manufactured most of our needs and wants, and enjoyed jobs in wholesale and retail sales. It was not a sin or disservice to become successful. It was a goal to make a lot of money, if not a fortune, which was everyone's dream. There was hope. There was a future in America for those who worked for it. I wanted a piece of it.

I marketed my furry mink bow ties, pens, earrings, flower pins, and more to department store buyers as well as small shop owners. I told them that the novelty items were made from fur produced locally, that carrying them in their store would help our economy. I pointed out the uniqueness of the novelties. I thought I knew it all. However, when I showed up in front of a fancy, high-end clothing store, and the owner saw me climb out of my old muddy pickup truck, dressed in faded jeans and my flannel work shirt, and watched me carry a cardboard box of "stuff" into her shop, nothing I said mattered. I learned that appearance was extremely important in sales. The potential buyers were immediately put off by my personal and product presentation.

I probably would have accepted the rejection because of my appearance if I hadn't needed a pair of shoes that were stored in the leftovers from my failed first marriage. They were somewhere in my dad's barn, mixed in with what furniture and household goods, clothing, personal items, toys, and junk I had managed to salvage and store. Mirror was also part of the salvage of my former marriage and was propped up against the leftovers from my former life and observed me rummaging about for my good shoes.

Mirror was pretty disgusted about finding itself in the heap of junk from my failed marriage in Dad's barn, instead of hanging in a place of prominence in my home. Not shy in the least, Mirror said, "Ugh, Gail, you look awful. You are not seriously contemplating a business in sales, are you? Are you really visiting upscale stores, trying to sell your investment in all those thousands of mink novelties, looking like that?"

I looked back at Mirror and decided I needed more than some better footwear to recreate myself. I went shopping at a store called Pick and Poke and bought a rejected business suit for a meager two dollars, along with a new pair of high-heeled shoes and a raincoat for a dollar each. At least Mirror wasn't a social liar. I could count on seeing the truth in Mirror.

I raced home to the mink farm, changed into my "new" outfit, and made a trip to my storage area for an old briefcase. Mirror was ecstatic and said, "Wow, that's better." I stood observing my reflection in Mirror and noted the neat hairdo, the better clothes, and now the old briefcase, which added professionalism to my appearance.

Mirror's observation was confirmed when I stopped at the little one-room country store on the corner across from the white clapboard country church in our tiny crossroads village. The proprietor was a petite, plump, seventy-year-old, white-haired woman who had become one of my original angels. Mary was no social liar either. She smiled broadly and said, "Oh my goodness, you look marvelous. Piffle-twash on those old-biddy buyers and their fixation on the superficial, but if that getup makes 'em buy, wear it."

The word "piffle-twash" became a staple in my vocabulary, and it was just one of the things I learned from that angel. The superior attitude of the hoity-toity buyers at the exclusive department stores toughened me. It taught me about rejection. It led me to create my first file of "asses." Mary has always resided on the angel side, as she encouraged my fledgling business and my pending status as a single, divorced mother in the 1960s when that was unpopular.

My introductory experience and early treatment in sales have been lessons and guides to how I treat those who come through my shop door selling their wares.

Chapter Twelve: Grampy, Family, and the Syrup Recipes

ENDINGS PRECEDED BEGINNINGS, AS they often do. All my grandparents overcame their struggles on earth, and the suffering and emaciating consequences of breast cancer took my mother to a better place in heaven before I could establish a business of my own.

Life was filled with terrifying uncertainty. Two little boys needed so many things. I no longer had a home, a kitchen, or a bedroom of my own. I didn't have a mother, grandparents, or a husband.

One day I decided that the kitchen in my father's home, my mother's kitchen, was arranged to meet her needs as she lived her final days in a wheelchair. It was not arranged conveniently for the cooking and baking I needed to do, so I rearranged it. I didn't ask my dad's permission. I didn't even think of doing that. I simply moved the canister set near the cupboard that held the spices, cocoa, vanilla, cooking oil, and other baking ingredients. I moved the toaster closer to the coffee pot and stove. It all made sense to me. It did not make sense to my dad.

"What the hell do you think you are doing to my kitchen?" he yelled. "Your mother had this kitchen a certain way, and that is the way it will stay. You may be here in this house with your kids, but that doesn't give you the right to move one single thing."

That's when I learned that grief causes a change in the griever's life and behavior that is foreign to their normal behavior. Dad had not adjusted to single life at that time. I also learned the importance of my independence. He was a hard taskmaster, but I benefited in the long term.

"I just thought that as long as I'm doing the cooking, I could rearrange things to make it easier and more organized for me," I countered.

"Let's get this straight right now," he said. "You and your kids are living here, and I'm okay with that. You need a roof over your head while you get your life back together. The rules here are that you ask before you make decisions. I expect you to cook, shop for groceries, clean the house, do the laundry, shovel the snow or mow the lawn depending on the season, put the mail on the table and the newspaper by my chair, feed the dogs, clean up after your kids, and keep this place neat and orderly. That being said and done, you won't owe me any rent for staying here. Of course, you will continue to work for me in the mink yard, and for that I will pay you by the hour. We'll get along better if we're both clear about this living arrangement. You also need to know that I'll watch your boys when it's convenient for me, but I am not a built-in babysitter. Do you understand where I'm coming from?"

I bit my tongue and held back tears because I had no choice and nowhere else to go. I couldn't depend on my old support systems. I had to search deep within myself and discover a strength I didn't recognize. The new business selling mink novelties was a door leading to self-esteem and personal freedom. Again, the endings preceded the beginnings and with a lot of learning in between.

I still visited Grampy every time I could, and he and I shared stories about our necessary living arrangements. My aunt, his daughter, had moved into his home to care for him after grandma died. Family took care of family; nobody went to nursing homes or senior living centers or received government help of any kind. Families still stepped up. That's how it was. My dad and I were no different.

One day as I removed my winter coat and hung it by the radiator in Grampy's dining room, he asked, "Gail, would you like a glass of wine to warm you up on this snowy winter day? I think it would be better than a cup of coffee. What do you say?"

We moved to the kitchen, and just then someone knocked on the front door. Grampy shuffled back to the dining room and opened the door to the minister from my aunt's church. The reverend was dressed in a long black topcoat, high zippered boots, black leather gloves, and a hat to match. Grampy took his hat and hung it on the wooden clothes tree, and while he waited to hang up the topcoat, he asked the reverend, "Would you like to join Gail and me in a glass of homemade blackberry wine on this cold wintry day?"

The reverend hesitated—because of his religious beliefs, I'm sure—but then acquiesced, saying, "I believe that would be fine, as it will warm my body as well as my spirit today." He followed Grampy to the kitchen and sat down at the table.

Grampy shuffled his ninety-five-year-old body to the cupboard and retrieved a bottle of blackberry wine he and my dad had made several years before. He carried it to the table and set it in front of the reverend. He shuffled back to the cupboard and brought three wine glasses toward the table.

The reverend had turned the bottle of wine around to read the handmade label, and he burst out laughing. Grampy looked puzzled and asked, "What's so funny?"

Reverend swiveled the bottle so we could see the label, which read, "For Shits." It was our family's remedy for diarrhea.

A short while later, as the reverend was putting on his hat and coat and zipping up his boots, he said, "Gene, have you forgotten something?"

Grampy paused with the reverend's gloves in his hand and said, "I don't think so. What do you think I forgot?"

"Well, Gene, I make these visits to you even though you aren't part of my congregation. I do so as a favor to your daughter. It costs me money to drive here, and it takes time away from the supporting members of my congregation. Does that jog your memory?"

It must have, because Grampy reached in his back pocket, got his wallet, and took out twenty dollars. Then he and I both saw the frown and furrowed brow on the reverend's face. Grampy quickly put the twenty back, sorted through some papers, and got a fifty-dollar bill. The good reverend snatched the bill along with his gloves. "See you next week, Gene. No wine next week though. It seems to fog up your memory."

That wine bottle label was perfect.

The next week when I visited Grampy, he said, "Gail, you know those fatty wens I get on my head and chest, the ones the doctors tell me not to worry about? Well, I have another lump like that on the back of my head, and your aunt took me to the doctor. This time he said that it was not just a fatty tumor. This one is cancer, and I don't have long on this earth."

I burst into tears. I could not imagine not having Grampy to visit. I could not fathom the emptiness I already felt, the sorrow, the ache in my chest, the denial I was about to voice.

Before I could say a word, Grampy said, "Now don't you cry. Do you remember when I asked you what the point of my life was without your grandmother? Do you recall when I told you that after seventy-two years of marriage I didn't have a purpose anymore? We all need a purpose. She was the love of my life. I lived for her, even when we fought, and boy, could we fight. It just about killed me when she wouldn't speak to me for a week at a time when she was mad, but how I loved her and her spunk. Now she's gone. There's no point to my life."

"But Grampy, I can't get along without you," I sobbed.

Grampy reached out, gathered me up in his frail arms, and whispered, "Now, now, girl. You have our memories. You have our experiences. You'll always have my love. Now stop it. I don't want you to cry. I need to tell you what I want to give you today so that when I'm gone, you will already have it."

"Grampy, all I want is you. I don't want anything else. I don't want stuff or things. I need you. I want you," I pleaded and cried.

Grampy shook me by my shoulders and said, "You're thinking only of yourself. I've told you that isn't a good thing to do. You have to think of others and what's best for them, and that includes me. Now get a grip on yourself and let me send you home with some memories. Did you drive your dad's pickup truck today like I asked you to?"

"Yes, but why did you ask me to do that?" I questioned.

"Because I want you to have my desk, the one I made. It's right here in the corner of the dining room, and if you don't take it today, your aunt won't give it to you after I'm gone. I want you to have it, with the paper clips and the pencils and all my stuff that's in there. I have two neighbor boys who will be here in a minute to load it up."

"Grampy, I can't do it. I just—"

"Now just be quiet, Gail," he interrupted. "This is how I want it. I know my daughter. I've left her a list of who's to have what, but I doubt she'll do as I wish. In the center drawer you will find an envelope with a list of things that I know you would cherish. Give it to her after I'm gone. I can't give the rest to you now because it will cause a war. She hates this desk because it's not a fancy manufactured one, but I put a lot of work into it. She'd just sell it for a few dollars, and I want you to have it."

The desk was loaded into the truck and then unloaded into my dad's barn with the remnants of my first marriage, where it sat for several years until it made its way to the farm I call home, where it still has a place of honor in my office.

Grandpa passed with little or no pain, in his sleep. He was right. I have a lifetime of memories, lessons, and his example of how life should be lived.

My aunt called all the grandchildren together at the funeral and announced that no one would be entitled to anything that had belonged to our grandfather and grandmother. She said, "I took care of them, and therefore I'll sell all their personal belongings at a household sale. If you want anything, come to the sale."

Twenty-two dollars to my name and first in line on the cold, snowy, blizzardy day of the sale, I shivered and waited. The door opened at 9:00 a.m., and I made a mad dash to the kitchen, where there was a table full of recipe books and grandma's recipe box. I took them all. Then it was a race to the dining room table for the photograph albums and on to the handmade rag rugs. I still had enough money to buy three salt-and-pepper shakers, and then my money was all gone.

All the things went into the barn with the desk. There they remained until I moved to the farm I call home to this day. They were then stored away in a closet for many more years.

One day, it was my good fortune to come across the recipe box, have the time to look through it, and discover the syrup recipes. For many years I made the syrups for only my family to enjoy. When I served strawberry syrup on ice cream to just the right person, the Sugar Shack business was conceived.

One more piece of the jigsaw puzzle of my life had fallen into place.

CHAPTER THIRTEEN: CONNECTORS AND REASONS

AS I LOOKED BACK, I recalled everything through the end of my first marriage, which included becoming a partner in my father's fur farming business, and marrying a second time to a controlling police chief who had the last abusive word when he committed suicide while I listened on the phone. All those experiences were now just memories.

Mirror said, "You sure moved up and on, and you didn't see that all those things that happened to you were lessons. They were building blocks in your education along the path to where God decided your future would be."

Mink farming passed into just a memory, and grape farming became the vehicle for my education. Men marched along through the educational process, unconsciously teaching me lessons throughout each relationship during my continual search for unconditional love.

At least I stopped marrying them. I tried business arrangements as an alternative to "for richer or for poorer," secured good health insurance in place of "in sickness and in health," and enlisted a financial planner to draw up a will to take care of the "till death do us part" section.

I bought and sold parcels of grape land, increased my business endeavors, held a commercial pesticide license (which expanded my ability to have a custom farming business), bought a grape harvesting business, and sold extra produce by the road. At home, I canned, put in the freezer, or preserved almost everything I grew other than commercial crops.

Mirror commented, "Remember your roots, your past, what made you who you are, because that is a critical part of you. Every business in which you became involved was somehow connected to past experiences. Those experiences became resources and building blocks in the bridge between your past and your future."

With the changes came anxiety, gender prejudice, and a variety of male candidates to fill my quest for unconditional love. The favorites, the steadfast teachers of basic principles, remained; the Master Planner, Grampy, and my dad were never far from my conscious thinking. Mirror reminded me that only the Master Planner could orchestrate the unusual events that kept appearing in my life.

Buying and selling grape vineyards was always exciting, and as opportunities arose, I made lists of pros and cons or reasons to take action. Again, Mirror made me realize that every transaction had a purpose by the Master Planner. I was unconsciously acquiring a contiguous strip of land between the interstate and the shoreline of Lake Erie. I did not, could not, and would not have believed the purpose if someone, even Mirror, had laid it out like a road map. It was just too unbelievable. Years later, a political economic development plan clearly disclosed the reason.

One day a man knocked on my door and said he was the son of my nearest neighbor, who was one of my favorite characters in life. He was old when I moved to my farm. He had Guinea hens, and they paid me an unexpected visit the first week I lived in the old house on the farm. They were a strange sort of chicken or turkey or some other kind of bird. I wasn't sure. They wouldn't go away.

Soon my neighbor showed up to claim them and took them back across the highway. I stopped at his house to thank him for coming to get them and for the education he had given me about them. He was a spry, thin old man who lived alone and owned a seventy-five-acre farm with grape vineyards and fruit orchards on it. He insisted that I take a tour, so we walked the whole thing as he explained the varieties of grapes and fruit trees. The open fields were producing acres of tomatoes, as he had leased the land to a commercial grower. The farm was beautiful. At the end of the tour, I asked him, "Would you ever sell this beautiful farm?"

"Absolutely, I would not," the old gentleman answered.

I asked him that question many times over the years as I bought farms two and three miles away. His answer was always the same.

Now his son was at my door and said, "My dad left a will and stated his wishes for how we should disperse his real estate holdings. He says in his letter of wishes that you expressed interest in buying his farm across the highway."

"Oh, I did want it, but I've bought other farms, and I don't think—"

He interrupted me. "You need to hear his wishes before you make any decision. He wants us to sell it to you for a third of its value. Ma'am, you were a favorite of his, and his instructions indicate he wanted you to have it for that reduced price."

I was flabbergasted. I did still want that farm. It was close. It was well cared for. It had a variety of fruit, almost everything that would grow in the unique microclimate along the shoreline of Lake Erie.

Mirror was listening and interjected, "You'd better snap it up, you fool. Don't let it slip away."

I had been about to decline the offer, but Mirror's insistence made me pause long enough to reconsider. "Okay. I'll see if I can find the money."

"No hurry, Mrs. Black. We'll not sell it then, and when you're ready, we'll do a land contract."

That farm was everything I needed. I could hunt there. I could pick all the wild berries I wanted in the woods. It was home to peach, pear, cherry, quince, and a variety of apple trees. It was a Garden of Eden in my eyes. My farm lending organization loaned me the money, and the sale was completed.

Mirror wouldn't let me be and said, "What would you do without me? You almost let that one get away. That farm is a no-brainer—close by and perfect for you."

I planted more grapes and continued to rent the open land to a tomato farmer. The deal was flawless, meant to be. Mirror was right.

Harvest season came in September of the first year I owned the old man's farm in the mid-1980s. I was intrigued, and one day I went to watch the picking process. The tomato farmer brought in a busload of migrant workers. It was so interesting to watch them fill cone-shaped baskets of tomatoes. They would run with a container of fresh tomatoes on their shoulder, race up a cleated ramp to a tractor trailer with a huge tank-type bin on it, and dump their load. Each worker received a chip for the basket from a supervisor at the bottom of the ramp. At the end of the day, the chips were exchanged for money. I watched with fascination. They worked so hard and fast. The acres of tomatoes were disappearing before my eyes. Truckloads left, and more empty trucks replaced them.

Before long, a big, old four-door Pontiac came slowly driving in. It passed me, the owner of the tomato crop, and the guy handing out chips for full baskets. The woman driving it finally came to a stop at the front of the semi that was half-filled with the fresh tomatoes destined for the canning factory down the road.

The woman, who had muddy bare feet, a long black skirt, and wild, blowing, long black hair, exited the car with a cash box and put it on a card table she retrieved from the back seat. She opened the trunk, removed the lids from coolers filled with food, and blew a whistle. The workers dumped their full totes and got their chip, and most of them produced a five-dollar bill, whereupon she handed them two slices of bread with a half a chicken breast or a leg and thigh between the slices of bread. That included all the bones, which they spit on the ground.

Toward the end of the line, some of the men handed her the money for a sandwich and then another bill that looked like a twenty from where I stood. She would take the money, lock the cash box, close the trunk, and climb in the back seat with the sunbaked, sweaty laborer. The door with tinted windows would slam shut. The car would bounce a few times. And then it was back to serving sandwiches until the next twenty-dollar bill.

Every day on that farm was a new education. The tomato plants got disked into the ground. The grapes got ripe, or nearly ripe, and there seemed to be steady traffic up and down the short dead-end road leading to my new farm. I thought that I now had a broad understanding of human nature, but it was nothing compared to what I was about to learn.

Chapter Fourteen: Community Activities

I ASKED MY YOUNGEST son to go pick some wild blackberries for a pie. He took his bicycle and set off with an eight-quart basket. In only a few minutes he came wheeling back down the driveway, skidded to a stop, and said, "Mom, I'm afraid to go over there. There's a guy with a pickup truck, and he's parked on the road into the Niagara grapes. He's smoking a cigarette and sitting on a sweatshirt on the tailgate."

"Okay. Put your basket in my truck, and I'll go with you."

By the time we got there, a little red car had parked behind the truck. I drove to the end of the dead-end road, past the turnoff where they were parked. We walked back to the blackberry patch and filled our baskets. After an hour or so, we were done, and the shortest route back to the car was through that parking road. We had to make our way through my new peach orchard, where I hadn't mowed the tall grass. As we stumbled through the high growth, we heard a rustling sound. I was taller than my boy, who was eight years old at the time, and I saw two people, a man and a woman, running ahead of us. Soon we stumbled into their nest, and in the flattened grass was a new hooded sweatshirt with the tags still on it. My young son pointed to it and asked, "What's a new sweatshirt doing here?"

I heard the car door slam and the truck roar to life as they sped down the road and back to their jobs following their lunch break. I said, "Oh, some folks were probably just looking for our good blackberry patch."

For days my son would run into the house about noon and declare, "They are stealing our blackberries again, Mom. You want to go throw them out? We could give them back their sweatshirt."

One summer morning I found a car with four flat tires, dented fenders, broken windows, and mud and grass hanging from it in the middle of the private road into my farm. Most of the end posts on twenty rows of grapes were broken. My workload had just increased significantly with all the necessary repairs. I called the county sheriff, and officers were soon on-site and calling in the license plate number. The owner's father arrived and declared that his son's car had been stolen and he wanted the responsible party arrested. Paperwork ensued, and a wrecker was summoned. I was showing the officers the damage to my posts, the ruts, and other damage I had found when another car arrived, and a young man climbed out. He started to say, "I'm so sorry, Mrs. Black. I'll—"

His father shouted at him, "You don't know anything about this. You were home all evening and all night. Your car was stolen, and they'll arrest the driver when they find him."

"No, I did this. I—"

"Shut up. Just shut up. I already told them you were asleep in your room. Somebody stole your car. Shut the fuck up," the father yelled.

"I did this. I'll fix it. I'll pay for it," the responsible young man insisted.

"You stupid jackass, you were asleep. Why are you trying to take the blame when I already have it handled?" the father kept insisting.

The deputy sheriff turned to me and asked, "Do you want to press charges and have this kid arrested?"

"No, sir," I answered. "You can arrest the lying, cowardly parent, but the kid is responsible. He'll fix the damage. He already accepted responsibility."

The young man continued to apologize, saying, "I got in a fight with someone. We chased each other all over your farm, Mrs. Black. I'll fix all of it and come and get you to inspect it when I'm done."

The parent left in a hailstorm of gravel and anger. The young man kept his word.

Mirror interrupted my memories by saying, "What about the episode at two o'clock in the morning? You can't leave that out. It is a sad commentary on parenting."

"You mean when I was awakened at two o'clock in the morning by a loud pounding on my front door? Are you remembering the morning that I tucked my handgun in my bathrobe pocket and peeked out a crack in the door? It was a young man I recognized, and he was being held upright by two others I didn't know."

Between attempts to shake off his helpers and stand on his own, almost landing himself in a heap on my porch, the young man said, "Gimme yer keys. I gotta has yer tractor. Our car's tuck in mud on yer farm."

"Whoa, boy, you're drunk. You can't even stand up on your own two feet. I'm not giving you the keys to my tractor. You can't even talk plain. I'll call your mother, and she can come and help you," I told him.

"Good God, nooooo. Don't call the ole lady. She'll beat my

ass. Ya know she buyed the car fer me. It's new. Shiny, purdy like you, Ms. Black. Just gimme the tract keys. I'll pull it out aself."

"No, I'm calling your mother. You are in no condition to drive a mule, let alone anything with a motor."

Swiveling his hips, he said, "I drive this motor purdy good."

I held up the phone so he could see it and pretended to dial. Then I closed the door and locked it. The last I saw of the three boys, they were wobbling away on my driveway. No danger—it was a muddy spring, and their vehicle was stuck. They weren't going anywhere. I went back to bed.

In the morning, after my coffee, I got the tractor and chains out of the barn and made my way to the scene. There was no shiny little car. There was, where it had been, deep ruts where someone else's tractor had dragged the car to the road. It had been buried at the end of one of my vineyards. In an attempt to get it out, someone had removed the end posts and braces from fourteen rows of grapes and laid them in the mud like a plank road. The area was strewn with empty wine bottles and beer cans. There was an array of male and female underwear hanging on the bushes in the area. It was a mess.

I pondered whether I should tell the parent. I decided not to. Then I decided to do it after all, so I got in my vehicle and drove to the kid's home. When I arrived, a Saturday morning coffee get-together was in progress. The drunken boy's father answered the door. I stated the reason for my visit and he said, "We're busy now. Come back later if it's important."

Anger rose in me in spite of my determination to be professional with this popular, socially active parent. I struggled with the decision, but Mirror wasn't anywhere nearby to advise me. I yelled, "Are you too busy to hear what your kid did to my farm last night? Are you too busy to make him take responsibility for the damage he did?"

"It couldn't have been my son. He was home and asleep all evening." This was the standard local parental response.

"No, he wasn't. He was at my front door at two o'clock this morning. He and two friends were drunk. He demanded that I give him the keys to my tractor because he was stuck on my farm."

Some parents do not realize that the best way to bring up a child is to let that child be responsible for his behavior and work toward repairing any damage he might have done. Such incidents throughout the years seemed like an endless parade of moral depravity.

A month passed without incident. I thought the few surprising episodes on my recently acquired property were just isolated happenings. But they were only the beginning of the live reality show and soap opera that would continue.

CHAPTER FIFTEEN: DIVERSIFYING

WHEN I CAME HOME for lunch one day, Mirror had some thoughts about the busy farm I had acquired. I was tired, dirty, and mumbling about the long hours and heavy labor. Mirror said, "You made a good decision when you bought that farm. Don't forget the gas well and the little bit of added income that brings to you. And remember the billboard sign and the rent you receive from the old guy who owns it. Now you even get paid for taking care of it."

"Mirror, if you only knew all the business, recreational, and farming opportunities that land offers to various members of this community, you would wonder how I got lucky enough to own it," I replied. I had removed old refrigerators and hot water tanks that people had dumped because it was an easy, cheap alternative to using the landfill. A local wrecker service had assisted me in removing an abandoned car and all the garbage strewn around it. That one had belonged to partying teenagers from a town twenty-five miles away. Countless other incidents of people stealing my grapes, dumping garbage, and having illicit affairs occurred frequently. I couldn't understand how all these depraved individuals found my farm. However, I still felt fortunate to own it, for entertainment value if nothing else.

Again, Mirror had planted a seed in my thinking. I began to wonder if the grapes were the only money-making use of the land. Then I began to wonder, as all grape farmers do, if the grape industry was sustainable and if I could ever make enough money farming them to retire.

Perhaps I had wondered out loud because Mirror spoke again. "You need to expand your business interests. You need to find an alternative for making money in case the grape market goes south or you have a crop failure. It's an insurance policy for your paycheck."

The newest agricultural adventure that I found interesting certainly did afford many opportunities to me. I just never dreamed that the journey I was about to begin would lead me into a quagmire of difficulty.

Chapter Sixteen: Searching for Opportunities

Industrial development was a great thing for our community. I was very proud of our grape processing plants, wineries, sewing factory, and small engine repair businesses, as well as larger manufacturing establishments that were all thriving. We were a vital, working, growing town. I thought about the public harbor on Lake Erie and the fishing and boating business that also helped our economy.

Mirror was right, as usual, so I began to investigate other opportunities. I could always build a bottled water business on a farm I owned twenty miles inland. It had an artesian well with pure water flowing from more than three hundred feet underground. It was the same aquifer used as a water supply for a nearby city. I'd had the water tested, and it was pure and flowed with enough volume to sustain such a business.

I started reading aloud from the list of pros and cons about a bottled water business, and Mirror said, "Not enough interaction with people in that business. I don't think filling plastic jugs and shipping truckloads of them to wholesale suppliers is your cup of tea."

"You're right, Mirror. What do you think about a fish farm?" I asked.

I had lots of time to mentally explore different ideas as I pruned and tied my vineyards. An alternate income source was a great idea, just as Mirror had suggested. I wrote a sketchy list of pros and cons. The fish farm idea was of great interest because I already had a worm business. I spent my rainy evenings picking up night crawlers and selling them to fishermen. Worm customers were another source of candidates for romance. Those men were complaining about the threat created by zebra mussels and the worry over declining walleye populations in Lake Erie.

Mirror pushed. Mirror reflected raised eyebrows and questioning eyes whenever I looked that way. "So Miss Farmer/Businesswoman, why aren't you doing something other than hemming and hawing over your fantasy ideas?"

I got in contact with a local small business development center, which soon connected me with a professor at a nearby university. He just happened to be doing research on the culture of walleye fry. We all worked together on a business plan as we explored using my latest farm as a hatchery location.

One critical component was a water supply. My farm had a registered creek, but not much water flowed in it in the summer months. I remembered the tomato field where I had planted cauliflowers a few summers before. That field had to have springs because the cauliflowers had thrived in a drought year. Once again, every new development or idea seemed to be connected to a prior learning experience in my past. Mirror was hopeful and supportive but couldn't let bygones be bygones.

"Hey, smarty-pants, do you remember when you made

that awful arrangement with the migrant workers when the tomato business went to pieces? They no longer had a job picking tomatoes and asked you if they could plant cherry tomatoes and cauliflowers in your vacant field. How'd that event transpire?"

"It was a long story that didn't end as expected," I said. "As I recall, a couple from south of the border drove down my driveway and asked if I'd let them plant those vacant fields. They said a local processor had promised to supply the plants and then, when the vegetables were harvested and delivered to them, to pay them twenty-five cents a pound for the cherry tomatoes and fifty cents a head for the cauliflowers. That processor agreed to supply not only the plants but the crates and containers for the harvest. The migrants were to plant, cultivate, care for, and harvest the crops. Mirror, you forget that those migrants worked for me in the vineyards in the spring. They were not total strangers, and I knew they were very hard workers. They had green cards and were becoming naturalized citizens. Their children were honor students and sports stars in their high school. I really liked them and wanted to help them. That is why I bought the tomato planter and put it on the back of my tractor. I drove, and they did the manual labor. We planted five acres of cherry tomatoes and fifteen acres of cauliflower plants."

Mirror added to my memory, "You bought the fertilizer and applied it for them, and in return they cleaned your house and took care of your lawn. It was a great way to help them help themselves."

"Then they suggested the idea of using the money from the fifty-five thousand cauliflowers, when they sold them, to buy a house and get their kids out of public housing. Mirror, I worried about the crime that was happening in their neighborhood. Their children were so bright and accomplished."

A rather thought-provoking, painful, expensive memory took over my present state of mind. With the money I'd spent on planting the crops that were now growing in my fields, the articles of clothing I'd bought for the kids, and the meals and wages I'd provided, my savings were dwindling. I lay awake at night worrying about enough rain to keep the cauliflowers growing.

Just about that time, a house came on the market a couple of miles down the road. Like lots of things in my life, the timing was significant, and the owner approached me privately. He needed money, and I thought the place was perfect for the migrants. The crops were growing rapidly. It was a drought year, and other farms were suffering with the lack of rainwater. My field was lush and green so far. That was how I discovered that spring water was keeping it moist.

I talked to the migrants when they came to tie the leaves up on the cauliflowers, to make them stay white as they grew. As my young son and I learned how to string special rubber bands up our arms and then pull up the leaves of the cauliflower plants and slip just one band on the plant to hold those leaves together and keep the sun and rain off from the developing white vegetable, I suggested I would buy the house, and then when their harvest money came in, I would sell it to them. I even found an attorney who would do the real estate transfer for cost to help them. That good man was another angel who has since gone to his reward in eternity (the saying "Only the good die young" comes to mind). I wrote the check for $19,000 plus costs. I was paralyzed with fear when I looked at the balance left in my checkbook. Nineteen thousand dollars was a lot of money in the mid-1980s.

Mirror reflected the mental recall in my eyes. "Then all hell broke loose just after you closed on that house, didn't it?"

My coffee got cold as I sat at my kitchen table remembering the sequence of events. Big Daddy, as the father of the family liked to be called, picked cherry tomatoes and took them to the processor. Of course, the processor wouldn't pay the promised price of twenty-five cents a pound and would give the migrants only ten cents a pound for the tomatoes they had already picked. That manipulative processor knew the migrants would take the ten cents because they had no other choice. That buyer said the market price for cherry tomatoes had dropped even though the drought had created a shortage.

On the heels of that deal, without consulting me, Big Migrant Daddy harvested one pickup truck load of cauliflowers. When he arrived at the processing plant to get weighed in, the load was refused.

Big Daddy called me to complain that the load had been rejected, and I questioned him about the cauliflowers he had picked. I didn't think they were big enough or ripe enough for harvesting. He assured me that they were fine, so I called another buyer that I knew and told Big Daddy to take them there. The second buyer called me back and said that he had inspected the load of produce. There were beautiful cauliflowers on top of each crate, but underneath, the heads were immature and of no use to him. He rejected the load the same as the first buyer had. I told him to send Big Daddy back here so I could see what the problem was.

An hour later, the pickup full of produce drove down my driveway. I asked Big Daddy to unload a couple of crates so I could look at them. Sure enough, the top heads were perfect, but the rest of them were the size of fifty-cent pieces, green and immature.

I looked Big Daddy in the eye. "You'll have to dump these. They're too small. You can't fool a produce buyer by topping the crates with perfect produce and then cheating him with the remainder. It doesn't work that way."

I remember being horrified when Big Daddy flew into a rage. He jumped on his truck and began to fling slatted wood crates of little cauliflowers all over the driveway as he screamed, "I no need cauliflowers, I no need cherry tomatoes, and I no need you!" He spun his wheels and tore up the driveway, never to be seen again.

Mirror was grinning in my reflection. "Miss Smarty-Pants, you'd just closed on that little house for them. I told you to get a signed contract with them, but you wouldn't. You said they were great, hardworking people, and you didn't need a contract. Your pocketbook was thousands of dollars lighter. Your field was still full of growing cauliflowers that would ripen just as your grape harvesting business became active. You had twenty-one farms contracted for picking. Your help had disappeared with Big Daddy, and you, smarty-pants, were in a pickle."

I remembered how furious I'd been with Mirror. "Mirror, you've always had an 'I told you so' mentality."

Mirror gloated and puffed up with righteousness.

"Okay," I continued, "I received a call from some acquaintances in Pittsburgh offering to come and cook for me during the six-week harvest season. They said they'd work for me in exchange for room and board so they wouldn't be bored. They were retired, and I regarded them as angels. They helped us pick and sell the cauliflowers and cherry tomatoes. They helped me move equipment from farm to farm in the harvesting operation, and supper was on the table every night when the work was finished for the day. Don't gloat, Mirror. The Master Planner was in control, as He always is."

I realized that rehashing my past poor judgments always gave me insight. The cauliflower incident had given me knowledge of the available spring water on that acreage. There is a benefit or a lesson in every misjudgment.

The lessons continued. Although Mirror was not aware, and the Master Planner had done the work, an alternate plan surfaced. A young couple appeared and needed a house. I didn't ask for references because I had known them for a long time. A few months later, they left in the middle of the night, owing a month's rent and leaving the house trashed. I fixed it all up and next rented it to a single mother with a daughter. She moved in with beautiful new furnishings. Each time I went to check things, the house was immaculate.

After several months passed, the neighbors began calling. "Who is in the house you bought in the middle of our neighborhood?" the man on the phone inquired in the middle of the night.

I had been sleeping the exhausted sleep of a farmer in growing season. I was foggy and said, "A lovely young woman with a teenage daughter. Why?"

"I'm calling you because no one on this street can sleep. If we can't sleep because of the big semitrucks rolling in and out every hour, every night, then you won't either. You need to stop this red-light district immediately," yelled the next-door neighbor of the pretty little house I'd bought on the quiet street.

I confronted my tenant, and she also left in the middle of the night. Soon, Rent-to-Own came for all the lovely furnishings. I learned to check backgrounds, get references, take security deposits, and a whole lot more.

The lady of the night, the truck drivers' friend, left owing me two thousand dollars in back rent. I filed a claim in small claims court. The case was processed months later. The case was heard several townships away because the local justice knew everyone involved. The new judge heard my story and then dismissed me, saying, "You can go on home. I'll get you the rent that's in arrears, and the court will send you a check."

Just before I finished presenting my case, the lady of the night, the truck drivers' friend, had entered the courtroom. She was dressed in a miniskirt, fishnet stockings, stiletto heels, and about thirty pounds of makeup, perfume, and hairspray.

I was dismissed by the judge, I walked through the plume of perfume and stood outside the courtroom door. I was startled by the click of the lock on that door. I flinched and started to leave as the situation became crystal clear in my mind. Instead of going home as instructed by the judge, I sat in my car and waited.

Thirty minutes later, the door opened, and the lady of the night exited, tucking her blouse into her skirt and fluffing her teased red hair back into place. I was pretty certain that the judge had personally collected my back rent, and I never saw a check from the court.

My lessons were completed, apparently, when my phone rang a few weeks later with an inquiry about selling the pretty little house. The Master Planner had taken care of it. I moved on, and the expensive education was used twenty years later when I bought another house and opened a bed-and-breakfast.

Mirror was still gloating over my mistake in judgment, and I said, "Mirror, just be quiet so I can continue thinking about the fish farming venture. You were right about the springs feeding water to that field."

Chapter Seventeen: Fish Farm Plans

THE PROFESSOR WHO WAS helping me thought the field would be suitable for a large pond or lake, which would be a sufficient water supply for the fish farm we were contemplating. The business plan and the research were finally completed, and it was time to get estimates for building the pond. The first estimate was over $100,000. I had already erected a large storage barn for my farm equipment, and it was also suitable for the indoor part of the fish operation. I had a significant financial investment in that building. The free gas from the gas well was close by and would provide the heat needed in cold weather. I looked for a second pond-building estimate. It came in at $96,000.

My business plan, the professor, and the experts advising me assured me that fish farming was covered under agricultural laws and regulations, and therefore no permits were necessary. That was positive information, but I was discouraged. I didn't have that kind of money to invest in an unproven business. I didn't want to borrow it either.

Mirror said, "Just tell all your supporters that you won't risk borrowing and paying interest on an unproven project; you won't move forward with the plan. You're right to be careful. You have always said that if something is meant to happen, it will."

I had invested more than a year in this endeavor. I had been excited about it. I had studied so hard to learn all I could about raising walleyes. The pole barn already existed. The road was there for the grapes, and I didn't have to spend a lot of money on assets already in place. I felt so disappointed. I dialed the numbers to call off the project. The people I needed weren't available, so I left messages. It was a Friday, and I didn't expect a call back from anyone until the next week.

On Saturday morning a young man knocked on my front door. "Mrs. Black, do you have any work for a bulldozer? I thought you might need some drainage ditches or something. I bought an old bulldozer, and I have been reconditioning it so I can go into the excavating business. I need a place to practice, and I'll work for the cost of the fuel."

Mirror exploded behind me. "See, I told you if it was meant to be, something would happen. Now take this guy to the proposed fish farm and explain about that hundred-thousand-dollar pond."

Two days later, I had a reinvigorated plan. I had a bulldozer on-site and a drawing, and the young man had measured with his laser gun to estimate how much dirt he would have to move. He began to create the water supply for my fish hatchery. He agreed to stay with the job until the fish runs below the pond were built. Gravity would feed them from the pond he was building.

My young contractor had lots of time delays and difficulties. The tracks would not stay on his bulldozer, and other parts broke repeatedly. It didn't matter. I could afford to wait for him. I had a new house to clean and paint. There would be potential renters to interview. I had plenty to keep me busy while I waited for the project to be completed.

It took several years to build the pond. The machinery breakdowns and the costs of parts and repairs were discouraging. In the meantime, I just kept on farming grapes, and I had that house to prepare as a rental. The young contractor was dedicated to his goal and kept making very slow progress on excavating a large crater on my farm.

CHAPTER EIGHTEEN: PAPER MILL COMPLICATIONS

SOON AFTER I STRUCK that deal with the young contractor, and while the work was being done, the local newspaper announced that a $210 million cardboard-recycling paper mill would locate in our town. The building site was just one-quarter mile up-water from the fragile beginnings of my fish farm in progress. I wondered if there would be groundwater contamination.

The announcement began a three-year battle to find and disclose the truth about this factory. Several interested neighbors were concerned about property values and the loss of potential tax revenue from lakefront land with the added view of a paper mill spewing out steam, dirty water, and odors. They began to investigate the trade-offs.

I continued to farm my grapes, work at the creation of my fish hatchery/farm, and listen to the concerns of fellow citizens. It wasn't long before that life morphed into doing only the absolutely necessary work on the grape farm. Paper mill concerns overwhelmed every area of my life. The investigation consumed most of my time.

I continued to pick night crawlers, sell bait, and sort out love interests. I was continually bombarded with information or misinformation about the looming paper mill. Someone brought me an environmental assessment form describing the project. I read it. I drove to the parent company and had a look and smell for myself. I took video footage, brought it home, and presented it to businesspeople, neighbors, politicians, and fellow citizens who were in favor of the project. All of them viewed the video with horror.

It seemed that those folks who were in favor of jobs and factories didn't live on the same side of town or downwind of the proposed paper mill. They wouldn't have to look at the mess of used, wet, dirty, rotting cardboard, and they wouldn't have to smell it or be affected by the mold spores coming from it.

The discovery that the promoters did not live near the proposed paper mill was not surprising. Most who were in favor didn't live within thirty miles. Concern grew, and it was suggested that an environmental impact statement was required under SEQR, the State Environmental Quality Review Act (New York State Department of Environmental Conservation). That legal safeguard was in place to guarantee public access to knowledge of all aspects of a proposed project. But the local development organizations in our county refused to comply with that law.

The political excuse for not following the SEQR law was that cardboard recycling is for the public good; the paper mill project was declared to be exempt from providing an environmental impact statement, or EIS.

I became really suspicious and used my living room to host a small group questioning the project. That was the beginning of three years of heated, dangerous, threatening, time-consuming, costly, mean-spirited, harmful, and dishonest public degradation and character assassination of the members of that small group. It was terrifying and unbelievable that tax-paying citizens could be persecuted for demanding honest answers to reasonable questions. Soon the group I had joined began to disprove many of the statements proffered by our economic development gurus.

Mirror monitored all our containerboard living room meetings. "Find out what the local politicians and economic development leaders are getting in return for their support of this project. You need to follow the money," it said. Mirror just could not leave things alone.

Some of our inquisitive members began an intensive information-gathering effort through the Freedom of Information Act. Others attended every public meeting where information about the development was being discussed. Others made it their job to disseminate any information our group gathered. I converted one bedroom in my home into an office for the project.

It became an all-consuming occupation for all of us. We felt that our health, livelihood, land values, future development, and quality of life were threatened. The more we sought answers to our questions, the more persecution we received.

People fired guns into our mailboxes, left threats on answering machines, and vandalized equipment and vehicles, and some of us were called economic development terrorists in public meetings. After three years of battling for truth and disclosure, it became necessary to bring a lawsuit against the agencies that were involved in bringing this project to fruition. Our lawsuit asked for an EIS, as required by environmental law. We did not sue for damages or costs. We simply wanted the responsible agencies to provide factual, truthful answers for this $210 million project.

We paid the costs of the lawsuit ourselves. To sue for costs would have been equivalent to making our fellow taxpayers pay for it. Doing that would have meant punishing them when their only mistake was unknowingly voting irresponsible politicians into positions of control.

We won on all three counts in the New York State Supreme Court. An environmental impact statement was prepared, and the politicians did not require the paper company to pay for all the costs. The taxpayers got stuck with a lot of that bill.

Among some of the highlights, questions, and findings explored by the EIS, a study on the Concord grape industry concluded there would be a 19.4% reduction in the productivity of Concord grape vines over a ten-mile radius. No grape farmer had a 19.4% profit margin, so it would spell the end of grape farms in that ten-mile radius. The reason cited was that moisture would be continuously discharged and added to the already high moisture from Lake Erie, causing fungal diseases that could not be controlled.

I remember the phone call I made at six in the morning. This friend, a farmer from a distant town, hadn't surfaced in my memory in years. He had taught me to square dance when I was eight years old and he was an awkward eighteen-year-old teenager. That memory was accompanied by an overwhelming need to call him on the phone even though I had not had any contact with him in fifteen years. I wondered why I was so possessed to call him right that minute. It wasn't even seven o'clock in the morning.

"Just look up the number and call him for goodness' sake. Haven't you learned to trust these spiritual leadings yet?" Mirror yelled at me through the front door.

I was on the porch having my morning coffee and was still a bit groggy. I spat back, "I don't have to look up his number. It's one that I will always remember from 4-H council meetings when I was the secretary and had to call everyone, Mirror. To answer your question, yes, I know where these feelings and thoughts come from. That's the Higher Power taking care of me."

While I dialed the landline phone (there were no cells back in the '90s), I expected to have to explain who I was (caller ID wasn't common yet either) and admit that I didn't know why I was calling.

I was wrong. No explanations were necessary. I wasn't in control, and here was proof that it was the Higher Power leading me.

My old friend answered on the first ring. He said, "What took you so long, Gail? I've been expecting your call for an hour. I know you are in a real battle over there by Lake Erie."

I sucked in my breath and was about to speak when he continued.

"I have the number for the New York State Department of Agriculture," he said. "If you call it right now, the secretary of agriculture will answer because his office manager doesn't come in until eight o'clock. He'll help you with the agricultural aspects of this paper mill intrusion into the largest juice grape– growing region in the country." He proceeded to give me the number.

"I'm speechless. How did you know about this?"

"It's my job," he said. "I'm involved with the local farm bureau. I keep up on these things. Just call the number I gave you, and this man will help you. Good luck, and stop and have a cup of coffee with my wife and me."

Those overpowering feelings I got were always right. I

needed to learn to trust them immediately. I couldn't do all these things on my own. That call is how a complete grape study was ordered for the EIS.

Some of the other findings in the EIS were as follows: The discharge stacks for the pollutants from the manufacturing process would be at the same height as the school and hospital windows. An engineering study listed the rules for discharge stacks. The ones that were planned would be so low that they would not protect the school and hospital air quality.

Ironically, the politicians had offered to build a wellness track around the paper mill perimeter for people with pulmonary diseases. "Was that so people with weak lungs could enjoy the high pollution and particulate matter in the air?" Mirror asked.

In another aspect of the study, the intake and discharge filters, screens, temperatures, and velocities were examined, and the discharge down Spring Creek—the registered, numbered waterway that traversed my farm and proposed fish farming enterprise—was projected to be three hundred degrees, with the velocity to scour the sides of the creek and kill any wildlife therein.

There were many, many more problems. Our small group found a letter from our county economic development team asking a local grape-processing facility to overlook any problems in the grape industry in exchange for the sewer plant upgrades they would enjoy. A vice president of that company agreed, and the Master Planner made sure we had the letter confirming the company's cooperation.

We also found that the water table on the proposed development site was only six inches below the surface. When we questioned that fact, we were called "economic development terrorists."

All those happenings indicated that a fish farm would

struggle down water from a factory processing used cardboard for the Canadian chemical industry. As a farmer I was well aware that chemical packaging was contaminated packaging. I couldn't imagine cooking up unknown varieties of contaminated cardboard and discharging the water and steam into our community and Lake Erie, which would receive those polluted discharges.

With the finding of the Supreme Court and the completion of the EIS, the paper mill abandoned its plan to build in our town.

Mirror was elated. A battle had been won, but the war was far from over. I became a target for blame.

Chapter Nineteen: Retribution

My pond contractor knocked on my door to ask me to come and check his finished work and okay the placement of the overflow.

We stood admiring his finished work on the new, still empty pond. The drainpipe was through the dike, the overflow pipe was in the deepest part of the pond, the peninsula was finished, and the graded slopes inside and outside the dike were perfect. There were no problems. The finished pond was the key to bringing this fish farming operation to fruition.

At that moment two police cars raced into my farm's driveway with their lights and sirens demanding attention. I couldn't imagine what officers of the law were doing on my farm.

Strutting, self-important officials yelled, "Stop. Cease and desist. This is an order. You will be fined for every day this machinery is on-site."

The legal document was duly served on me, and I told the young bulldozer owner-operator to take his machine home and then come to the house, and I would pay him. The pond was done anyway. The final payment brought the total price of the new pond excavation to $10,000. It was a far cry from $100,000, and for that I thanked the Master Planner.

The legal notice said I could not fill the finished pond with water. State authorities had declared that I was building that pond in wetlands without a permit. I wondered, Didn't they know that farming fish was a type of agriculture and exempt from the permitting process?

This sort of reminded me of the mink farm fiasco that had begun with the "cease and desist" order from an elected town board a long time ago. I hadn't thought of that in eons, but as I grabbed my phone book for the numbers of the agencies advising me, I remembered the full event in detail. Now I fully understood the sickening, unnecessary frustration my dad had felt, caused by the power and greed of overzealous small-town politicians. Not much had changed in approximately forty years.

First I called my advisor, the university professor, who was directing and instructing me on the fish farming operation. At his suggestion, as I remember, I called one of several state permitting agencies. Within an hour, because we both had topo maps, the man on the phone determined that the pond was *not* in a wetland. He further said, "What is the problem anyway? You are creating wonderful wetland habitat. I would think everyone would be thrilled. Is it possible that someone is harassing you for some reason?"

I explained the situation over the paper mill. Even though the idea, business plan, and implementation for my fish farm were flawless, I had not counted on crooked, mean-spirited, self-serving, get-even politicians who would attempt to foil my endeavor.

Weeks later, Mirror reflected the disbelief in my eyes as the powers in control won the battle. The pond stood empty and useless, and the fish farming dream ended as a nightmare.

I said aloud, "Don't worry, Mirror. They may have won this battle, but the war goes on and on. I have the Master Planner directing me. I'll be okay."

The pond sat empty for several years. The Sugar Shack fruit syrup business replaced the fish farming dream. Sure enough, the Master Planner worked to steer me toward a different goal. Those passing by on the interstate highway viewed the empty pond as a large crater. Local kids with four-wheelers and neighbors with snowmobiles used it as part of their trail rides. I told the story countless times to people from everywhere when they visited my shop.

The town fathers felt justified. If they couldn't have a stinking, dirty, polluting paper mill adjacent to their school and hospital, with smokestacks at less than good engineering height, spewing out contaminants not fit to breathe and creating an unhealthy environment for the grape industry, then I couldn't have a pond and fish farming business. They couldn't imagine any personal gain from helping the struggling walleye population in Lake Erie. They could not comprehend that fishing and tourism would bring untethered dollars into our struggling community.

The Sugar Shack gift shop became a stage upon which to share and learn many lessons. People visited from near and far and from all walks of life. They told horror stories about self-serving politicians and economic development scams in their own towns across this great nation. They confirmed the need for people to question, educate themselves, and seek motives when politics and money were involved.

It was time for me to examine my current situation, learn from past experiences, and move forward in my business life while I watched for more political snakes in the underbrush.

CHAPTER TWENTY: SUGAR SHACK AND ADVERTISING

I HAD ACQUIRED FARMS in a contiguous strip between the paper mill site and Lake Erie. That was a major problem for the economic developers because there is a law protecting against eminent domain in agricultural districts in New York State. Therefore, my farms had been in the way of the paper mill's need for a Lake Erie water supply and wastewater disposal. I had also refused to be bought off by the developers when the paper mill promoters offered me $785,000 for my farm with the agreement that I would shut up and go away the day the paper mill started operation.

I had been an outspoken leader of the opposition to the paper mill, and the townspeople had been made to believe that I was responsible for their loss of the 132 promised paper mill jobs. It was generally believed that I had stolen their opportunity for economic success.

I was asked to leave public meetings, thrown out of a chamber of commerce meeting, and snubbed in the grocery store—all that on top of the pond issue. It was okay. In fact,

I told Mirror, "It's an honor to be able to stand up for what's right and win the fight, and even if there is retribution, at least I know I did what I believed was right for the health of Lake Erie and my community."

Mirror smiled.

The unsettling part was that there were twenty-seven other folks in the same camp who were oftentimes smarter, better planners and harder workers in the battle against the paper mill. They didn't seem to be the target of any paybacks. In most cases their lives went on without incident.

The one exception was a licensed engineer who had dissected the engineering studies and broken them down so that the rest of our small group would understand them. He also had been active with public speaking and letter writing in the environmental review process. He was targeted financially and in many of the same ways that I was. He suffered a heart attack that many of us believed was from the stress. I lost only the prestige of serving on some committees and boards of directors. I was no longer needed to lead the local cancer drive, and I was discarded, along with my opinions, as a director for the local town counseling service. But in the master plan, I can now see that the loss of those volunteer jobs freed up a lot more time for me to pursue the fruit syrup business.

Soon after the win in the state supreme court, the other targeted businessperson suggested that I start to make and sell fruit syrups. He is one of the angels in my memoir *Asses and Angels.* The Sugar Shack was born against all odds and all my beliefs. Even Mirror was a bit skeptical. The original building, the little shed where I produced maple syrup and later used as a sales room, was torn down, and a new addition to my barn was built. I was offering my value-added, farm-raised fruits as syrups for pancakes and more. I also sold our maple products in the new addition.

Then I had another idea. The Master Planner allowed me to see the need to add Lake Erie shoreline tours to the farm and wildflower walk. The teaching and learning aspect of the Sugar Shack now included visual and verbal lessons on Lake Erie's waters, including an expanded knowledge of water depths of the Great Lakes and other local lakes. My tour guests were curious and enthralled by the knowledge of the source of the water flowing past my house and its destination and effect on climate and culture in our area. Some lessons were difficult, some were fun, and all of them were educational. The lessons in my life continued.

Chapter Twenty-One: Glass Bottle Crisis

THE FLEDGLING SUGAR SHACK fruit syrup business was booming. I could hardly keep up with picking fruit, making product, printing labels, and selling fruit syrups. I was flying high.

I bragged to Mirror, "I'm a genius. I get my bottles free because I'm not afraid to work hard. I just go to the local colleges, hospitals, and every place there are juice vending machines and pick up the used glass bottles from the garbage cans. It's not much work to wash and sterilize them, and they are free!"

"Oh, stop it. You just never learn. You get so stuck on yourself that you forget that the higher you fly, the farther you fall." Mirror glared and looked disgusted as the words of wisdom flowed out of the reflecting glass.

"That's all you know, Mirror. Take a good look at me, and you'll see a very smart businesswoman on her way to the top with free glass bottles she saved from the landfill. I'm off to make my rounds gathering them right now. See you later," I bragged as I slammed the front door shut.

The truck radio was blasting out some great country music

as I pulled up at the local state university's juice machine. I jumped out in a flash, a five-gallon pail on each arm, like I'd been doing for three years, eager to get the used empties and move on to other local vending machines for more.

Something was wrong. The machine was in a slightly different place, and it looked kind of funny. I grabbed the huge waste container to pull it toward the truck and nearly fell backward. It was light. I had expected it to be heavy with glass bottles. To my horror, there were fewer than a dozen glass bottles, and all the rest were plastic. The same scenario repeated at all my recycling locations. Glass bottles were to become a thing of the past. Didn't these juice makers realize that plastic bottles were not impervious? Didn't they know that plastic bottles were made from crude oil? Didn't they know that plastic contributed to the carcinogens in our environment? Didn't they care?

Mirror saw the horror on my face when I raced in the door soon after I'd left. "Aha, I told you not to be so smug and self-assured. What happened?" Mirror asked.

"Just listen, and you'll hear the whole story when I get this juice plant manager on the phone. Then I won't have to repeat it all to you and tolerate your superior attitude about being right all the time," I growled as I waited for the ringing to stop and the secretary to connect me.

Once the pleasantries were finally finished, the real conversation began. "Sir, my name is Gail Black, and I noticed that your company has changed from bottling in glass to bottling in ten-ounce plastic bottles. I'll get right to the point here. I make a fruit syrup product to sell on my farm, and I collect and sanitize your used glass bottles. I use them for bottling maple syrup as well as the fruit products I sell. When I went to collect them, I saw that some of your vending machines now contain plastic bottles. Will you have any glass bottles leftover when you complete the changeover to plastic?"

The volume was turned up on the speakerphone when he answered, so that I could hear him as I paced around the kitchen table to relieve my worries. "Well now, Miss Gail, it will be a full year before the changeover is completed. Why do you ask?"

"I am interested in buying whatever glass you have left," I replied. "Will you please keep my name and phone number on your desk and call me when you know a time frame?"

"I will, Miss Gail. Do you think you will still be interested a year from now?" he queried.

"Sir, my little business depends on those glass bottles, and I sure hope I'll still need some in a year. Thank you for your time, and please call me," I pleaded.

Mirror was just waiting to discourage me. "Oh, Miss Smarty-Pants, you're the eternal optimist, aren't you? You know he'll throw away your name and number and laugh while he does it."

"We'll see," I whispered as I thought, *I'm a farmer. I planted a seed. If I didn't plant it, nothing would grow. If I plant it, there is always a chance.*

Chapter Twenty-Two: Phone Call

A YEAR LATER, ALMOST to the day, I answered the phone, and a man asked, "Is this Miss Gail?"

My heart skipped some beats as I caught my breath. "Yes. And I bet this is a man with some glass bottles." I punched the speakerphone button so Mirror couldn't miss the call.

"Miss Gail, I did as you asked and put that scrap of paper with your name and number on it under a glass paperweight on my desk. I have glass bottles. Do you still want them?"

"Yes, I do. I'll take them. How many do you have, and how much do you want for them?" I asked, naive as I was.

"I'll answer your questions in reverse order. We're going to landfill them, and whatever it would cost us to do that is what we will charge you. I have 120,000 bottles. Unfortunately, you would have to take them all and be responsible for removing them from our warehouse immediately or within a couple of weeks at least," he said.

I began frantically figuring how many bottles I had used the first, second, third, and now fourth year I was in business. There was an increase of about 25 percent each year. I was multiplying and figuring how many years it would take me to use 120,000 bottles.

Mirror knew that without the bottles my business was doomed. I was done. I couldn't continue and use plastic. I didn't believe that my product would stay stable in plastic. I had complained about the plastic jugs I filled with maple syrup because they smelled of the plastic when the hot syrup filled them. I was sure that chemicals were leached into the syrup. I hated plastic. I used pints, quarts, half gallons, and gallons in glass for maple products when I could. Mirror was watching me closely as I frantically figured and planned.

Finally, the man on the phone said, "Are you still there?"

"Yes, yes, I'm still here. I was just doing some calculating. Yes, I want all of them. You said I have two weeks to get them. Could you possibly give me a month? I have to arrange transportation and storage, and I believe I'll need that long at the maximum. I don't want to mislead you and miss a deadline."

"Thank you for your honesty. I'll make the arrangements and get you a final price, Miss Gail. Good luck with your business venture. You're a brave woman," he said as he ended the call.

Mirror yelled, "Brave? Hell no! You're just plain stupid. Do you have any idea what 120,000 bottles look like? Your barn is full of tractors and equipment. Where are you going to put them, under your bed?"

I ignored the comments. I was already looking in the phone book for trucking companies. I knew Mirror was right. I had no storage. I could, however, buy a used over-the-road trailer, have it filled, and park it beside the already full barn.

The next two days were filled with phone calls to salvage companies as I tried to find a roadworthy trailer. Finally, I found one 250 miles away that would make the trip to the juice plant. Then I found a fellow farmer with a licensed tractor who would haul the trailer loaded with glass to my farm. I calculated that I would be able to bottle my products in glass until I was seventy-five years old. I would not have to buy any more bottles.

The arrangements were made, and the fun began.

Chapter Twenty-Three: The Haul

THE SALVAGE COMPANY DELIVERED the trailer to the loading docks of the juice plant. The license was valid for one more week. The title came the same day the trailer was loaded, and the farmer showed up on time with his Kenworth to haul the forty-eight-foot trailer loaded with glass to my farm. I went to watch the loading and hauling. The glass bottles were on pallets about four feet square and were layered with thin cardboard to a height of approximately eight feet. They were packed solidly into the trailer with no room to spare. Not one bottle was damaged in transit, and we set the trailer in place on my property. I anticipated that it would be a tricky maneuver to unload a pallet at a time with my forklift. It was, but I did.

The problem occurred when the juice company pointed out that a dozen pallets hadn't fit in the trailer and insisted that I remove them to my farm immediately. Soon I had my pickup attached to the trailer I used to haul thousand-gallon tanks of maple sap. I had ratchet straps from my harvesting business, and off I went to make the first of several trips to retrieve the remaining glass.

I had four pallets of 5,500 bottles each strapped down four

ways as I pulled that trailer home. There would be three more trips, and I was congratulating myself on my ingenuity and resourcefulness. I was so proud that I could haul the glass home and unload it with my forklift, by myself. After all, I thought, I was only five feet tall and weighed only ninety-five pounds. I was almost sixty years old and pretty damned proud. I didn't need a man to succeed. Then I heard the siren and saw the red flashing lights. It was me getting pulled over.

I knew I'd had it; I was caught. I looked down at the speedometer, and it said I was doing seventy in a fifty-five mile-per-hour speed zone. I pulled to the side of the road, and the young officer approached, ticket book in hand.

"Miss, do you know why I am stopping you?"

"Yes, sir. I was probably speeding, but I don't know why because I had the cruise control set at sixty," I answered honestly, knowing full well that my mind had been on something other than my driving.

"That's one reason, but the other reason is that you have an unsafe load. You are hauling glass, and if you have an accident, there will be glass all over the highway, and others could be hurt. You can't haul glass on an open trailer. I'm going to write you up for that along with the speeding," he said with a superior edge to his voice.

"I beg your pardon, sir, but I don't believe there is any such law covering farm products. My load is wrapped in plastic with heavy strapping on each pallet. I have secured the pallets four ways with ratchet straps, and the load is safe," I said.

"Miss, don't tell me how to do my job. I said your load is unsafe. Therefore, it is unsafe, and I will ticket you. End of story."

I was suddenly hot. I was mad. "Sir, with all due respect, please turn so that I can copy down your badge number. I also would like to have your supervisor's name. I see this as harassment of a farm business. I have orange triangles on my trailer to identify that it is part of a farm business."

"My badge number is not your concern, miss. You do not need my supervisor's name. Stay in your vehicle while I write your speeding ticket. I'll cut you a break and let you finish your trip with the glass this time. However, if you break this glass on the highway, I'll see that you pay for the cleanup," he snarled.

I didn't need a speeding ticket. I assessed the situation. This cop did not have a sense of humor or an ounce of kindness that I could see. I instantly decided to test my judgment and people-reading skills.

As he started to walk to his car, I was ready to lay the truth on him and see what happened. "Sir, would you like to know why I was speeding at seventy miles an hour?"

The young, surly, sour officer pivoted on the heel of his shiny black shoes and glared at me. "There's nothing further for you to say that will change things, but I would like to know why an old woman with a truck and a trailer full of glass would be speeding."

"Well, you see, I had the cruise control set at sixty, like I told you a minute ago. I had to pass some gas, and it just wouldn't happen. I lifted one cheek of my ass, pushed real hard, and finally farted. When that happened, I must have pushed down on the gas pedal with my right foot."

The poor young man threw his hands up in the air, dropped his head, dropped his ticket book, and said, "Go on your way."

I did, with a smile on my face.

The Sugar Shack became a stable part of my existence. It developed a life of its own. It demanded a certain amount of commitment and time every day, which gave structure and purpose to an otherwise chaotic time that involved one crisis after another.

Chapter Twenty-Four: Advertising

No business endeavor can succeed without advertising. When the Sugar Shack opened, I put an ugly homemade sign at the end of the driveway. It was directly above one that said "WORMS," which had been stuck in the ground for years. At the bottom of the new sign were the words "FREE TASTING."

Soon a new customer arrived at the door and said, "I had to drive in and see this place. I never saw a business that offered free tastings of worms."

As soon as I was finished with the free tasting of fruit syrups, I hurried up the driveway and down the road, where I turned around and approached my signs. Sure enough, as I drove along, the signs appeared to say, "FREE TASTING, WORMS." I immediately became acutely aware of roadside advertising.

Mirror offered a suggestion. "Go buy a large container of gummy worms to add to your tasting menu. You need to find some humor in everything you do. Don't be so serious. If you'd taken me up the driveway to look at the approach to that sign, I'd have seen it. Just keep on thinking you are so smart, smarty-pants."

I laughed. What I learned was that most signs had too much

information on them to be read and absorbed at fifty-five miles per hour. Immediately, I moved the signs farther apart.

It was interesting to me, in hindsight, that I had that experience just a few weeks before I was offered the opportunity to buy the twenty-foot by eighty-foot billboard sign that was located on my farm near the empty pond from the failed fish farm. Such signs are known as "boards" in the advertising industry.

When that farm along the interstate highway had been offered to me at a much-reduced price because the owner had died and left that request in his will, I had become more aware of the large billboard on the property. The closing papers had included a lease agreement with a man from Ohio, who owned a sign company and had boards in several states. After I purchased the farm, he soon stopped at my house to discuss his lease agreement for the land where the sign was located. I offered him a slice of fresh elderberry pie as we talked.

He savored the pie and enjoyed a cup of freshly brewed coffee. "Do you know anyone who might be interested in overseeing the installation of new ad copy on the board?" he asked. "I need someone who might want to keep track of the seven large lights that illuminate that sign at night and who would cut the brush and wild grapevines that keep growing on the structure."

"I can do that," I volunteered before Mirror could advise me one way or another. "I'm always working on that farm, and those things won't take up much time."

"I'll increase the lease payment by fifty percent and visit you once a year, provided you have elderberry pie each time," he offered with a smile.

The following year, I served him another piece of elderberry pie, and he said, "I have to tell you how I came to install that board on your farm in the first place. I own boards all across Pennsylvania, Ohio, Indiana, and Illinois, and as I was driving on this interstate highway, I noticed the long view across the fields of grapes and tomatoes and decided to exit and check out those fields. I met the property owner, signed a lease agreement, and spent the night in a motel. The next day, as luck would have it, there was a town board of directors meeting, so I stayed. I spent the day preparing my presentation and then applied for a permit to erect the billboard.

"The town supervisor and board of trustees granted me the permit on the spot. I was really excited about a new board and its location in advance of the state line and development there. It was a perfect location. It was fantastic. I immediately began construction plans and hiring. It wasn't long before the contractor was on-site, digging holes and installing the framework. I came out from Ohio to check on the work, and while I was standing there talking with my contractor, the local police car came screaming up the road, lights and siren going full blast. The mayor and police chief bolted out of the car, papers in hand, yelling, 'Stop the work right now! Get those men down off that structure. The town supervisor and the board made a mistake, and you can't build that sign in our town. We'll fine you if you continue.'"

I made a mental note that those were almost the same words that had been spoken to me over the pond excavation, except that it was a farm pond and exempt from needing a permit under agricultural law. "What did you do?" I asked.

He looked over the top of his glasses with raised eyebrows. "I said, 'Gentlemen, cool down. Put your paperwork away. You can't just change your minds, especially after all the paperwork is filed with the county clerk and the work has begun.'"

"What then?" I asked.

"Well, the police chief threatened to arrest me, and I laughed at him. He got back in the car and turned off his attention getters, and he and the mayor left after telling me I'd not heard the last from them. The whole deal went to court, and they lost. I never quit working on the board, and here we are. For some reason I thought you might find that story amusing."

I was blown away by the similarities between his story from thirty years ago, which included threats, bullying, and attempted misuse of power, and my own recent experience with police cars and officials. It amounted to the same method of operation, just a different project, day, and year.

A few years passed, and the Sugar Shack grew along with my custom farming business and vineyard acquisitions. I was considering some options to reduce my workload when the billboard owner called.

"I'm getting old," he said. "I'm calling to tell you that I'm selling all my boards in New York and Pennsylvania, and I want you to buy the one on your farm. A commercial sign company is buying all of them except that one. I pulled it out of the package because you need to have it."

"Oh, Harold," I said, "I don't know a thing about the billboard sign business. I don't really think I want that sign."

"Not so fast," he said. "You need that sign for your new fruit syrup business. Knowing those power-hungry politicians in your town, it might be the only sign you'll be allowed to have. You really need it. Trust me on this one."

Mirror was on high alert, with familiar whispers of hope and suggestions. "Ask for details. Get the price and annual costs."

"How much do you want for the sign, Harold?" I asked, only because Mirror was glaring at me as I looked into the reflection.

"I've thought about that, and I want you to have it. I'm willing to hold your hand, so to speak, and teach you how to market the sign. I'll connect you with my advertising company in Tennessee. I've already talked to the gal who handles all my accounts, and she will personally guide and teach you for two years. I want two years' rent from you. That means that you won't be getting your usual check from me, and you'll owe me the income you receive on it from renters for the next two years."

"I'll get back to you in a couple of days, sir," I said, stalling.

Mirror was reflective and anxious as I hung up the phone. "You just keep falling into it and coming out smelling like spring sunshine. Call the farm lending folks and borrow the money. Pay the man and seal the deal before he changes his mind or kicks the bucket."

I made the call, and the check arrived the next day. I spoke with Harold, and when I hung up the phone, I owned a billboard sign facing the westbound lane of the interstate. He was happy to have his money up front, and two years later, I had the loan paid.

I received a very good education in outdoor advertising. The most important fact I learned was that ten words was the maximum that people could read and absorb at seventy miles per hour when they passed a sign. My two years of help from my friend's marketing company went by, and then I had to find my own clients needing signage on the interstate. I continued to hire the painters to keep the copy on the board up-to-date, and I took care of all the other maintenance chores.

My friend Harold kept in touch and had one more suggestion. "Gail, call the state authorities and explore the possibility of being included in their attractions signage program. It's duplication but also insurance. Believe me, repetition in advertising helps name recognition. You need to do it."

Three years later, a representative from a local chain restaurant contacted me. "I really need that sign because our eatery in town is not visible from the interstate, and we feel we are missing a lot of business. It would be great for the village if we could entice interstate traffic to exit and visit the downtown commercial area."

We struck a deal and signed a contract, and I had the board face repainted with the restaurant's logo. However, there was a problem. When cars exited the interstate, there was no further directional sign. Traffic didn't automatically flow to the establishment because travelers didn't even know where the nearest town was.

The restaurant's spokesperson was disappointed, but I remembered studying state and local sign ordinances a few years before. I hadn't understood the need for that knowledge back then and was surprised that it was important now. All the events seemed to be like jigsaw puzzle pieces. I never could have planned how using my custom farming business could affect my billboard sign business years and years later. I was benefiting from the experiences of someone else, and the education was free.

Mirror, of course, had to point out that another diamond in my backyard was being mined. "Miss Smarty-Pants, this is just another example of recognizing, weighing the pros and cons, and then acting on opportunities as they materialize. I notice you don't let many slip by you."

Mirror was just as surprised as I was when the next situation presented itself. I was about to use past lessons to solve a present problem in this merry-go-round of unforeseen events.

CHAPTER TWENTY-FIVE: THE IMPORTANCE OF INSURANCE

APRIL 1 IS ALWAYS a chance to have a bit of fun. Laughter encourages a positive outlook in life and business. On this fun day, getting the best of my boys is always challenging. There are times we play pretty rough, and sometimes they win. There have been years when I've lost track of time, and Fool's Day has sneaked up on me.

It was just such a day when my son offered to conduct a tour of our maple syrup–making operation for a family from San Antonio, Texas. The car with Texas plates came slowly down the driveway on that misty Monday morning just as my insurance agent arrived to go over all my policies. I was at the kitchen table with car insurance, liability insurance, product insurance, business and property insurance, and even health insurance papers stacked high. I had a long list of questions. The cost was increasing every year. I wanted answers and ideas about how to cut costs without jeopardizing my financial liability. I was curious about wind insurance, earthquake coverage, flood and fire, theft and vandalism, and lots more.

My insurance man was unpacking his briefcase and rubbing his hands with anticipation about the fat check I would write before he left. I was pouring him a cup of coffee, reminding myself to be nice and polite. Premium increases were standard practice every year. It was difficult to be complacent when the insurance industry was intent on depleting my checkbook balance. I wanted protection against risk, but only reasonable protection. I didn't want to be frightened and coerced into buying coverage against scary and highly improbable risks.

Mirror kept whispering, "Be a lady and try to be reasonable and polite. His agenda is to sell you all the insurance he can talk you into buying. Yours is to keep the cost affordable. Stay calm, Miss Smarty-Pants. Don't be a know-it-all hothead."

We began with the business insurance, and we were discussing coverage on the physical building, including the equipment and processing supplies housed therein. I had the actual numbers; the insurance agent had only projections and scary scenarios.

Suddenly, the front door burst open, and my son yelled, "Insurance man, come quick. The garbage truck just took out the barn and the Sugar Shack."

I hadn't heard any crash or rumble or the hollow thumps of the dumpster being emptied. I'd just looked at an estimate paper and noticed that the current date was April 1, so I said, "Yeah right, son. Happy April Fool's Day to you too."

"No, no, come quick. I'm telling you, the garbage truck hit the barn. It's still there, and the barn is broken. The Texas folks thought it was an earthquake. They ran out of the sugar house and left," he said, talking fast and animatedly.

I walked to the front door to look out, expecting to see nothing, but there was the gigantic garbage truck stopped at the corner of the cement-block building that houses my business. I gasped. The insurance man then walked out to have a look. Sure enough, the stinking truck was just sitting there. We made our way across the parking lot and saw that the truck's boom was against the very corner of the structure's roof overhang. The driver just sat there, stunned.

"Oh my God," I said, "the cement blocks are all cracked and broken, and there goes a bird flying through an opening."

My insurance agent looked shocked and in disbelief. Suddenly, he realized the reality of the situation. "I've got to get my camera. We need pictures of this." When he returned, he began snapping photographs immediately, from every angle, and he circled the still stationary truck. He took picture after picture of the boom against the building and the broken blocks that looked like stair steps. Then he noticed that the whole roof had been knocked back a few inches and was just barely hanging on the block walls.

The truck driver hadn't moved, but as his picture was being taken at an angle that showed him, the truck, and the damage, he suddenly realized what was taking place. He put the vehicle in gear and roared away.

Closer examination revealed a leaning chimney, falling pieces of mortar and cement, broken doorjambs, broken windows, and some product knocked off sales shelves. The shingles were rumpled up on the back side of the roof. The steam stacks from our new maple syrup evaporator were leaning precariously to the east.

We made our way back to the business of insurance policy renewals at the kitchen table. The coffee was cold. The Texas customers had fled in fear. The truck driver also had fled in fear. There had been no accident report or driver's license information gathered. I said, "I'm going to call the sheriff's department and get an officer here to file an accident report.

That driver left the scene of a major accident, and there is extensive damage."

Mirror, who hardly ever swears, said, "Holy shit!"

The insurance agent called the company that owned the trash business and informed the owner.

"I wondered why the driver parked the truck before his route was done," said the owner. "He came in the door, threw the keys on the desk, and left without saying a word."

The agent smiled. He didn't have to invent any scary scenarios to justify the increased cost of insurance or the inflated premiums or come up with reasons to expand my business coverage. The garbage truck incident had taken care of all the fear he didn't need to invent. This fear was in my face. It was real. He asked, "Aren't you glad you have full coverage, including your inventory?"

Six months later, he had proven his worth. I had learned another valuable lesson. He had handled all the negotiations with the garbage company, fought for the money to pay for emptying and storing the contents of my business, and recovered the loss of income during the time it took for the completion of repairs. Finally, I had a stonemason on the premises, and the birds were no longer able to build nests inside my business. The bonus was acquiring a new friend when the local owner of the trash business did all he could to make the accident right.

Mirror and I just braced ourselves for the next episode in the life of an entrepreneur. We wouldn't have to wait very long.

CHAPTER TWENTY-SIX: SIGNS

As I REMEMBER IT, I received a call from a local businessman. He asked, "Mrs. Black, do you still do custom farming?"

"I do," I answered.

"I have a tiny triangular vineyard, not an acre altogether. It's across from the interstate exit. It's small, but I need someone to take care of it. Would you be interested?"

I didn't agree immediately. Mirror was always eavesdropping on my phone conversations and had some advice. "Check out the sign laws and find out if you can put a farm sign right there across from the exit. If you're farming that little vineyard, I think you qualify for a sign there. You probably don't even need a permit."

After doing some investigation and reading the local sign ordinances, I was told that I could legally erect a sign with directions to my businesses, which included the Sugar Shack. There was synergy in all my businesses, it seemed. Soon I had contacted all the controlling, permitting agencies, and my sign was in place. It directed traffic away from the nearby downtown center of commerce.

I assembled all the paperwork, facts, and ideas and called

the chain restaurant rep. "Sir, I believe I have a solution that will bring the thruway traffic to your restaurant. I believe you need to attach your logo with an arrow pointing to your location at the bottom of my new sign across from the interstate exit."

Soon the logo was in place, and I expected that the village and town fathers would be appreciative. They should be thrilled to have a free boost in advertising that would send hundreds of cars into their downtown shopping area. I even fantasized that the chamber of commerce would call to thank me. Ha. Not.

Instead, some of the chamber of commerce members and town board members began to complain about my sign at the interstate exit. Because it had been very successful, other businesses had installed expensive, attractive signage of their own. There were now signs advertising restaurants, gas stations, lodgings, convenience stores, and more. To me and many other businesspeople, it was an indication of a growing economy in our local community.

"Flabbergasted" doesn't begin to describe my surprise when the local building inspector cruised down my driveway in a cloud of dust. He jumped from his car and breathlessly declared, "Mrs. Black, I need a check for twenty-five dollars."

"Okay, Tom, I'll go get my checkbook, but what is this for?" I inquired.

"I'm privy to a lot of meetings, and I hear a lot of stuff," he said. "Gail, you and I haven't always agreed on all that I do and require, but you've always treated me well, and we've always come to mutually satisfactory agreements. The powers that be aren't through with you yet. They're still mad and blame you for losing the paper mill. I believe your sign at the thruway exit is their next target. I want to be absolutely sure it is legally permitted. You don't really need the permit, but it's insurance for you," he said.

"Tom, thank you. Why would you take your time to look out for me? I appreciate your cooperative attitude ... but why?"

"I wasn't going to tell you, but I'm terminally ill. I don't have long, and I like the honest way you conduct your business. That's one reason. And I believe the signs are good for the business community on Main Street. I also believe in doing the right thing. That's all. Oh yeah, one more unsolicited suggestion for you, Gail: Get your business listed on the interstate's attraction board, both east- and westbound. It will be harder for the locals to control that, and it would hit both directions of travel."

I wrote the check and shortly thereafter received a letter confirming what Tom had said during his visit, including his belief that the local reigning political powers wanted to put me out of business. He died about a week later. One more angel had gone to his reward.

Remembering that my sign mentor, Harold, had given me similar advice about the attractions board, I contacted the interstate authorities and set the process in motion to become an attraction at the nearby exit. I met most of the criteria since I was only one mile from the exit and practiced the required hours of operation. The few, but expensive, remaining adjustments I needed could be accomplished as soon as the permit was approved. The cost of making the signs plus the yearly rental fee of eight hundred dollars brought the price tag to over three thousand dollars, but the cost was worthwhile when I considered the safety net it afforded my fledgling business. It also followed the idea of repetitive advertising in business name recognition.

My Sugar Shack business listing on the interstate attractions sign reduced the stress I felt when the next bomb was dropped by the local politicians.

Chapter Twenty-Seven: Common Sense in Advertising

IT WAS NO SURPRISE when the local chapter of the chamber and the town board suggested that all the signs at the thruway exit were ugly. The building inspector had warned me.

A member of one of the planning committees had taken a trip out of state and presented a new idea of beautification in roadside advertising for our town. The planning committee member described the idea in a presentation to the town board, saying, "We need to remove all those individual signs across from the interstate exit. I saw a wonderful way to advertise local business on my recent trip down south. It was a tall treated post with hand-cut arrows attached helter-skelter, and each arrow had the name of a business printed on it. The individual arrows pointed in the direction of those businesses. Instead of a half dozen individual signs, it was uniform and equal. The signs across from the local exit now are all different colors and sizes. They are unequal, and I think they look messy."

The town supervisor and board members all nodded in agreement.

I remember listening in amazement. I had tried to discuss this sign issue with individual chamber and town board members who had no comprehension of the purpose of roadside advertising. I asked to speak.

"A signpost with a business name on an arrow is not a substitute for a descriptive business sign," I said. "First, let me tell you my definition of a good sign. It should contain minimal but pertinent information. Second, that information should be a snapshot of the business it depicts. That snapshot should entice the traveling public to visit that specific business."

Some board members crossed their arms over their chests or behind their heads or leaned back in their chairs. One executed a fake yawn and closed his eyes. Another said, "A signpost with the name of a business on a directional arrow is all we need." He looked at the planning committee member and said, "Thank you for this terrific idea. We'll see that those hodgepodge signs are removed." He and the planning committee member smiled and nodded at each other, and the town board thought the issue was settled.

I wasn't about to let it go. "Case in point—you want to put up an arrow pointing to the right, and you want to print 'Sugar Shack' on it?"

"Yes. One that says 'Drive-In' and one that says 'Sugar Shack' and so forth," the town supervisor said in a condescending, irritated voice.

I continued to hold my ground. "With all due respect, do you think the traveling public will automatically know what the drive-in or Sugar Shack is? Will they think the drive-in is a band, a movie, or a hot dog stand? Do any of you even know what a sugar shack is in a midwestern city?"

Several board members shook their heads.

"It's a whorehouse. But here, and all over the northeast, it's a maple syrup operation."

There was stunned silence. The board members were all awake and at full attention now.

"To make my point clear, a roadside sign should be a snapshot of the business it represents, which entices passersby to visit that business. It should not be a generic arrow with a name on it, mixed in with a lot of other arrows pointing every which way, with names that have meaning only to local residents. I believe the idea here is to attract tourist dollars, which are more valuable to our economy."

The sign controversy surfaced every now and then over the next few years. Then one day I received a registered letter from a state agency directing me to remove my sign from a state road at the interstate highway exit in our town. I called the town offices, and they claimed to have no knowledge of that action.

My next call was to the main office of that state agency in Albany. After working my way up the chain of command, I connected with someone in authority. I asked why the letter had been sent, how much time I had to comply, and what the consequences of noncompliance would be. Finally, I asked, "Were duplicate letters sent to all the other sign owners at this particular location, as well as every location where such a proliferation of signs appears along the length of the interstate?"

The supervisor said, "Mrs. Black, the letter was sent to you because we received a complaint about your sign."

"Who complained?" I asked.

"I can't disclose specific names. I will tell you that all the other sign owners at your exit, in your town, received letters too. You'll all be fined for noncompliance. The letters were sent only to your local exit."

"Why is it illegal to install and display business signs at our exit and not at all exits on the interstate?" I asked.

"We only enforce the code or law when asked to do so by local officials or the interstate authority. In this case, a local official wanted the signs taken down."

"What local official?" I asked.

"Look," the authority said in a frustrated, impatient voice, "I don't make the rules, and I don't do the enforcing. I can only tell you that my paperwork says, 'She doesn't like the signs, thinks they are ugly.' That is why you all got the letters. The local official doesn't like the signs and thinks they are messy, not uniform. Good day." The official hung up on me.

My next call was to my state assemblyman. He was very understanding and took a few weeks to investigate the situation while driving to and from the state capitol and checking other exits. He reported that there were individual business signs at almost all the exits. He stated that he was frustrated with local political muscle, especially when it hampered business growth in our state.

I spoke to some of the other sign owners, and together we determined that at that time there were very few female officials for miles around. All of them vehemently denied making a call to the department of transportation for the purpose of removing our signs.

Newspaper articles appeared in local papers, and all elected and appointed officials immediately pledged their help. There were no further articles or reports of efforts to remove the signs. The signs remained for a time. The issue seemed to be resolved, or at least in a neutral holding state of existence.

Chapter Twenty-Eight: Political Muscle at Its Worst

THE SUGAR SHACK PANCAKE restaurant I started years ago to promote and use my homemade fruit syrups was running smoothly on Saturday and Sunday mornings. Our business was drawing in customers from cities across a two-hundred-mile radius. We trained our waitresses and staff to encourage folks to put a star on our wall maps indicating their hometown. We asked each person paying their bill to sign a guest book.

The experience was confirmation of how one small business like ours could draw tourism from other areas and then encourage that clientele to shop and spend time in our town and county. We offered tourism information and suggestions to all who would listen. We gave away dozens, perhaps hundreds, of county vacation guides and brochures from other local businesses. We regularly encouraged our customers to spend time at a new farm and craft market. We called it our "turn the other cheek" effort, and it provided an opportunity to educate our young employees on the importance of supporting other businesses in our community. It was the right thing to do. We felt pride in being able to give back to our local community and in helping other businesses prosper. It felt great to be helpful and supportive.

Mirror wasn't asleep. Mirror was always listening and said to me one Sunday afternoon when I had finished the pancake business payroll, "You know, Miss Smarty-Pants, you're getting too big for your britches. Your dad used to say, 'Pride goes before a fall.' I heard you telling somebody out there that you promote this area more than anybody else does. I heard you telling them and showing them your book of news clippings and telling them all how great you are. Your dad also said, 'Brag was a good dog, but Hold Fast was a better one.' You're due for a real shocker."

I didn't want to hear that. "Mirror, you're out of line again. I have the maps, the guest book, the empty brochure rack, and the empty bin where the vacation guides are available to all. I can prove my worth. Nobody's going to give me any grief, so shut up."

Mirror reflected the superior tilt of my head.

"I also have several thick three-ring binders filled with letters, pictures, and positive comments about the Sugar Shack. It confirms that we are giving great customer service when people say their visits were the best part of a vacation or road trip. So there, Mirror. I know I'm good."

I had the last word in the argument, but little did I know, nor would I have suspected, the undercurrent of wrath, jealousy, and hatred that was about to descend upon me.

Chapter Twenty-Nine: Disappearance

The pancake room at the Sugar Shack was filled with conversations and mouthwatering aromas one Sunday morning. People waited for seats, made reservations several weeks in advance, and took our suggestion to combine a breakfast visit with a trip to other venues that were of interest to them. Business was great. Customers were departing with smiles and full tummies. I didn't think it could be any better.

Angels appeared every now and then at the Sugar Shack, and one set of them came for breakfast on this Sunday. When they were finished, they asked me to join them at their table. As I sat down, the gentleman asked, "Have you ever considered having music during the hours you're open?"

I was surprised by the question. "No, but it's a terrific idea. Why do you ask?"

"Would you let us set up our four-piece folk music band in your gift shop and play for your clients?"

"I'd have to know how much that would cost. You see, there's not a very large profit margin in a weekend pancake restaurant. What would you charge me to do that?"

"It's not what we would charge you; it is what you would charge us to let us do that," he said.

"I don't understand what you're talking about," I said. "Normally, an establishment pays a band to provide entertainment."

"We're retired musicians from a local educational institution, and we'd just like to play on Sunday mornings for a couple of hours. We'd do it for free, or we'd pay you if you want."

"Would you play for pancakes?" I asked.

The answer was yes, and the group played for several years. Their music fit our rustic country atmosphere, and our clientele loved it. When children were present, puppet horses and jointed wooden men danced to the rhythms of the fiddle and the bass. Many times the musicians played rhythmic, musical spoons. It was mesmerizing entertainment for all. The group sold some CDs, but basically they just loved to entertain and share their delightful music with all who listened. It was a gift to me, my business, and my customers.

These musicians were also a gift to our entire county. They've donated their time and talent at local venues for years. Like our tours and our syrup tasting, their giving behavior reinforced my belief that the more you gave, the more you received in return, in business the same as in life. Customers came from afar for the music and pancakes, and our area prospered as a result. Angels come in all forms.

Pancake customers came and went. Many stopped at my gift shop counter to pass the time of day. Then one day a man asked me what had happened to my sign at the interstate exit. I told him that nothing had happened to it, thinking he was referring to all the controversy over those signs.

He said, "No, I mean, why is your sign gone? We came in from out of town and couldn't remember which way to turn, so we were looking for your sign with the arrow, but it wasn't there this morning."

"I don't know," I said slowly. "It was there last night. I'm going to go and look because I can't believe it isn't there."

I asked one of the waitresses to cover for me at the counter while I went to look. Sure enough, it was gone, and so were all the other business signs. All that remained were piles of fresh sawdust where all the posts had been chainsawed off. I raced back to the Sugar Shack and called some of the other business owners. They knew nothing about the missing signs or even that they were gone. I was pretty mad and excited when I called a law enforcement agency and asked to have an officer come by immediately.

An officer was dispatched to my shop, and when he arrived, he asked, "Do you have anyone you suspect might have done this? Do you have figures on the value of the missing signs? Who do you think might be responsible for their disappearance?"

I was shaking mad and immediately thought of the politicians who didn't like them, but I calmly said, "A fair estimate of value is an average of one thousand dollars each. There were at least six of the large ones and about four smaller ones."

"Where would you start looking for the signs? Let me ask you again—who do you think might have cut them down?" the officer persisted.

"I'd start with the guy in charge of the grape vineyard. I lease those grapes as part of my custom farming business, so my sign is fully permitted, but I think some of the others just pay him to have their signs there. The town has asked him to get rid of them in the past, but he makes money, so he hasn't done anything about it. Maybe somebody had a grudge against one of the sign owners, so I'd check with them also," I told the policeman.

The uniformed officer took the information on the other sign owners and the landowner, including that he was elderly. I gave him an address, and he went off in his police car to begin the search for the thief. It was about 8:00 a.m. when he left, and he was back by 11:00 a.m., but in a different vehicle. He was smiling as he got out of a full-sized van, not a regular police car.

"The information you gave me was right on target," said the officer. "I knocked on the grape farmer's door, and when he opened it and saw my uniform, he grabbed his chest, took a very deep breath, and said, 'Don't arrest me. I'm an old man, and I can't go to jail. The signs are gone. Go look for yourself. I had them taken down in the middle of the night, last night. They're gone. I hired a guy from another town to do the job, and he even took them away and hid them. Please don't arrest me. I did what the town official told me to do.'"

The officer continued, "I couldn't believe it. I got a full confession without even asking a question. That old man was scared to death that he was going to jail, and he said, 'A town official came to see me yesterday and said I'd go to jail if those ugly signs didn't disappear right away.'" The officer shook his head. "What kind of creeps do we have running this town?"

"I never would have dreamed such a scenario," I gasped. I was livid.

The restaurant was silent, its customers intent on listening. We were all in shock.

"Will you and the other business owners sign an arrest warrant for the old man?" the officer asked.

"I don't know about the others, but I won't," I said. "Now if you want to find out which official threatened him and arrest that creep, I'm in. I won't go after an old man who was coerced and threatened into this act. I don't think the others will sign a complaint either," I stated.

Later on, it would turn out that I was right. We all agreed that it was the town official and the forces behind him that should be charged with the theft.

The officer asked me to come out to his van and look at the signs and take mine. He said he would return all the others to their rightful owners.

I finished for the day and went into the house. Mirror was waiting. "Can you believe the nerve of the politicians? Even you never dreamed they would stoop that low. You were too confident and proud with your bragging about what you could do for this town. It'll get you—or they will—every time."

Mirror and my subconscious always had identical opinions on everything.

The only private business sign that remains across from our interstate exit is that of the landowner's business. It is said that his sign remains because it was grandfathered in, but some will always wonder if it remains as a payoff for compliance. Glittering in the headlights, after dark, from that time to the present, are so many "official" reflectorized town, county, state, and highway directional signs that it takes several minutes to sort them all out. None of them points to any business. Not one of the present signs indicates a healthy business climate in our rural town or identifies the public harbor on Lake Erie. There are no signs that point in my direction except the ones associated with my interstate attractions program. That angel Harold had given me good advice concerning the safety of the interstate highway sign program.

Mirror mumbled, "Small-town politics knows no ethics." Mirror continued in an assertive voice, "You do understand that when folks can't make it in private business or in a job in private industry, they run for office and suck the hind teat of the political system." As usual, Mirror's observation probably wasn't far off.

Soon after the signs disappeared, the chain restaurant's representative came to inform me that he would not be renewing his contract for my billboard. He said that from the day their logo and arrow had been attached to my sign across from the interstate exit, his employees had counted license plates from a dozen different states every day in their parking lot in town. The day the signs disappeared, not one out-of-state license plate could be seen. That decline in business continued daily from then on. He considered repainting the billboard to say, "Exit now, turn left," but he didn't feel it would be effective.

CHAPTER THIRTY: STILL TRYING TO HELP

THE ADVERTISING WAS SOON to be replaced on the billboard sign. I remembered the argument my advertising mentor, Harold, had used to convince me to buy the sign in the first place. He'd said, "You never know when those asses will curtail all your other advertising. You have a unique business that needs exposure to the 6.5 million people traveling this interstate every year."

With that in mind, I began to plan the repainting of the billboard with my own Sugar Shack copy. I was upset at the loss of business in the village, so I extended an olive branch once again. I offered half the board to the community for an ad that would entice travelers to exit and visit our gorgeous town. All I asked the town board to do was come up with ad copy and pay for painting it on the board. There would be no monthly rental charge.

Mirror was right there with targeted comments. "Certainly, you don't expect anything creative from the group running this town, do you? Remember, they think a post with business names on boards is advertising. It ain't going to happen, Miss Smarty-Pants."

"I do. You underestimate them, Mirror. In their hearts they have the community's best business interests at the forefront. You wait and see. They'll come up with dynamic ad copy and the few hundred dollars for installing it on half the sign. I won't charge them a monthly rental fee, and they will change their attitude. You're smart, but you don't give the politicians credit. They marketed themselves well enough to get elected. You know, and I think, that they are all about their own agendas, money, power, and control, but I'm offering them the driver's seat here. You wait and see." I still wanted to think they meant well and was trying to convince Mirror and myself of that.

"Ha" was the only response I got from Mirror.

I continued to contact the various organizations that were supposedly moving my community forward, asking for the requested ad copy. They could never come up with any ideas. In frustration I said, "Mirror, maybe you were right. The painters are coming in a week, and time is running out. Apparently, there is no creativity among these elected officials. I even waived the cost of painting for them, but nothing."

I continued to complain about the lack of cooperation, and one of my sons said, "Mom, why don't you just add a line to your own copy? Just add a line that says 'Explore Our Town.' You're paying for it anyway. The elected officials obviously aren't interested in drawing thruway traffic into the village, so just do it for them."

I did just that.

Mirror couldn't let the issue die and asked repeatedly if I had received a thank-you note from the politicians in charge.

"Mirror, I've told you before—it doesn't matter who gets the credit as long as the job gets done. Now let's move on."

Multiple visitors in my gift shop asked me what there was to explore in our town, so I knew that they were travelers using the local exit and that the sign was creating interest and being read.

Two businesses closed; the rest struggled. The local officials and economic development people continued to declare that they couldn't imagine why business was declining in our town. Smart business owners took active roles in the chamber of commerce. Some won seats on the town council and village board. I continued to find ways to stay in business in spite of the constant political hurdles. I remain hopeful that the old-style politicians will retire and more new people with no personal agendas will be elected.

Today there are just as many signs at the exit, but they are official state directional signs or local generic ones that point to nothing except the existence of a village. It appears that business is out of business in our town.

This limited understanding and unwillingness to learn about roadside advertising was apparent in other venues as well. We would soon see another example of the same prevalent marketing ignorance.

CHAPTER THIRTY-ONE: FARM AND CRAFT MARKET

THE SUGAR SHACK FRUIT syrup business had been created because my friend Stan had seen my anger and depression following the successful battle to prevent the containerboard paper mill from locating in our pristine grape farming community. Stan had proved his unselfish, entrepreneurial prowess by encouraging me to open the Sugar Shack retail business. He, too, had fought the good fight over right and wrong as he used his education and licenses to improve the quality and honesty of our community.

When our small group was struggling to find the truth about the impending industrial development in our community, he asked how he could help. He followed up with professional opinions and statements based on his knowledge and experience. He was persecuted and fined and had his property reassessed and his taxes raised as punishment or retribution for his involvement in our quest for an environmental impact statement. He never wavered. He never gave up in his attempts to improve our community.

At his suggestion we founded the Excellence Council and tried to take a proactive approach to finding solutions for economic development in our dying town. Our small group agreed with Stan when he said, "It is not acceptable to say no to what we consider dirty industrial development unless we find alternative solutions for advancing the economy of our community. We all need to do what we can do in our own sphere of influence."

I remember how the farm and craft market project came into being. In our small group, we did not always agree on everything, but we respected one another and worked together for the good of our goal. At least that's how it worked for a little while. Personality, ego, power, and control are strong human motivators. Even the most sincere among us found being altruistic difficult or nearly impossible.

On the other hand, the new farm market idea was a basic, wonderful, well-meaning, opportunistic, small business incubator project from its inception.

I remember when Stan came knocking on my door, a lot like he had when he suggested I move forward after the paper mill project ended, with creation of the fruit syrup business. He wasted no time with small talk and said, "Do you have a few minutes? I have just come home from a buying trip for my gift shop, and I found a wonderful concept for this area."

"Come on in and tell me all about it," I said.

"If I talk too fast, stop me," he said. "I'm so excited. I can't wait to tell you. I saw a sign for some kind of market thing. It said there were hundreds of businesses, and it was only open on Saturdays. It was Saturday, so I turned around and went back to investigate. There were a lot of buildings surrounded by parking lots, so I went in. I saw all these little shops, or displays or vendors—one after another—selling all kinds of things. I started walking through and found a huge variety of goods. Many of them were homemade, but others were strictly resale, like kitchen gadgets or wines or decorations or packaged food. Admission and parking were free. I spent several hours exploring all of it and talking about how wonderful it would be to have something similar around here. Honestly, Gail, it was like a small business incubator where wannabe business owners could try out an idea and learn and practice accounting skills, marketing, customer service, and more. So now I'm here, and I want to know what you think. Do you think we should invite the people who originated this idea to come and explain the concept? Do you think we could introduce this idea here? How would you do it? Are you interested?"

He was so excited and enthusiastic as he described many of the businesses involved and the concept of being open only one day a week. I had never heard of anything like it, and I reassured him that I was in. Together we decided to talk to our small anticontainerboard group about it, reinforcing the idea that we didn't want to say no to development of one kind without suggesting an alternative.

The group met again in my living room to brainstorm this concept. We concluded that we needed an article in the newspapers and a public meeting at the town hall.

I was having an adrenaline rush when my bubble was struck with something as sharp as the point of a knife.

Kathy, one of the original group members, said, "Gail should not be mentioned in this plan. If we have a meeting, she should not be present. She's poison in the opinion of this community. Her involvement will kill the deal."

I was devastated. These were my friends and cohorts, my fellow planners, my extended family. I was in shock. I was broken by the rejection. I couldn't believe that this group sitting in my living room, as they had for the last several years, knowing me and my thinking process, my sincerity, and my desire to help our community grow, could nod in agreement and exclude me completely.

It was merely the beginning of the separation anxiety I was to experience. All things happen, sometimes in strange sequence, to mold and make us or to take us along our journey to our purpose in this life.

Chapter Thirty-Two: Public Meeting

THE GROUP SET THE date and chose the location. Details were assigned to members of our small group. The public meeting was advertised in numerous local papers. Many opinions were voiced, and it was finally agreed, by popular vote, that I should have a quiet, innocuous part in the event.

Finally, I was stationed at the back of the auditorium. At the last minute I received a set of lined pages attached to a folded document. I was instructed to get the signature of each person who was paying a twenty-five-dollar membership fee to join the group exploring the viability of a farm and craft market in our town. The money collected would go for legal fees and costs incurred to implement the plan and file the business name. More than one hundred people wrote checks or paid cash to join. Stan and the people who ran the market he had visited did the presentation. It was very professional and successful.

At the end of the meeting, I handed Stan an envelope containing the lined pages in the document showing the potential members' names, and the cash and checks.

Stan asked, "Gail, do you have time to take this to the

county clerk's office and file the business name along with this list of new members? It needs to be done first thing tomorrow morning, and the money needs to go in a special account at the bank. I can't do it because I have another commitment." He gave me all the details, and I agreed to take care of it.

Mirror the doubter was waiting when I got home. "How'd it go? Did anybody show up? I bet they didn't. I bet they hid you in a corner too."

Mirror wasn't going to bring me down. "The attendance was great, and over one hundred people joined the effort," I said confidently. "Yes, I was at a table in the back corner of the auditorium. My presence didn't seem to deter anyone from joining. I hope all my buddies noticed that. I'm going to file these papers and deposit the membership money in the morning." I threw the envelope on the kitchen table.

"Aren't you even going to look at who signed up, count the money, and see if it jibes?" Mirror asked.

I was tired, but I saw the value in that advice. I pulled out the document first, looked at the signatures, and then proceeded to refold it properly, pulling the cover page to the front. To my horror, printed on it were the words "General Partnership Agreement."

I grabbed the telephone, dialed Stan's number, and screamed, "What in the hell is this form I had everyone sign?"

There was a pause before he answered. "A general partnership agreement. Why?"

"Stan, you can't do this," I shouted. "Because of a personal experience where I recently lost a lot of money, I just finished a course on business entities at the state university campus. This is dangerous for every person who signed it, including me. I won't file it with the county clerk's office tomorrow. It's awful."

"You calm down, Gail," he said in an authoritative manner.

"You're not a lawyer. You took a course. You are not qualified to discuss this, and you will go and file it, or I'll come and get it right now."

I said firmly, "I won't give it to you. Possession is nine-tenths of the law, and I have it. If you file this thing, I believe that any person whose signature is on it can, for example, borrow money, and all the others who signed it are responsible for that action. I know what I'm talking about, Stan. You can't do that to the unsuspecting people who signed this. I had no idea what it was. I trusted that you did and that you understood it. I'll not be associated with this type of scam."

"I'll pick up the package in a few minutes," Stan yelled.

"Don't bother. I'm going to bed, and the door's locked. If you don't believe me, I'll set up a meeting and get an attorney to explain it to you and our core group."

"Gail, be reasonable. You're not a lawyer. You took a class. Your little bit of knowledge is what's dangerous. There'll be no more meetings in your living room, none."

"Okay. There are only about twenty of us. I'll get a local restaurant reserved for next week and get an attorney to come and explain business entities. Would you believe him?" I asked.

"Wednesday night would be fine. I'll call everybody. In the meantime, I'll come and get that package," Stan said.

"I'll put it in my safe," I said, and there it stayed until the meeting.

The dinner meeting was well attended, and the attorney gave a thorough education on various business entities. He also offered to file the necessary paperwork immediately to create a corporation with a board of directors. He explained that would eliminate the risk to all members and allow money and business to be done legally. He stated that he would do that for reimbursement of filing costs and would donate his time. He said that he would prioritize it and that the work would be completed within approximately a month.

Discussion was lively. Everyone was relieved that the general partnership agreement would not be filed and that we could keep the list of names and the membership fees and move forward in a safer direction. We voted unanimously to move forward as agreed that evening. The attorney went home, and Stan was to deliver the paperwork he needed. I felt comfortable and gave everything I had in my possession to Stan to deliver to the attorney. The comfort was short-lived.

Early the next morning, the attorney called to tell me he had been fired. He was no longer involved, nor would he be filing corporation papers for the group. That was the very last communication I ever had with him. It was the last meeting about the farm and craft market that I ever attended. I was never notified or invited to any more.

Months passed. Word of mouth had it that the group thought my involvement with the paper mill project tainted the group's reputation, and they wanted nothing more to do with me. Finally, over a year and probably many thousands of dollars later, the official farm market project was announced. Important names, obviously not including mine, were mentioned, and those people were thanked for initiating the idea. I slunk around town and hid in grocery store aisles as I shouldered the blame for the loss of potential jobs at the not-to-be paper mill. Publicly, I was castigated, shunned. However, privately many members of the original group thanked me and said they missed my input.

I continued with my grape farming, custom farming, and fledgling fruit syrup business. I found validation in the tourists who stopped at my shop when traveling the interstate and main state and county highways. Many of those who visited my farm business sent unsolicited thank-you notes, cards, and gifts for the service they received. I was humbled by the respect and appreciation I received from strangers who stopped by and became friends in many cases.

However, when I laid my head down each night, my last thoughts were confusion, shame, and regret resulting from the public shunning I was receiving.

Mirror reminded me that my feelings were filled with self-pity and were unfounded. "What's the matter with you? Are you upset because you're not in control, not receiving the publicity and appreciation that you think you're entitled to? If that's the case, you're just as bad as your ungrateful critics. And, Miss Smarty-Pants, while we're face-to-face, I've noticed that you're still lonely. What's the matter, no pleasure to mix with your business?"

"Mirror, advertising opportunists and politicians don't interest me. End of conversation," I grumbled.

Mirror was a hard taskmaster.

Chapter Thirty-Three: Opportunities

Kathy, the lady who had originally declared me unfit to be connected with the market project, knocked on my door. When I opened it, she said, "Don't throw me out. I come offering an olive branch. I'm chair of the committee to find two suitable sites for the new market. The involved county agencies and local promoters will make the final decision. Knowing that you really do have the sincere best interests of our town and this project at heart, I want to ask you for something."

As I stood at the front door listening, Mirror was directly behind me and whispered, "Look out—it's a snake in the grass, a wolf in sheep's clothing!"

I listened to the whisper and said, "What can I help you with, Kathy?" I did not invite her into my home.

"I have been doing most of the investigating for a proper location for the new market now that we have backing from several county agencies. I believe your farm is the perfect location for this project. I'd like to ask you for a proposal for its sale to us. It should include acreage and amenities like roads, buildings, water supply, and anything else that is on your farm bordering the interstate highway. The property you own has a billboard sign facing the highway, at least one gas well, and grape acreage along with some timber and a registered and numbered creek. Is there anything else, Gail? The visibility of the completed farm and craft market would be huge considering the millions of folks passing by. That is more valuable than any advertising could be. That alone could make the project a success. I can pick up your proposal in a couple of days. Thanks, Gail."

"It's not for sale," I said.

"Now, Gail, there is always eminent domain," Kathy countered with a raised eyebrow and know-it-all grin.

"I told you, it's not for sale, period. It's in an agricultural district, and I actively farm it. It is not for sale or for the taking," I said, planting my feet wide apart and crossing my arms over my chest.

Mirror hissed, "Good girl."

Kathy sighed. "I must have misread you, Gail. I never saw you as selfish and always believed you had the good of the community at heart. Think it over. You know where I live."

Mirror growled. "She never saw you as anything but a pushover and a threat to her quest for power and control. She always wanted to take credit for any morsel of information that would be in the newspapers, no matter who unearthed it."

Business and pleasure are always mixed in my life. In my book, *Asses and Angels,* a ten-year relationship with a man who became my business partner instead of my husband abandoned me for an old girlfriend. My lack of legal knowledge, choice of the wrong law firm, and my business partner's scheme to take my farm were errors made by me. It was an expensive lesson.

Hardship and turmoil had filled my life in the months since the end of that business partnership. My partner and significant other had taken more than his share with him in many ways. He had left with my heart, my dog, most of my money, and a lot of my property. He had wrought emotional havoc to the depths of my being. I wondered why the Master Planner was allowing this mess.

I rested my head against the door I had just closed with a bang after Kathy left and watched the tears puddle on the floor. All the work that needed to be done by two was now being done by one, me alone. Selling would give me rest and relief, the end of worry.

Mirror reflected a combination of anger, sadness, and self-pity but had nothing to say.

I climbed the stairs to my office, pulled open the filing cabinet, and brought out the expensive appraisals recently completed to satisfy the dissolution of my general partnership agreement with my last man-friend. The appraisals were current. Because of them, I had traded other properties and made up the difference in values with a cash payment to the partner/significant other in the legal dissolution of that, God forbid, general partnership agreement. It was a terribly upsetting and financially devastating memory. It had been a very expensive lesson and the reason I signed up for the class on business entities at the local college.

I thought about the grapes, pond, almost fish farm, billboard sign, gas well, gravel road, woods, tree stands for hunting, fields, snowmobiling, hiking, and wildlife. I started to cry again. I enjoyed that farm, which was a bonus garnered from my long workdays and my constant labor.

I also thought about the debt and the workload I was carrying since the end of my general partnership agreement. The thought made me cringe. It was a heavy load.

The appraisal folder was on my desk, waiting for me, unopened. On the wall there were photos of containerboard meetings in my living room that included Kathy, who I had thought was my friend; pictures of grapes being planted on the farm; a photographic, chronological record of the pond being built; various pictures of different advertisements displayed on the billboard; and other mementos. I saw how the long shelf in my office bowed under the weight of the containerboard project files. I looked out the window and recalled how I always looked across the grape vineyards in the winter when the leaves were gone; I could see my beloved farm. Now I was thinking about selling it.

Finally, Mirror came to life after Kathy's shocking visit and yelled up the stairway, "Don't sell it to the enemy. Don't sell it to the enemy."

I closed the door to the office and went for a walk in the woods. It was quiet and peaceful with no pressure. Nature calmed me, cooled my temper, and prevented me from impulsive action.

As I came in the door after a long walk on the threatened land, I told the reflection in a very worried Mirror, "I'll sleep on it."

Sleep came immediately as I lay my tired mind and body down. Sleep was an escape and procrastination. The last thing I did before drifting off was the first thing I should have done. I prayed, "God, your will be done."

Things always seemed to go in the right direction when I had sense enough to quit trying to micromanage the master plan. Sometimes, however, it took a while to understand that.

CHAPTER THIRTY-FOUR: TO SELL OR NOT TO SELL

I AWOKE KNOWING THAT sleep had cleared my mind. I drank my fresh coffee as I watched Mirror reflecting on the situation. Coffee in hand, staring at the sad eyes in Mirror, I said, "The decision is clear to me after sleeping on the offer. Selling the farm would lighten the workload and erase my debt. It's a no-brainer, Mirror."

Mirror looked back at me in disbelief and sadness.

I climbed the stairs to my office, more hot coffee in hand, and opened the file. Searching my records, I compiled a list of investments to determine the actual value of the farm. I had purchased the sixty-five acres with grapes and a tomato lease. I had bought the sign, built the thirty- by fifty-foot pole barn, graveled the roads, constructed the pond, planted more grape acreage, cleared more land, and made a field around the gas well, creating easy access for the daily gas well tender. I had built drainage ditches, cleaned fence lines, and had the timber evaluated. The value of the farm that day far outweighed the actual costs.

After much soul searching, weighing the pros and cons, and realizing the reality of the debt and workload, I decided to offer it to the market committee for the actual amount of money I had invested. It would erase my debt.

Mirror was comatose.

I wrote up the offer and delivered it to Kathy that day. No words were spoken. I held out the paper, and she snatched it and closed her door.

Days passed, and I heard nothing. I spent hours walking the woods and creek bed on that farm. I imagined my life without the burden of debt, the taxes, and the upkeep, labor, and responsibility. I felt such relief. My partner was gone. My workload and debt would soon be gone. It was done. I was relieved but very, very sad.

Perhaps I could find a part-time job as a school bus driver. I still had all the licenses. I could always wait tables, but that was strenuous work for someone my age. There had to be work for me somewhere. The debt would be gone.

Chapter Thirty-Five: The Master Planner

SIPPING MY STRONG BLACK coffee and taking a few extra minutes to savor the anticipated relief from work and debt, I was startled when the phone rang. Mirror was calm and quiet but remorseful a lot of the time. This was a relief from Mirror's judgmental advice, now that the decision to sell the farm was history.

I answered the phone, and Kathy's voice cut through the peaceful calm with grating clarity. "Just wanted you to know that the committee settled on a thirty-acre piece of property owned by one of the other committee members. We don't want yours."

I started to answer, but she had already disconnected.

The burden of ownership, responsibility, and aloneness slammed onto my shoulders, collapsing me in a heap on a chair by the phone. I was mixed up, my emotions confused, as realization of the burden of debt, work, and worry weighed me down once again.

I looked up just as Mirror said, "Whew. That was a close call. You took the high road and made a sacrifice for the good of the community and, I suppose, your physical and mental health, and the Master Planner rewarded you by finding a way for you to keep your farm. Don't be scared. It was going to be okay before the offer, and you've lost nothing. It's their problem. Wait until they realize their market will draw even more revenue away from their precious downtown area."

Mirror was reflecting a grin from ear to ear. The smile was infectious, as smiles usually are, and this changing reality began to set in.

Mirror continued to assess the situation. "Let me get this straight. They bought a piece of land offered in classic political style. They bought from a committee member dumping a useless piece of property way off in the boonies for an inflated price and paid for it with public money. The political vehicles camouflaged as helpful county agencies made the decision, and as I see it, it is probably a "you scratch my back, and I'll scratch yours" kind of deal, isn't it? The land is that garbage thirty acres five miles out in the woods, where the snow is mountainous, right? Does it even have water, sewer, or roads, let alone a gas well, buildings, drive-by traffic, and a billboard for advertising?"

"All the lack of things you mentioned, but a third of the money, Mirror," I answered.

"Miss Smarty-Pants, thank the Master Planner. Hold your head high and be thankful you are not besmirched by that kind of a political deal. Count your blessings. You'll be okay," Mirror comforted me.

I got the tractor out of the barn, thanked the Master Planner with every turn of the steering wheel, and worked the land on my farm.

Chapter Thirty-Six: Fighting for Improvement

The Sugar Shack became a popular place with tourists, but few local customers could be lured to the shop in the early days. Surprising things happened. Looking back at my notes and old yearly guest books, I saw the records of that history. I answered questions from travelers passing by who happened to stop at my farm shop. I was participating in more of the master plan.

Tourist information was the number one inquiry. Without thought, I sent my customers to Main Street, even though many there would not speak to me. Tourism downtown was good for the tax base. It was good for the economy. As I continued to ask the tourists what their interests were, to target my directions accordingly, it was obvious most of them were traveling on the Seaway Trail, designated as a National Scenic Byway. I wondered why I had never seen any signs or news articles about Route 5, which traversed the entire northern border of our county along the Lake Erie shoreline. No one ever mentioned or acknowledged its existence.

The Sugar Shack had a steady growth pattern, about 25 percent per year. A clear pattern of tourist travel began to develop. I received letters regularly from people who visited my little farm business, and I began to organize them in three-ring binders. By putting them in plastic sleeves, I could keep them preserved and in chronological order. Many different states were represented by the unsolicited thank-you notes, and I felt humbled by messages from my customers saying their stop at the Sugar Shack had been the highlight of their vacation. Most of these travelers were following the Seaway Trail that began at the New York-Pennsylvania border and continued past Niagara Falls, along Lake Ontario, and then followed the St. Lawrence River toward the northern border of New York State.

I polled my customers and learned how they happened to stop at my business. I had them identify their hometowns with stars on a wall map. Soon the importance of the Seaway Trail program in New York State was obvious, as was their ultimate destination; 90 percent of my business's customers were traveling to and from Niagara Falls. The other 10 percent came from cities within two hundred miles. I noticed a complete lack of local clientele.

Cousins I had never met arranged to visit and stayed with me for a couple of weeks. I was delighted. I found that early morning hikes along the Seaway Trail and the Lake Erie shoreline were an inspiring way to start the day, and my cousins enthusiastically agreed.

One morning, a woman was unlocking the local tourism information booth as we passed, and information signs were being set out. My cousins wanted to know what was in the little cottage as the volunteer finished with the opening.

I needed to prepare breakfast, so they visited the volunteer, checked to see if my brochures were displayed, and inquired about the Sugar Shack and what it had to offer as I walked on home. They were strangers to the area and did not know the volunteer, and it was a wonderful way to investigate the success and method of operation at the information booth.

When we sat down to enjoy a country breakfast and rest from our brisk walk, we discussed the brochures my cousins had picked up at the tourist information booth. They mentioned that the volunteer had told them not to bother with the Sugar Shack. She had said, "Oh, don't waste your time going there. It is just some little old lady who makes homemade stuff."

I was horrified but not surprised. My cousins further revealed, as they displayed all the brochures and a tourism guide the volunteer had hand-selected for them, that she had said, "You need to get on the interstate just around the corner and head east to Niagara Falls. That's where all the good experiences are. We just have some old grape farms here."

My temper flared. I was incensed. I could feel my blood pressure rising. "What a stupid circus. The monkeys running this show haven't got a clue about tourist dollars and the value of them in our town's budget. Just the sales tax return would be helpful." I sputtered on and on.

Mirror spoke to me in a soft but firm voice, saying, "It's not your circus, it's not your show, and they're not your monkeys. And it's not your cousins' fault. Do something constructive. It really isn't the volunteer's fault. Nobody trained her or explained the purpose of the tourism booth. Just take care of it. Just find a way to help them run their circus."

I stopped the tirade immediately and looked up the phone number for the town offices. When I calmly, in as sweet a voice as I could muster, asked who the volunteer was, the town official said, "Oh, I couldn't tell you that."

"Okay, perhaps I should tell you a story." Then I repeated what my cousins had told me about their visit at the information center.

The silence that followed was broken only when I spoke again. "I'm wondering, ma'am, if you would like to gather the volunteers and have me train them."

Silence again.

"You see, it is my belief that tourist dollars are extremely valuable in our economy," I continued. "Just the increase in sales tax revenue from tourist spending would help our local economy. It is also my belief that it is counterproductive to send tourists away from our local businesses, out of our county, when there is a plethora of opportunities for entertainment, dining, and accommodations right here locally. With a bit of training, some brochures, and personal recommendations, all the businesses and our tax base could benefit."

Still there was silence.

I kept on going. "If training isn't an option, perhaps an article or letter to the editor in our county newspapers and periodicals would help disperse the information. Some insightful communication in the newspaper might also help the attitude of our citizens. They could be more welcoming and friendly, don't you think?"

"I get your point, Mrs. Black," the woman finally said. "I'm not sure if your ideas would be accepted."

"It's worth a try," I insisted.

"Let's shoot for Sunday morning in two weeks. I'll put up a notice at the information booth. We'll see if anybody shows up for your so-called training session," she said. "I'll be in touch with a time. Will you have handouts for those who agree to come?"

"Yes, and a gift from the Sugar Shack, as well as brochures

and gifts from all other businesses in town that are willing to help," I responded.

It turned out that there was an interest. Eight volunteers showed up at the training session held at the volunteer booth. Each one was given a gift and packet of local and county business brochures, as well as free handouts with maps for trails and parks.

The meeting was not covered by the newspapers. To my knowledge, no mention of the time and effort that those frontline volunteers invested in their gift to our community was ever made. No thank-you notes were sent to them for their interest in learning or for the time they spent trying to improve our economy.

It was a sad commentary on small-town power, control, and politics. It was another nail in the coffin of rural small-town growth, especially in our hometown.

Mirror made a point with a question. "Nobody thanked you for caring and trying to fix their disinterest, did they, Miss Smarty-Pants?"

Perhaps years and gentle persuasion would bring growth and improvement.

Chapter Thirty-Seven:
Unexpected Credibility

I KEPT LOOKING FOR fertile fields of possibility, planting idea seeds, and cultivating and fertilizing any new sprouting growth. I found that I needed only the tiniest bag of commercial fertilizer. But horse manure seemed to be the choice of local politicians, who applied it with such vigor that it killed most sprouting new ideas.

I poured a cup of my wake-up staple and sipped the hot black coffee at my kitchen table while I enjoyed the bright sunshine of hope and determination. I was feeling particularly strong and optimistic about the world at my feet, so I perused the daily news offerings in a local paper. Otherwise, I didn't let that opinionated, often misleading bit of political spin ruin my day.

It was a great day in my neighborhood, and as I turned to an inner page of the newspaper, I noticed a tiny article about a contest being held for the best usage of Route 5, which had been designated as the Seaway Trail.

The National Scenic Byway program included Route 5 as

it entered New York State and traversed the most northern border of our county, leading to Niagara Falls. The scenic byway traversed Lake Erie, Lake Ontario, and the St. Lawrence River, with the ultimate destination being the northern border of New York State. Because it was a national and state designated program, it was a huge opportunity for name recognition and attention for our local communities. The signs along Route 5 identified the route as the Seaway Trail, but no local articles or political attention focused on the state and national recognition of our fortunate location on Lake Erie and the Great Lakes. Those deep waters were home to an international border with Canada. No recognition of Barcelona Harbor as a safe harbor on that international waterway ever surfaced either. All the grants, loans, and allocated financial benefits in our county appeared to go to the south portion of the county, where most of the financial support for our tourism industry was generated. That area was the pinnacle of interest for people benefiting from public financing. It was truly the pig's ear. The north county, where Lake Erie sparkled like a diamond in the summer sun, railroads and state and interstate highways connected the eastern and western portions of our great USA. Millions of travelers traversed the northern portion of our county. It was truly the silk purse.

Mirror interjected, "You can't make a silk purse out of a pig's ear, Miss Smarty-Pants. I see where your thinking is headed."

"Mirror, you are right to a point. Sometimes, I think you can dress up a pig's ear with political spin and make folks believe it is a silk purse. We have an actual silk purse with our location on the intercostal, international waterway that connects the Midwest with the Atlantic Ocean. Our local leaders appear to many of us to be unaware of—or they choose to ignore—the world of international ships and impressive sailboats passing by our coastline."

Mirror kept on with the observations. "So you found an article about a contest for the best promotional usage of Route 5? And now your delusions-of-grandeur mentality is letting you believe you can change the backwoods thinking of this area? You're an idiot, Miss Smarty-Pants."

I chose to ignore Mirror and continued to read the news article, which listed the contest categories in which participants could enter. Winners would be chosen from different sections of the byway that ran from the Pennsylvania/New York state line and followed Lake Erie, the Niagara River, Lake Ontario, and the St. Lawrence River through New York State. I determined that my category of interest was "Best Business Use" in the western section.

Excitement consumed me. "You know, Mirror, I could win that contest. I run a great tourist business, and people from all fifty states visited and put stars on my wall map this year. They signed my guest book, and a lot of them wrote me letters. I want to find out what I have to do to enter. It's time the north section of this county got some recognition and attention. Maybe, just maybe, I can get that done if I win this contest."

Mirror was always skeptical of my ambitious dreams and repeatedly called them delusions of grandeur. "Miss Smarty-Pants, you are getting too big for your britches again. It won't happen."

I made phone calls in spite of Mirror's skepticism, and soon a packet arrived with the requirements and rules for entering the contest. I met all the qualifications. It would be a short job to fill out the application, include pictures, and write a detailed description of why I felt I should win. Including proof of any unique offerings or practices available at my business was extremely simple. I had guest books, maps, Lake Erie shoreline tour descriptions, and a picture of my sign offering free tastings of syrups made from the fruits on my farms. I had coined the saying "Our farm sunshine bottled just for you" and had included it on my bottle labels and advertising since opening my business in 1993.

I went right to work on the contest, and as I assembled the necessary components, I reread the material. At first, I was very confident, but that was followed by disappointment. Then I was certain that applying would be a total waste of my time.

"Mirror, I can't believe I missed this requirement. It says here that I need a supporting letter from someone in authority in my community. I'll never get anyone in this town to write a supporting letter for me, no matter how great I think I am."

Mirror groaned, "Delusions of grandeur, remember?" However, I could see a glimmer of possibility in the reflection. "You could ask the mayor," Mirror continued.

I argued with Mirror, pointing out that the mayor had been on the opposite side of the recycled paper mill controversy. "You're dreaming if you think he will support me. You're just crazy to even suggest it. It isn't going to happen, Mirror."

Memories flashed through my brain, reinforcing the feeling that I should abandon the application. I knew it was a crazy, dead-end idea to ask the mayor for support. It was one of Mirror's worst suggestions.

Mirror spoke again. "Okay, genius, what's your other choice?"

Looking through that reflective surface, I could see no field to plow, only the same old brush-covered wasteland with no possibility of cultivation. I recognized that a brush-burning strategy was necessary, knowing that at worst, the smoke would blow away.

I planned my approach to the mayor, remembering that I needed to acknowledge his power, control, and importance. Those things were easy and honest to highlight about him. I made the call while Mirror grinned away at me and reflected my skeptical attitude.

"Mr. Mayor, this is Gail Black. I know we have had our differences over issues in the past, but you and your wife used to be my good friends. I am calling to extend an olive branch. I'd like to let bygones be bygones."

I held my breath during the few seconds of silence.

I then proceeded with my planned discourse. "Mr. Mayor, I learned a lot of things from you when I was your campaign manager a number of years ago. I also learned a lot more during the paper mill conflict. One of the most important messages I found in the paperwork I accumulated during that fight, written by a career-politician friend of yours, was how to win a conflict. It was the same advice you gave me when I was your campaign chairman. Let me quote as best I can—'select two hundred leaders in the community, convince them of your point of view, and then turn them loose on the naysayers.' You're the only leader I am able to find to write a letter of support for me. I want to enter a state and national contest that I believe will bring positive press to western New York, and I need a supporting letter from you in order to win this contest. It would bring attention to Route 5, the Seaway Trail that parallels the interstate east to west through our town. I believe that, with your support, I can bring more tourism and attention to our area and thereby increase the tourism dollars it receives."

I heard him exhale loudly before he answered. "Put the tea kettle on," he said. "I'll be right down."

When the mayor arrived at my house, we shook hands, had

a cup of tea, and discussed the letter content. He agreed to let go of past differences of opinion. The mayor looked over my application for the Resource Interpretation Award. He wrote a letter stating how my business promoted tourism in my town, my county, and New York State. Hopefully, this would lead to the success of my entry.

The statewide contest application process, my limited advertising budget, and my desire to grow my business in spite of all the local opposition had me on high alert. The simultaneous learning experiences, my new fledgling attempt at a positive attitude about trusting politicians, and my inexperience in the world of advertising were all about to be tested.

Mirror was always there, pointing out the possible errors of my ways. "Miss Smarty-Pants, aren't you embarrassed by the lurking advertising issues? There is an outside chance you might win this contest, get your picture in the paper, and be honored at a fancy luncheon, but you've got a lot to learn. You're a farmer at heart. Tourism is brand-new to you, and there are many experienced leaders following proven avenues to success. Some of your angry temper outbursts might even come back to haunt you. Do you really think you will get any credit for bringing a small bit of glory to this area? Be careful who you trust and where you spend your money, girl." Mirror was right on top of it.

Mirror was often a prophet and caused me to recall the misfortunes of my ill-fated, often impulsive, uninvestigated misadventures. Mirror jogged my memory, which led to my recognizing the Master Planner's lessons in my life. Each time I thought I was going to graduate from the school of hard knocks and perhaps go on to achieve a doctorate degree, Mirror and I found more quagmires of difficulty.

Chapter Thirty-Eight: Vigilance

A FELLOW BUSINESS OWNER appeared at my Sugar Shack with his briefcase in hand. Julius was an imposing man. He was a salesman staying at a local campground and also had business and political aspirations. He was tall, handsome, and well dressed. His briefcase was genuine leather and sported a digital lock and the latest technologies; it was obviously his mobile office. He moved with a superior air and spoke with authority. I felt slightly intimidated and was very aware of the beat-up farm work shoes, stained jeans, and worn sweatshirt I was wearing when I came in from pruning apple trees to greet him.

The gentleman said, "Mrs. Black, it was suggested to me that I should include your little business in this cooperative advertising brochure I am assembling. If you can't afford to be included, I'll understand. It was against my better judgment to come here because I know a tiny business like yours needs to watch every dollar. However, there are several business owners who are sharing the cost of printing a combined brochure to advertise their businesses, as a way to cut costs. I have experience in all facets of this matter, so I have been hired. Hence, I'm here."

Mirror screamed across the lawn, "A put-down from a smooth talker and slick operator. Beware of all this."

I heard the noise from Mirror but ignored it. "Thank you for coming. I was just thinking about my advertising program. Show me what you have."

He punched in the code on his expensive briefcase, and his portable office sprang to life. "You see, I have some samples here of other cooperative brochures. This proposed one will be printed on white paper with green ink. It will contain stories about the area interspersed with appropriate ad copy. In other words," he said, as he obviously talked down to me, to make sure my stupid little farm mentality could comprehend his highfalutin ideas, "the cover will have a story about maple syrup and then your ad. The cost is three hundred dollars payable upon your order placement. You would need to supply only your ad copy. We will create the story content."

Misguidedly thinking I knew a lot about advertising, I asked, "How many will you print?"

"One hundred and fifty thousand flyers," he replied.

"Isn't that an awful lot?"

"Each member business will receive a supply and be responsible for the distribution in their area," he stated.

"I don't understand. If these are all local businesses, don't we all have the same area?"

He looked at me like I was the stupidest human he'd ever been forced to visit. "You and you alone will give them out to your customers. Each business will do the same. There will be a minimum of fifteen businesses joining this cooperative effort, and each will distribute ten thousand flyers anywhere they would like. It is a privilege to be invited to participate."

"Okay, I'll join. I'll get my checkbook, and it will only take me a few days to get the ad copy ready," I said.

I had never had a brochure at that point. I had no experience with that advertising venue. This smooth-talking man made it sound like a no-brainer.

A few weeks later, Julius came by and dropped off a carton of brochures, and I couldn't wait to finish with my customer so I could examine them. When my counter was clear, I eagerly opened the carton and pulled out a few. The first thing I noticed was how flimsy they were. They seemed to be printed on unusually thin paper—not even regular typing paper. They were folded, and the paper was difficult to hold straight enough to read. The front had a background picture of a bright green tree-lined street. Superimposed on it was the story. I began to read: "Western New York is the home of some of the best restaurants in the ..." I had to unfold the paper to look for the rest of the article. There was no indication as to where to find the remainder of it. There was no continuation. I searched and searched, but there was no additional story. Then I noticed misspelled words and a misspelled business name. The flyer was awful. It was a disgrace to the intelligence of the businesses it advertised. I never found any mention of my business.

I heard Mirror's hardly audible voice say, "Too trusting again—you are just too trusting. When will you learn not to pay for things before you see them?"

I made phone calls to other advertisers involved and to the slick salesman suggesting that he pick them all up and redo them. It was too late. Most had been delivered and then distributed. I put my carton in the attic where I kept supplies. I used it as a reminder and a teaching tool about what I should do before writing a check.

I didn't realize at the time that this experience was a basic lesson that I would use for many years to come. Stiff paper, bright colors, eye-catching pictures, unique logos, and a diligent distribution company were essential. A final edit was imperative.

I felt stupid and depressed that I had been a victim of this ignorant charlatan who had talked down to me, made me feel important because I was asked to participate, and gained my confidence and my money with bullying bluster.

I was somewhat comforted by the fact that this was not the only segment of my advertising plan. I still had the main piece, the most important one for my clientele because I had identified them as tourists. That ad was in a major tourism publication. It covered the bases, so to speak.

Chapter Thirty-Nine: Backup Plans

THAT DAY'S MAIL CONTAINED a fresh-off-the-press copy of a widely distributed advertising handout in our area. I had placed my ad copy in it after agreeing to the cooperative brochure. At least I wasn't out all the way around, or so I reasoned with Mirror as I set the newspaper-type publication on the kitchen table and grabbed a cup of coffee.

A folded map was included with the publication. It was similar to the ones used at local campgrounds, and as with those, I had paid a handsome price to be included. I opened it with excitement and anticipation. It was the only affordable backup after the debacle of the cooperative flyers filled with errors.

Mirror said, "At least all your eggs weren't in one basket," and grinned at me with confidence.

All the lovely lakes in our area were portrayed in bright blue. The exception was the largest lake, the one that encompassed the whole northern boundary of our area and bordered my farm; this international lake was gray. It was one of five Great Lakes, Lake Erie, and was of great importance. I looked for the listing of my business along its shoreline. It wasn't there. I searched for other nearby businesses and found them missing also. There were no businesses located on Route 5, the Seaway Trail, according to this map. Upon closer inspection, at the edge of the map, I found them all on a list with driving directions to a nearby city sixty miles away.

Mirror said, "You're making awful noises and slurping your coffee and coughing. You're all red in the face. Why are you pounding the table with your fist?"

"It's just too much. This ad was my safeguard," I said as the tears and shaking started. "I don't have any more money for advertising. I spent my whole budget on these two avenues. First I received my order of that flimsy, damned cooperative brochure, which obviously wasn't edited, and now this awful map with business locations in wrong places. Nobody edited this piece of crap either," I moaned. "I don't believe it!" I screamed. "You should see this thing. Amish country is highlighted in gray like Lake Erie. The area is bigger than Lake Erie, and it's shaped like a breast with a nipple." Mirror was the only one listening.

"Don't wait around," Mirror advised. "You know what happened with the brochure. You were late getting your supply, and all the rest were spread all over everywhere. Call up the people in charge of this publication and stop it from being distributed while you stand a chance."

I was fuming, and my temper was nearly out of control. I didn't even think of changing my work clothes. I grabbed my pocketbook and the offending map, and on my way out the door, I said, "I'll do better than that. I'm going to the office with this piece of crap to tell them they need an editor and some supervision. I'll never give them another dollar if this is the way they perform."

I got madder with every mile I drove with the offending

paper beside me on the seat. As I rushed through the office door, I yelled, "I want to see whoever is in charge here!"

"The office is in the back. I'll see if anyone is there. Whom shall I say is calling?" the receptionist asked.

"Never mind announcing me," I growled as I pushed past her and into the hallway. I knew I'd never get an audience if she revealed that an awful-looking, red-faced, angry woman in a pair of overalls, torn sweatshirt, and muddy boots was waiting. I had already learned lessons in appearance.

I beat her to the doorway where a light was shining through the opening. I glanced back at her so I wouldn't hit her when I slammed that door shut. She looked frightened and almost in tears.

A good-looking, neat, intelligent-appearing advertising executive looked up from some paperwork. His smile vanished once he had time to analyze my appearance.

I didn't wait to be greeted; I just slapped down the folded paper, ripped it open, and asked, "What kind of a piece of shit is this anyway?"

"Excuse me? You are?" he asked.

"I'm from over by Lake Erie at the Sugar Shack. I paid a high price for an ad in this piece of crap. I demand to know why my business is over here on the edge of the map, along with all the other businesses on Route 5, with directions that point to a destination sixty miles away."

His only response was a blank stare.

"And furthermore," I continued, "why is Lake Erie gray when all the other lakes on the map are bright blue? Don't you even know Lake Erie is one of the Great Lakes and of international interest?"

His attempted answer was barely audible. "I didn't realize—"

I interrupted, "And there's more. Why is Amish country highlighted in gray and in the shape of the profile of a woman's breast?"

The poor, unsuspecting, unworldly, inexperienced young advertising rep said, "I wasn't aware of any of that."

"And why aren't you aware of it?" I demanded. "You're in charge, aren't you? I would have expected you to edit this paper before it went to print, or at least to have delegated that task to someone qualified to do it. This map brings you thousands of dollars in advertising. My business can't be found by following the map. People will go to the wrong destination. I'll lose business, and my income will be negatively affected. I want a full refund. This is despicable, a disgrace. I only know about the obvious stuff and things that pertain to my business, but I don't think you give a crap."

I was so upset from the brochure fiasco and from counting on this publication to justify my advertising budget that I ranted on. "Just in case you don't know, I'll tell you again: Lake Erie is one of the Great Lakes and is world-renowned. It's the whole northern border of this community. Were you afraid that if it was blue, like the other lakes, people would find it more attractive than those smaller lakes? I would guess that is why it's gray. You hoped it might get ignored, right?"

The obviously flustered ad executive said, "Calm down. You're overreacting. It's not the end of the world or a big deal. I can't refund your money because the piece is already printed and distributed. The money is spent. Just calm yourself down."

I grabbed up the paper, slammed the door to his office again when I left, and went home. I was still fuming. I was incensed, and there was no recourse. There was, again, nothing I could do. Of course, it was no big deal to him. He did not depend on customers who spent money directly with him; he worked for a salary at an advertising agency.

Some things a person can't anticipate. My meager budget for advertising was spent, and the value for each of those hard-earned dollars had vanished. It was a bitter pill. It was an expensive lesson in my business education, one I never forgot, but the drama was a long way from over. A business owner can never be too vigilant and must never be too trusting.

CHAPTER FORTY: ASSUMPTIONS AND MISUNDERSTANDINGS

THE FOLLOWING DAY, I won the Seaway Trail contest. Included with the notice was an invitation to an awards ceremony and the ceremony program. I was to be awarded a prize and certificate at a special luncheon meeting at a lovely, exclusive local hotel. The invitation said that I could invite a guest, and our lunch would be complimentary. I called the mayor because he had written the supporting letter for my application. He agreed to meet me there for the ceremony.

Arriving fifteen minutes early for the luncheon and wearing a new business suit and shoes to match, I stood tall and moved with confidence. My hair, makeup, and accessories were perfect. I had learned about appearance. The large room was already filled with politicians, dignitaries, news reporters, and advertising executives and more people of importance. The back portion of the dining room was a reception area with wine, cheeses, and a table filled with brochures and advertising publications. Seaway Trail magazines and other National Scenic Byway advertising pieces were included. Stacks of flyers containing my first attempts at printed advertising were also on the table and reminded me of the embarrassing disappointments I had paid for. I immediately felt my blood pressure rise, but I walked away and got some wine and cheese.

Mr. Mayor approached me and asked if I had seen the newest maps, magazines, and brochures. He asked if all the various promotional printed materials were available for him to take to his real estate office for clients. I debated for a second about whether to point out the obvious flaws in my ads but took the high road and said, "There are many different flyers, magazines, newspaper inserts, maps, and handouts over by the wall on that long table. There's a sign indicating you can take as many as you like."

I walked over to the display and pointed out the many options before I went to the head table and took my place of honor. My anger was replaced with a feeling of pride that my small shop could bring statewide recognition and honor to our area. It was such an adrenaline rush to win and be recognized as successful in tourism; it was especially sweet after the ostracizing I was receiving from my town over the nonexistent paper mill.

My lovely, uniquely designed, hand-painted plaque would be hung in a prominent place in my gift shop. I knew Mirror would say, "Such highs and lows, such highs and lows. It's unbelievable. Don't fall off the pedestal, sunshine."

After all the handshakes and congratulations, a short speech, and photographs for the newspapers, Mr. Mayor and I carried his supply of paper advertising offerings to his car. He would distribute them to new home buyers and folks passing through his businesses. I thanked him for the letter of support he had written on my behalf, acknowledging that it was the reason I had won. It was a short conversation, after which we went our separate ways. I thought the tide had turned and life was on an upswing. Wrong.

Three days later, the mayor raced down my driveway in a swirl of dust and skidded to a stop. He exited his car red-faced, waving a letter at me. "Get in the house right now. I want you to read this. I'm so mad I'm going to call for that guy's resignation," he yelled as I crossed the lawn from my gift shop to the house.

The letter was from the advertising executive responsible for the editing of the tourism handout who had attended the recent luncheon. It was copied to every politician, elected official, and business owner in the county. In essence it said that I had specifically taken the mayor, who was also a legislator, to the table of displays at the Seaway Trail luncheon, and that I had pointed out the shortcomings in the printed materials where I had invested most of my advertising budget. It said I had blamed the advertising executive specifically. It attacked my integrity and business credibility, naming me and my business.

The mayor said, "You never said a word to me about any problem in your advertising. This letter is a lie. I studied the printed materials to see if I could tell what the rant was about. Could you explain all this to me?"

I said, "There are a lot of errors in several of the publications. Businesses are in the wrong places, and there are inconsistencies in the color of lakes, incomplete stories, and highlighted areas that are an embarrassment."

"Show me," he demanded as he handed me his copy of one of the publications in question. It was filled with erroneous details and descriptions for all the local destinations, attractions, and retail offerings.

I opened the publication to the map and showed him the

Amish country teat. When he finished laughing, got over being horrified, and finished his angry rant, I showed him the color of the lakes. He did a repeat performance. I then showed him the businesses listed in the last paragraph with directions indicating they could be found in a city sixty miles away. With misspelled words, faulty directions, and misleading descriptions, the publications were worthless to many of the businesses depicted in them. The errors would cost local tourism businesses huge financial losses.

The mayor's reaction wasn't pretty. This was no laughing matter to him either. He was sincerely disgusted and offended by the damage the publication inflicted on local businesses, mine included, and the tourism economy.

"Gail, you don't deserve this letter. I have already asked for an apology from this self-important person. I demanded that duplicates of the written apology to you be sent to each of the other letter recipients at once. I hope a lesson is learned about assumptions, about the content of conversations observed but not heard."

The apology for smearing my character arrived a couple of days later. The thought crossed my mind that grant money was available for the advertising community and this executive in question. Perhaps the leader of this advertising company was anticipating some of that. The mistakes would negatively affect that financial support. He wasted no time in complying with the mayor's demand for an apology.

Mirror watched me open the letter. I read it out loud, folded it up, and said, "I'll save both letters and think about the way I reacted. I really wasn't a lady when I went to that office to complain. I think I need to try to fix the relationship."

Mirror gave me an incredulous look. "Do you really think you need to become friends with this jerk?"

I scowled back at my reflection in Mirror, combed my hair, changed my clothes, and went to the offending office once again. This time I let the receptionist announce my visit. I formally accepted the written apology, and shook hands with the advertising executive. We agreed that for the good of all our interests in the traveling public, we needed to put this issue away.

I felt no repercussions and was treated fairly from that day forward. Forgiveness is healing for all parties. The young, incompetent advertising guru learned about editing, taking responsibility, and second opinions and has become a great leader in our community. The traveling ad salesman moved away. I was thankful for the incident because my business became noticeable to many powerful entities in the area. Business thrived, and I enjoyed some financial gain from new clients who were intrigued with the drama.

Upon winning the Resource Interpretation Award offered by Seaway Trail Inc. for the western section of the Seaway Trail, I was also privileged to be invited to serve as a Seaway Trail board member. I additionally was interviewed, photographed on my antique tractor, and featured in an article on the front page of *Business First*, a well-known business newspaper in Buffalo, New York. Down the road and a few years later, I was honored to find my picture in a neighboring town's paper under the heading "Following the Golden Rule through Life." That photo caption was the best compliment I ever received, and it was followed a few years later by another honor, when the county executive appointed me to the county commission on small business as a board member. These honors and articles have been continuous to the present time. I was delighted to be featured with a three page article and photographs in the 2019 summer issue of a national magazine, *New Pioneer*.

In addition to farming the grapes, running the harvesting business, and keeping the Sugar Shack shelves supplied with my ever-growing list of syrup varieties, I enjoyed several public speaking engagements. I tried to remember that unpleasant events, along with recognition and rewards, were learning tools. I started a scrapbook and kept notes to reinforce those lessons.

Mirror chided, "Don't get to thinking you're famous; you're just notorious. Your mother always said, 'Fools' names like fools' faces always appear in public places.'"

I ignored Mirror. There was no room in my life for negative thoughts.

CHAPTER FORTY-ONE: MEN AND WINDOWS

THE MUNDANE CHORES OF everyday life groaned on. I worked harder and longer each day and accomplished my grape farm goals. Fertilizer had to be ordered, and I knew, like any woman, that bargains could be found if I shopped around among the farm supply businesses.

My fertilizer needs came by the ton, not the pound. On the mink farm many years before, I'd learned that the more of anything you bought at one time, the cheaper the price you were quoted. On my search for nitrate and potash bargains, I visited all the suppliers for miles around throughout the grape-growing region. Usually, I found garden seeds, plants, tools, and such in my travels. Once in a while, I found an extra-special offering. I enjoyed the interaction with the farming community.

As usual, one of the largest farm suppliers was offering a closeout sale just inside the door. This sale was on a pile of windows with wooden frames. They looked out of place among the displays of seeds, chemicals, implements, and other boring work-related items.

It was obvious the sign had been hastily created with a red marker. It screamed, "Eighty percent off." Most windows at that time were aluminum. Vinyl windows were the newest offering. The older-style windows in this pile were made of wood and glass. They were plain, double-hung wooden windows. But a sale was a sale. Eighty percent off was a real deal. The sign caught my full attention. I filed the information in the "ask about it later" section of my brain.

In the next aisle, I saw a very successful neighboring farmer, an icon, an inspiration to all, and the very same farmer who had been instrumental in my difficult farm machinery purchase years earlier. He was an old friend, and I was delighted to see him. I asked about the best price for fertilizer and the suppliers who would bundle the fertilizer with my chemical spraying needs, and he had a suggestion.

"Gail, why don't you buy into the railroad carload of fertilizer with my buddy and me? We buy a boxcar-load of nitrate and get it delivered to the local siding. We cut out the middleman and get the wholesale price. I think you could save a lot of money now that you grow over forty acres of grapes."

I agreed on the spot. "I'm interested, and I appreciate the offer, so count me in." I was pleased to reduce my cost and felt honored to be invited to participate with these highly successful neighbors. The railroad siding was only two miles from my farm. I always loaded and unloaded all the fifty-pound bags I bought by myself, so that aspect would be no problem. My friend said he would let me know when the railroad car would be positioned on the siding and ready for me to unload my portion.

I noticed the pile of windows again when I was leaving the store. My truck was empty, and I didn't have to haul any fertilizer. The windows were a real bargain, and I had just saved hundreds of dollars, so I bought them.

I headed for home, careful not to hit any bumps in the road

or turn any corners too fast because of the fragile cargo in the back of my pickup truck. A cup of coffee at my kitchen table was on my mind.

At home I was mentally savoring a successful fertilizer shopping trip, a huge financial savings, and delivery of my product close to the farm until Mirror reflected my subconscious doubts. I had needed to share my pumped-up state of mind, and there was no one to listen except Mirror.

After I finished bragging about all my great deals at the farm store, Mirror said, "Well, Miss Smarty-Pants, what are you going to do with those useless old wooden windows? I bet you'll just let them sit in a pile and rot." The old naysayer continued, "And when that boxcar of fertilizer comes, you know those guys won't call you first. They'll unload theirs close to the center door, and you'll carry your part from the far corners of the load. They'll be somewhere laughing while you carry every bag that is half your weight. How many tons will you get? And there are forty bags in every ton. Good luck. You're brilliant."

My temper flared. I knew Mirror was right. I remembered just how the boxcar unloading process worked. I'd had years of experience on the mink farm.

I formulated a plan while I stacked and stored the windows for some future fantasy project. Mirror had reminded me of the many railroad cars loaded with fifty-pound bags of mink feed, and it was a tiring memory.

I raced back into the house. "Mirror, this isn't my first rodeo. I know all about boxcar loads of stuff. I'll call my farm mentor and ask for the number on the seal, and when that car is placed on the siding, I'll break the seal and get mine first. I'll watch. I'll know it is in position before they do. Watch me."

"Good plan, but we'll see," Mirror replied.

The railroad car was on the siding at daylight one morning soon after that. I had driven my stake body, dual-wheeled truck to see if it was there. I had the number and seal information on my dashboard, and I compared the details. Sure enough, everything matched, and it was the right boxcar. I put on my work gloves, backed up to the door, broke the seal, and unloaded my portion with a few steps for each bag, making several trips back to the farm. Then I went by the diner where the old farm boys always wasted the best, early hours of the day having coffee and sharing the local gossip. They were pretty surprised when I announced that I'd taken care of the seal and unloaded my portion. Heads swiveled to confirm the load on my truck. I was done. I sweetly thanked them for helping me.

Back at the farm, I unloaded the last of the fertilizer and stacked it in front of the pile of windows. The nitrate would be piled and replaced yearly many times in front of those old windows until I found a purpose for them.

Eight years later, the farm store salesman stopped by with his yearly free calendar offering. "Gail, I remember that a number of years ago you bought some windows that were on sale where I worked. What did you ever do with them? I was going to buy them, and you took them before I could get it done."

"I didn't do anything," I said. "I still have them. I probably shouldn't have bought them, but I can never resist a real bargain. I have fantasies about opportunities, and only occasionally do they come to fruition. Why do you ask?"

"I'd buy them if you want to sell them. I'd pay you double what you paid at the store." The windows went home with him.

Four years later, I was building an addition to the barn to house a new evaporator for maple syrup production, and I remembered those windows that I'd bought and sold. They would come in handy now. It was always like that. After I got rid of something, I needed it.

I called the salesman and asked if he'd used the windows. He said, "I thought I was going to build a sunroom. I didn't do it, so I still have them. Why?"

"Do you want to sell them back to me? I have a project going, and I could use them."

"Sure, and I'll sell them for just what I paid you. They're actually in my way. My wife will be thrilled to be rid of them," he offered.

The salesman even delivered the windows. Mirror commented, "Windows and men—the more you're around them, the more clearly you can see right through them. Remember that, Miss Smarty-Pants."

"Mirror, you should add politicians to the windows and men," I replied. As usual, Mirror was spewing out prophecy.

Chapter Forty-Two: Mixing Business and Pleasure—Again

It SEEMED THAT SOME lessons were difficult for me to learn. They just had to be repeated over and over again. I was successful in business, and my sons were developing into great young men in their own right. I had lots for which to be thankful. I was thankful, but I was also lonely.

My relationships with men were somehow in cycles of around ten years each. I calculated that I had forty years of unsuccessful relationships in my portfolio. I was busy with my grape businesses and the Sugar Shack, and I still picked worms at night. It was a way to fill the lonely summer evenings. It brought in fishermen who also became Sugar Shack customers and returned to shop with their wives and families in many cases. Once in a while, a single guy became a candidate for dating as I mixed a little pleasure into my businesses.

I owned a boat and loved to fish for walleye in Lake Erie myself, so I could converse easily with the men who came to buy my night crawlers. Pete was a summer resident of a nearby campground and a steady customer. He asked me out and then to go fishing with him on his boat. We began to date. A few years passed, and the arrangement seemed to be congenial.

Pete was a big, rugged guy with an offbeat sense of humor. He was retired, self-supporting, and busy with a part-time business in which he operated his bulldozer and backhoe to do odd jobs on local farms. He was a plumber by trade and found more work than he wanted.

We fished and hunted, roller-skated, and danced. Our families became friends with each other. Pete visited regularly from Cleveland during the winter months, when he wasn't a resident camper nearby. Soon he was extending his visits to weekends and then weeks at a time. He often brainstormed business decisions with me. If I was shorthanded, he filled in.

Pete and I found compatibility in our personal, social, political, religious, business, and everyday lives. He filled a lonely void in my life. Slowly, his life, business, and equipment infiltrated my life and farm. Then he suggested that because his machinery was on my farm, perhaps I could include it on my farm owner's insurance policy. He used that machinery for my benefit on my farms, so I didn't see a problem. Soon he was charging personal purchases on my local store accounts. When we were shopping, he would often throw clothing, tools, parts, and more into my cart, promising to pay me later. Because he had been instrumental in the expansion of the Sugar Shack, helped me move and set up my display at craft fairs and festivals, kept my equipment in good running condition, and took care of building and home repairs, I didn't see a problem. I benefited from his extensive knowledge, expertise, and business contacts.

Mirror, on the other hand, never missed a thing. "Don't you think Pete is spending a lot of your money, smarty-pants? Isn't that a repeat of what the last guy did? Isn't that a little bit of a red flag?" Mirror asked.

"Mirror, you can find red flags in every relationship, friendship, or business deal. I'd never do anything if every red flag got in my way. Forget it," I said.

"Pete seems to have a lot of friends who stop by every time you're away. Isn't that a red flag?" Mirror persistently asked.

I shrugged off Mirror's nit-picking, worrisome questions. Pete and I were several years into a comfortable relationship. We were a couple. He stayed at my house a lot and took on major projects for my benefit.

"Mirror," I said, looking deep into Mirror's reflection, "think about all the improvements Pete has instigated and completed around here. There are the plumbing and heating systems at my bed-and-breakfast property, the expansion of my sales room at the Sugar Shack, the addition of the kitchen and pancake dining room, plus all the help he gives me at festivals and shows. I'd have spent a lot of money on all those things. I've been awfully lonely for a long time. It's all okay. Don't worry. The arrangement is fair and exclusive. The real bonus is that I'm not alone. It's just a little bit of pleasure mixed in with my business."

Mirror looked doubtful and worried, not convinced that I was right. Time passed, and routines continued. I should have looked longer and harder into Mirror's concerns.

One day I came home from shopping, and Pete and his friend were in the Sugar Shack. I wandered over with some supplies for the restaurant, entered through the back door unannounced, and heard Pete talking. "Hell yes, I get a little on the side. I never get caught; not even a suspicion arises. I take care of business here at home regularly, and then I take my dirty laundry back to Cleveland, stay with my sister, and enjoy a little strange. That's how you get away with it. Why, I've seen more pussy than a toilet seat," he bragged crudely in his rough man-to-man language that I had overlooked. Whenever he embarked on his crude discourses, my cheeks always flushed, and I found reasons to leave conversations.

I stopped dead in my tracks. I nearly dropped the dish soap and window cleaner I was carrying into the restaurant kitchen. I stood frozen, a peculiar kind of cold creeping over me. I listened for more and felt guilty for eavesdropping. Then I remembered Mirror and the red flags. Could I have been wrong about Pete? Was I really hearing this stuff? Was it true, or could it just be male testosterone telling big stories?

The conversation continued, and Pete said, "Come on, Buddy. Let's get the meat you wanted out of the freezer and into your car before the old girl gets back."

They went out the front door. I crept out the back door and into the maple syrup evaporator room, where there were windows through which I could see my freezers. I kept whispering over and over, "This conversation just can't be happening."

Sure enough, Pete and his friend had my freezers open, and they were filling boxes with sausages and bacon from the restaurant supply. Walleye frozen in water, chicken, pork chops, and several packages of frozen fruit from my farm disappeared from my personal freezer. It all went into the trunk of Buddy's car. What a Robin Hood Pete was.

I went back to the Sugar Shack kitchen, and soon Pete came in, saying, "I didn't hear you come in. Where's your truck? When did you get here? Can I help you unload or carry things?"

"Won't be necessary, Pete. I've got it all unloaded, and I'll see you in the house," I replied as I worked to keep my shaking hands from showing.

Mirror was waiting when I walked into the house and said, "Wow. How enlightening. You never saw that coming. Have you noticed that you aren't crying? Isn't that amazing, girl?"

"Mirror, I'm cold, angry, shaking mad, disgusted, and feeling dirty. I'm not sure all the talk was real. Maybe it was just male testosterone talking; maybe it was big talk to make him feel good. Who knows. But I now know enough to recognize a liar and a thief," I said.

"You wish it was just big talk, but you know better. You know Pete is crude, uncouth, and even vulgar at times. Remember when he said, 'I'm not the plumber, I'm not the plumber's son, but I'll plumb the hole until the plumber comes'? What are you going to do about all this?"

"Look, Einstein, I don't have a clue yet. I'll let him explain himself when he gets in here," I answered Mirror.

Mirror was just plain nosy sometimes and continued to prod me. "You just said you'd recognize a thief. What do you mean by that?"

"The barn door was closed, and you missed something. Imagine that. Mirror, I'm not sure what I saw, but Pete and his friend were filling cardboard boxes with restaurant food like potato cakes and meats. Then they moved over to my personal freezer and took packages of chicken and pork and sauerkraut and fish and fruit. Maybe Buddy paid for the stuff—I don't know. I mean to find out when Pete gets in here."

"All I heard was Pete bragging about his sexual exploits in other locales. What about that, missy?" Mirror asked.

"Stop it. Shut up. I'll take care of all of it. Trust me. Just be quiet."

"Right," Mirror said, dragging out the word. "'I'll take care of it—trust me' is a common refrain around here. Pete uses it many times a day when he slaps you on the ass and avoids explaining where he's going or what time he wants his dinner on the table. You go, girl. You're a genius."

I made a pot of coffee, poured a cup, and began the weekly book work while I waited for Pete to come to the house. I suspected that he wondered what I'd seen and heard. The only answer to my questions was the swirl of dust following his pickup truck out the driveway. The voice mail on my phone said, "I have to go to Cleveland to Mom's. She called and said she has a bad leak in her plumbing. I probably won't be back tonight."

A few days later, Pete returned, came in the house whistling, and presented me with new faucets for my kitchen sink. "While I was getting stuff to fix Mom's leaks, I saw these new faucets and bought them for you. I'll install them in a few minutes. In the meantime, remember that I'm 'Tit Feeler P. Hot Nuts,' so come here and let me do what I do best," he said nonchalantly. I was repulsed.

He worked on the faucet installation and brought me up-to-date on his family news. His mom was in her eighties and had hip problems. He informed me that he had promised her a new bathroom downstairs to make life easier for her. He had always been good to his mother. However, I remembered that this was not the first time he had claimed he was installing a first-floor bathroom for her. It was the second time. I remembered using the new bathroom he had installed a year before.

The latest suspicions about his Robin Hood behavior also made me recall that each time he returned from Cleveland, he had antiques and expensive trinkets that he said his mother had given him. I was instructed to never display any of them, including a very old family Bible with generations of his family history written on the pages. He said seeing them would bring back difficult memories to his mother when she visited. Instead, he always sold the items, including the family Bible.

Thanksgiving was less than two days away, and Pete's relatives would be joining us for dinner. Names would be drawn for Christmas gifts. Dates and plans would be made for the holiday festivities, and it was not the time of year to rock the boat with confrontations.

Chapter Forty-Three: Bold Evidence

The holiday season was upon us. Our pancake restaurant was out of control and extremely busy with family reservations and folks shopping after they ate. We hired extra waitresses. Kathy was an older woman and an experienced, excellent waitress. She was thin, good-looking, energetic, and friendly. She was Pete's recommendation, someone he knew from one of the local campgrounds where he did contracting in the summer. She was great about helping in the kitchen, getting supplies from the freezer, and doing anything else that was necessary. She was a treasure. Her husband was ill and would never be able to work again. She needed the job I had to offer.

One busy morning, she ran to the barn to get a box of potato cakes from our commercial supply. Soon after she left, the staff told me they were running low on bacon too, and I said I would get it. Instead of going the usual route through the seating, I took a shortcut out the back door and through the maple syrup evaporation room. It was the same route that I had taken when Pete and Buddy were emptying my frozen foods into Buddy's car.

I was on a mission and not very quiet. I suspected nothing.

I was only after supplies in a hurry. I was approaching from an unexpected direction when I burst through the back door. It was dark by the freezers, and the light switch was next to them. I hurried around a tractor, toward the light switch. They saw me. What I saw completely incapacitated me. I could not move.

"Oh my God!" the lovely new waitress screamed as she struggled to pull up her too-tight jeans. "Oh my freaking God! It's not what you think," she yelled.

Pete was using his large body to block the view of her naked ass. I'd already seen the freezer rocking to their beat, seen Pete bent over her, and I was shaking from head to toe. He said, "Gail, this is not what you think at all. I was just trying to help her reach the things she needed in the bottom."

"The bottom of what, Pete?" I asked.

"I was helping her get the stuff out of the freezer, damn it, the bottom of the freezer. Don't be stupid and disgusting," he yelled at me.

"Get out. Get out now, both of you," I said with a cold calm.

The woman who had pretended to be my friend, who was such a great waitress, pleaded with me, saying, "It's busy in there. You need me, and I have a dozen tables in progress. Please, Gail. Let me finish out the morning, and we'll all calm down and talk about this later. Sometimes you only think you see something. It's not like the lights were on. It's dark in here, and you didn't see anything going on. I wouldn't do something like that." She was crying and trying to explain away what I'd seen as she buttoned and snapped her clothing and tried to straighten her disheveled hair.

I fired the waitress and went to get her final check.

Mirror wanted to know what I was doing in the house when

I entered. As I looked at the reflection of my eyes, I said, "The new waitress is done. I caught her stealing from me."

A few weeks passed amid the tensions between Pete and me. It was New Year's Day, and the holiday festivities were nearly over. Pete and I had reached a cease-fire in our war, and he suggested that we drive to Niagara Falls and visit a new casino in Canada. It would be a distraction from the growing unhappiness. He insisted that it would give me special, firsthand information to pass on to my customers traveling in that direction. For me, the trip was better than fighting.

We arrived there at 1:00 p.m. He showed me around the first floor, briefly demonstrated how the slot machines worked, and pointed out where the snack bar was located. We listened to a band and watched some couples on the dance floor. He gave me a pocket full of change for the machines before he hurried away to use the restroom. "If I lose you, meet me in the lobby in a little while," he said.

I had no luck and didn't enjoy the machines with the flashing lights, loud bells, and clanging sounds. I wandered off, got a cup of coffee, listened to some more music, explored other floors, and finally wandered to the lobby to find Pete. Four hours later, he showed up, and we rode home in silence.

On January 2 he announced that he wanted me to buy him out of the additional bed-and-breakfast. His investment was half the purchase price. "I want to invest my money elsewhere. You have become unreasonable, and you refuse to sleep with me lately, so I'm going to remodel my mother's kitchen. I'll use some of the money to buy the materials until she can repay me."

Mirror dragged out that word again: "Riiiiight."

It was the solution to my problems. I made an appointment with my attorney to have a land contract drawn up. When the lawyer asked what had happened, I explained that we had an informal business relationship in which we each had contributed half the price and costs of the latest bed-and-breakfast. We had agreed that I would do all the decorating and furnishing. He would update the plumbing and heating, but I would pay for all the materials. It had seemed fair at the time.

He now wanted me to buy him out at 25 percent more than he had invested and justified that by saying this would compensate him for his labor. Each year we had divided the net profit, so I felt he had already been paid. That was not the end of his demands. He wanted to appreciate the value of the property, which would allot him a 50 percent gain on his money in three years.

Mirror was constantly screaming at me when I walked past. "Not fair, not fair. Don't do it, Miss Smarty-Pants."

We finally settled on a 30 percent gain, worth every penny to get rid of him. I gave the attorney the details along with a brief description of life with this man.

The attorney said, "I'll go file this today at the county offices. I'll put everything else on hold. Get rid of him. I disliked him from the beginning. He is crude, crass, and uncouth. You deserve better, Gail."

Once again, business and pleasure, work and romance, had mixed like wind and snow to create a blizzard, an impenetrable wall of difficulty.

I was right back to sole proprietorship on all fronts. The workload increased significantly again. I was alone one more time.

Chapter Forty-Four:
Manipulators Never Change

THE FARM AND CRAFT market was about to open for business. The acreage chosen instead of my farm had finally been drained and landscaped and had roads and parking lots installed around one building. The original founder, who seemed to radiate entrepreneurial talent and who also had encouraged me to create the Sugar Shack, came to my door with a special invitation. He wanted to show me the new enterprise. Stan was very proud of the progress that had been made from the time he brought the idea to my kitchen table until that day. The concept had reached fruition.

I was still stinging from being eliminated from the process. I was still angry because I had been further rejected after submitting my farm for consideration as the location of the farm and craft market.

I declined the invitation. A couple of weeks passed, and articles about the grand opening appeared in the newspapers. I was curious but still angry.

Mirror, never without an opinion, said, "Better for you

personally if you forgive and forget. Those negative thoughts use up time in which you could be moving your life along happily."

On the Sunday prior to the grand opening, I went to have a look. Stan welcomed me with a proud smile and began to guide me though the building while explaining all the vendors' little shops. It was an enchanting scene. I stood looking at the rows of individual, creatively decorated spaces and noticed that the very first one, just inside the main door, was vacant. It was also the last shop a customer passed when leaving.

I asked Stan, "Who is going to fill that spot?"

"No one wants that space. That's the worst spot in the whole market. It is the first one you see and the last one you pass when you leave. The draft from the opening and closing doors is a problem. Folks don't want to spend money at the first business they see, and their money is all gone when they leave. We'll probably just put benches or tables or something else in there."

"Really? What's the rent on that space? Is it discounted due to its drawbacks?" I inquired.

"No discount. Three hundred dollars a season for every Saturday, plus all the holidays when we are open," Stan answered.

"I'll get my checkbook. I'll take it," I said, surprising myself.

"Are you sure? It's really a crummy booth space. I hate to see you waste your money, and all the other booths are filled up," Stan said. I thought he looked panicked and was trying to discourage me.

"I happen to think it's the best spot in here, and I'll take care of all the drafts from the open doors," I said. I handed him my check, and he marked a receipt as paid in full. I'd depend on my son's problem-solving abilities. With his creativity and promise to work most Saturdays, we'd make this work.

I had a history of vending at craft shows, fairs, festivals, and church bazaars, and I was confident that this space was great. With my son's help, I erected my four-walled, tapestry-roofed display shed. We screwed antique wooden grape crates to the walls for shelving and stocked the fruit syrups and maple products already juried and itemized in our contract. There was a market rule that no item would be duplicated by any other vendor, and we listed all the maple products, fruit syrups, fruit spreads, pancake mixes, gift bags, potholders, and grapevine wreaths. I appreciated the fact that every vendor had the opportunity to sell with no competition.

We bottled more maple syrup in jugs from the barrels of syrup we'd stored from our own maple production. Sales were brisk.

I was completely surprised when the market created a new vending space at the other end of our row. The new business was a maple syrup vendor, in violation of the exclusivity clause in our contract. I was sure there would be no problem when I pointed it out to the committee that juried in products and approved contracts. After all, this market was not run by politicians. The folks in charge were other business owners and vendors. The board of directors had worked long hours to craft the rules. I just had to make them aware of the violation.

I immediately filed a complaint stating that this new vendor violated my contract for the exclusive right to sell maple products—that is, syrup, cream, sugar, and all other maple products.

"Now, Gail, don't be difficult," I was told. "You need to know that the other vendor represents other county maple producers and sells everyone's production. You can take your maple products to them, and they will sell for you for a portion of the sale." The chairman of the vendors' committee thought he had explained the perfect solution to my complaint.

"Why would I do that when I sell all I can produce myself without paying a commission to them?" I asked.

The board member, also a former supporter of the paper mill project, asked, "Do you always find conflict in your business relationships?"

"This isn't a conflict," I insisted. "It is a violation of my contract, which is a legal document. This issue is only about my contract with the market. Stop trying to cloud the issue and make it something it isn't."

"We'll consider your complaint and make a decision soon," he said.

The next week, my son and I noticed that one of the workers from the competitor's booth was sitting at a bench near our booth, only a few feet from our sales window. He had a notepad and was writing something every time we waited on a customer. Within a couple of hours, our competitor was offering free tastings paired with our exact sales pitch at the other maple booth. There wasn't an original idea in any of their heads; they had just stolen someone else's sales pitch. When I brought this to the attention of those in charge, they condescendingly said, "Now, Gail, you do know it is a compliment when someone copies you, don't you?"

Because we were situated in the first booth customers encountered, we adjusted our sales method and closed each sale immediately instead of suggesting customers pick up their maple products on their way out. By implementing that small change, we were able to maintain our volume of maple sales. We stayed for the year, finished our contract, and put up with the decision of the board that allowed our competitor to stay.

Although the vending conflict was angering me, during this time we became friends with Jay, an outgoing, smiling, gray-haired older man with magnetic blue eyes. He made it his business to walk past our booth and visit a bit each time. We learned that he grew and preserved the fruits and vegetables he needed to feed his family. He seemed to be intrigued with our products. He was a small man with a huge presence and a compelling personality.

An interesting history emerged as I spoke with Jay each week while I stocked the booth. I knew he seemed familiar, but there was a distinct difference in his appearance from when I had seen him in the past. He was a friend of Pete's.

When I was acquiring the bed-and-breakfast properties and Pete was updating the water supply, plumbing, and heating equipment, he had hired a contractor to dig some water and gas lines. Jay was that man. He did not resemble the man dressed in heavy workman's clothes who had dug water lines at my bed-and-breakfast locations. As we visited, I found out that Pete had operated his bulldozer at several local campgrounds. I needed two septic systems installed, so I asked him to look at the job and give me an estimate.

The day he came to measure, do perk tests, and lay out tank and line locations, he assured me he was approved by the county health department. I invited him into my shop, conducted a free tasting, and listened to him recall how he loved to garden and can and freeze the produce. I gave him a bottle of wild raspberry syrup to take home for his family's ice cream. He was a personable, credible, nice businessman.

A few days later, as I expected, a truck drove in, and I waited for Jay to come to the door with the estimate for the two septic systems. The checkbook was in my hand, and I was ready to sign the contract, but it was a woman in a truck very similar to

Jay's. I walked out to the truck, stuck out my hand, and said, "You must be Jay's wife, and I'm glad to meet you. I see you have the paperwork, and I have my checkbook right here."

"You the one who makes the syrup?" she asked in an unfriendly voice.

"Yes, I am. Would you like to come visit my shop and have a sample on some ice cream?"

"I'm not interested in you, your shop, or your syrup. You shouldn't be offering my husband samples. He's a married man. Here's your estimate," she snarled as she slapped the papers into my hand.

Mirror said, "Better find another contractor, girl. This one is just trouble waiting to happen."

I did just that. Two septic systems were installed by Jay's competitor, inspected by the county, licensed, and soon in operation at the Sugar Shack and my house.

We ended our contract at the farm and craft market and increased our show and fair schedules. It was a better fit for my business since I could choose the weekends I wanted to vend and have the others free.

Mirror reminded me, "You never know when your business will intertwine with your personal life. They say never mix business with pleasure, but no one can control the fact that business leads to pleasure in many cases when you meet someone special. Sometimes the seeds you sow will sprout and blossom with flowers you never imagined. The future may surprise you. Be prepared, smarty-pants."

Life went on, and crops ripened. We harvested, processed, and sold my farm fruit after it was made into syrups (referred to as value-added products in the business world). My new septic tanks worked fine, and I forgot all about the unpleasant folks I'd met along the way. My business flourished without my participation in the farm and craft market. I lost track of the nice man we had met there, and I never saw his disagreeable wife again. That woman's problems did not become mine. Running my farm businesses, the bed-and-breakfast houses, and the Sugar Shack was my life.

"Mirror, I don't need any bouquets or flower gardens or complications in my life. I get up, work hard, get tired, and go to bed. It is enough, I guess."

Chapter Forty-Five: Ponds and Hope

LIFE WAS RACING BY like a tornado. Some days it felt like I was whirling from one business and its problems to another and another and another. It was a major job just to keep track of the grape farm and its labor and financial records. The grape harvesting business, which included hiring a crew for only six weeks, plus scheduling the delivery of tons of grapes from twenty different farms to four different processors, was also a full-time business during the fall. At the same time, the Sugar Shack involved daily customers, sales, product inventory, raw products and processing, bottling, and labeling twenty flavors of fruit syrup. Keeping on top of the inventory and records for all the businesses and managing the bed-and-breakfasts, along with the maintenance of the forty-two acres adjacent to them, left me no time for fun. My sons were a great help in their spare time but also worked full-time at other employment. The hours, days, weeks, months, and years flew by. The one constant problem was my loneliness, and there was no time to change that.

Pete had been gone for a long time, and I missed having a companion, but not him. I dated, skated, and went to a few dances alone, but there was no one I wanted to see for more than a date or two.

Mirror had been pretty quiet but heard me complaining as I talked to myself. "I can hear you, girl. I think I heard you say you miss Pete. How in the hell could you miss that lying, cheating, stealing piece of crap?" Mirror asked.

"I'm just overwhelmed with work and worry," I confided to Mirror. "I get up early and go to bed late. I plan and organize and work as hard and long as I can, but it is just one problem after another. Now the pond at the latest bed-and-breakfast has sprung a leak. It's the one Pete built, and I know that he buried trash in the dike. I told him not to, that it would cause it to leak, but I wasted my breath. I'm afraid the dam will break, and I'll lose all the water. It's the water supply for that business. If I lose it, I'll lose the income from my summer rentals. I'm beside myself. I don't know who to call or what to do," I sputtered. Mirror must have misunderstood my grumbling about Pete and mistaken it for missing him.

"Think back, girl," said Mirror. "Remember the little man Jay? Didn't he have a bulldozer and excavator? Wasn't pond building the reason he began working at the campground nearby? Didn't they hire him to build a pond for a water supply? Didn't Pete say that is where he learned to build ponds?"

"You're right about all that, but I have no idea how to contact Jay or where he lives. Besides, he has that mean, terrifying wife. I don't know if I dare ask him to look at the problem," I reasoned out loud.

The leak was getting bigger every day when I checked it. I was tired and stressed and decided to go to McDonald's for a coffee and burger for my supper. Entering the parking lot, I saw Jay pulling out onto the highway. I hadn't seen him in over two years, but there was no mistaking that pretty new pickup truck with the cute man behind the wheel.

Suddenly, I felt compelled to follow him. I raced around the building and out onto the street, trying not to lose sight of him. He caught a green light, and by the time I got to the light, I had to stop. When I could continue, he and his truck were out of sight. I raced forward in the direction I had seen him go, and there, about a mile ahead, was the truck of interest disappearing over the crest of a hill. Off I raced, breaking all speed limits, throwing caution out the window. I had to catch that truck. I had to fix that pond.

The race was on. I'd crest one hill just as his truck disappeared over the next one. Finally, a stop sign came into view way up ahead, and his truck had to wait for traffic. I caught up, pulled to the right of his truck, and rolled my window down while indicating for him to do the same.

"What do you want?" The terse greeting from the person I remembered as a nice man was short and to the point.

"I need to speak with you about a leaking pond dike on my farm," I answered.

"Pull over there in that gas station." There were no pleasantries or friendly overtures in our exchange as he spoke and pointed.

I backed my pickup into a gravel area; he chose to drive in. We were driver's door to driver's door, with about two parking spaces separating us. I envisioned just speaking through the windows, but he got out. I opened my door and stepped down on the ground, looked up, and met his stare.

Something electric happened. Our eyes locked. Neither of us spoke for a few seconds. He took a step in my direction, and I felt terrified, not dangerously terrified but terrified like I was about to jump off a cliff without a parachute. I stopped and turned midstride. I watched him over my shoulder and quickly got back into my truck. He never took his eyes from mine and walked purposely to the side of the truck. There was electricity, anticipation, suspicion, curiosity, and something that I could not identify. Suddenly, I couldn't remember why I had wanted to speak to him. I saw aggression in his body language and locked my doors.

He stepped up to the window, still staring, and said, "You wanted to speak to me about a pond?"

I lowered the window a crack so he could hear me. "Yes, I have a leaking pond."

"And?" he questioned. Now his eyes were smiling but still not friendly. It was more like he was irritated but intrigued.

"It leaks. I need it fixed. I hear you're the best in the business. I didn't know how to contact you. I saw you at McDonald's. I followed you. I didn't know how to stop you. I didn't know how to find you again. I need to talk to you." I rattled on and on.

"Who are you?" he asked. "Where do you live?"

He obviously didn't recognize me. I was disappointed about that, but I gave him my name and address, and he said, "I can't really hear you. Open the door."

I opened it and turned to face him, sitting sideways in the driver's seat. To my chagrin, I felt that damned electric charge even stronger and realized I had put my feet wide apart on the running board.

He instantly moved into the space between my knees. Our eyes locked, and he said in a bored monotone, "I'll be there to look at it in the morning." He turned, got into his truck, backed out, and drove away.

I was shaking. I suddenly recognized the feeling that surfaced from my past. It was attraction, sexual connection, desire. I remembered sitting with my knees apart, door open, and shook my head back and forth. I tried to clear the images from my memory.

All the way back home, I kept thinking about how this was not a new feeling. I had experienced it before and often enough to make me wonder if I was a nymphomaniac. As I drove, the full realization of his marital status loomed. What the hell was I doing?

When I walked in my front door, right in the face of Mirror, my eyes revealed the story of my inner thoughts.

"So you finally met somebody, didn't you?" Mirror observed.

"Absolutely not, Mirror. That part of my life is over. I'm not going there ever again. It is always a disaster. All the men I meet are mean bastards sooner or later. I just found the guy who fixes pond dikes," I lied in self-denial, while mentally reminding myself again and again, *He's married.*

The next morning, as I walked out of the kitchen with a cup of hot coffee in my hand, I heard Mirror say, "Good morning, sunshine. You're up and dressed, and your hair is shiny-clean and looking good this morning. Six o'clock—now isn't that interesting? You sure—" Mirror's sentence had to hang in limbo because that smiling, handsome guy was knocking on my door.

"Hi. You sure are punctual," I said, greeting Jay with a huge, stupid grin.

"Do you want to show me the pond and explain the problem in person?" He got right to the point, and his blue eyes were even more intense in the morning light. There was no smile, not even a smirk. His eyes penetrated my very soul and roamed over my height and breadth with curiosity and interest. The deep character lines at the corners of his eyes did not smile; they just hungered. He had moved so close, only inches from me, and he looked straight into my eyes.

"I'll take you there. Let me get my keys, and you can follow me," I said with a forced smile and an offhandedness that wasn't genuine. I was not riding in the same vehicle with this married man.

"Nope, you might as well ride with me," he said. "There's no sense in both of us driving." This time there was a flirtatious wink, and his whole face moved from a poker-game blank to a wide, sunny invitation of hope.

My legs were shaky, and my lips were trembling. I just wanted to kiss him, even though I knew it was an irrational compulsion. He was married. His wife was dangerous, and my morals were at stake. I would fight the feelings I had. That decision was firm, but the logic of driving only one truck was compelling.

Mirror weighed in on the situation as I was closing the front door. "Come on, girl, you know this is stupid behavior. Look at you. You're drooling, and for what? Look at him for heaven's sake. He doesn't weigh 140 pounds. He's just a couple of inches taller than you, and his hair is white. His jeans have patches over the holes, and the patches he sewed on his shirt don't match the shirt. Didn't I hear you whisper that he's married as well?"

"But Mirror," I whispered, "he sparkles and shines, and his smile lights up the world. Did you see him wink at me? Look, Mirror, he's holding the truck door open for me. It's been a long time since anyone held a door for me. Its just a three-mile ride down the road. I'm not doing anything wrong."

"Oh, for heaven's sake, get a grip, girl. He is just being polite. You must be starved for attention," Mirror said judgmentally.

Soon the pond inspection was over, and I was at home again, climbing down out of the tall pickup truck and wishing I had more pond dikes to examine, when I noticed he was already around the truck and offering me his hand to help me down.

"I'll be back in a few days with the estimate. It's possible to repair it, even make it safer and the pond a touch bigger. I'll see you in a few," the man said, and then he was gone.

I began to refer to Jay as the raggedy little man when I talked to Mirror about him. He reminded me of the nursery rhyme called "The Raggedy Man."

It had been over thirty years since such strong, lustful feelings had overtaken me. I knew I was too old to be experiencing this rush. Why, I was ashamed of myself to have no self-control over such things at sixty-five years of age. He was a married man. Sometimes it is a good thing that no one can see the reaction that rebounds from every interaction we have in business with the opposite sex.

Chapter Forty-Six: To Chase or Be Chased

MIRROR WAS ALWAYS AWARE of my confusion when difficult situations presented themselves. Offering advice I didn't want to hear, Mirror said, "Most of your girlfriends were done with this kind of sexual desire and crap a few years ago. They just want a good-looking, wealthy man to take care of them. You're such a shit. Can't you get control over this? Years ago, I heard you pray that your overactive sex drive would diminish or go away. That didn't happen. I thought it was better now, but oh my God, you're still at it, and you're old. How old do you think this ragged, patched, white-haired tiny old man is? And Einstein, he's married. Remember?" Mirror continued to badger me some more. "I bet he's way older than you are, and you know the little rhyme you made up about that when the commercials were on TV. It was offbeat ad copy you didn't dare print or use. How'd that go, girl?"

"I'd forgotten about that too, Mirror. I think it went something like this: 'We have a new gal at our agritourism gift shop, the Sugar Shack. Her name is Violet. We feature agriculture tours and free tasting of our syrups. Stop by and enjoy samples and tours with Vi—agritourism at its best. If you aren't satisfied, we have another sales lady. Just see Alice.' You know how I love to play with words like Viagra and Cialis, don't you, Mirror? However, I don't think this guy needs either of those products. He's married. There's not an ounce of fat on him, and he runs when he walks. No decline there. By the way, he is seventy-five years young. I asked him when he was running up and down the pond dike, taking measurements for the repair."

My trails for my farm and wildflower tours were covered with debris. The winter winds had blown trees and limbs across them, and it was tour season again. I was up early the following morning with a trail-clearing agenda on my mind for the day. It was still very early when I went out to the barn. With no companion or help, I had to start early. I finished putting bar oil and the gas mixture in my chainsaw and pulled the cord to start it. I pulled the starter rope again, and nothing happened. It barely turned over. I checked the choke and the tightness of the chain and pulled again. Then I pulled again and again and again, until my arm muscle twitched. I couldn't even get it to turn over. Frustrated, I tried the choke in different positions and sprayed starter fluid in the carburetor. I needed to get those trees cut up. I was getting more angry and frustrated. I cussed and swore and used terrible obscenities—ones that not even my dog should hear. I called that piece of machinery every name I could remember hearing or reading.

Then, right behind me, at quarter to six in the morning, in my own barn, on my own farm, when it was barely daylight and I was all alone, I heard someone say in a throaty, masculine, unmistakable voice, "What's going on in here? What's the racket all about?"

I jumped two feet. I had thought I was alone in my barn on my isolated farm. I recognized the Raggedy Man's voice.

I was dirty, covered in grease, oil, starter fluid, and gasoline. My language was not fit for the dog to hear. I hadn't combed my hair either.

I managed to calmly turn around and look into those incredible blue eyes and say quietly, "My chainsaw won't start, and I have tried everything. I need to take it to the repair shop and find out why."

Jay said, "Let me see that thing."

I handed it over. He pulled the cord once, and it purred into action. I might have known. I figured I had it all primed up and warmed up, and of course it would have started if I had pulled it just one more time. *Sure it would*, I reassured myself. But I knew better. I just couldn't pull the rope hard enough to start the cold engine. I reached for the running saw and said, "Thank you. I almost had it started anyway."

Jay held onto the saw with a death grip. I tried to remove it from his hand, but he kept hanging on and wouldn't release it. He said, "What's a little lady doing with a chainsaw anyway?"

I explained that I needed to clean up my trails for a tour later that day. He asked me to show him what it was that I needed to cut.

I said, "It isn't necessary to show you. I will take care of it later."

He started out of the barn with the saw in hand and began to walk toward the woods.

Finally, seeing that I was not going to win, I said, "The trail that needs clearing is over this way," and we walked past my house and pond to the blocked trail.

He started the saw again and began to cut through the tree trunks that had blown down across my nature walkway. I yelled over the noisy saw, "I can take care of that," but he kept on cutting.

The chunks of wood that he was cutting were piling up in his way, so I bent over and removed a couple and then a couple more and began to stack them so that I could split them for firewood later.

I glanced up at one point, and those startling blue eyes were fixed right on my butt. I was so surprised and embarrassed that I started to back up with the wood to stack it. I was shaken. I was drawn. I was obsessed with this white-haired, blue-eyed, well-coordinated, raggedy little man.

The saw stopped. The trees were all cut, and the wood was stacked. Jay said, "Do you have any coffee made?"

"Yes. It's in the kitchen. I'll go get you a cup," I offered.

"Oh, you don't have to. I'll just tag along and get it myself."

When we walked in the front door, Mirror whispered, "You might as well bite the bullet and find out a few things about this old guy."

It was a great idea, so I asked, "How come you showed up so early? Doesn't your wife fix you breakfast in the morning?" I was visualizing that mean woman who had delivered the septic system estimate years before, and I wanted him to know I was aware that he had a wife.

"I don't have one of those anymore," Jay answered.

"You mean you don't have a wife anymore? How about a girlfriend or a significant other—do you have one of those?" I asked, pushing on with my inquiry.

"Nope, I don't have any of the above. So what kind of music do you like? Do you dance?" he asked as we entered the kitchen.

"I love country music, and I love to square dance," I said. "Not the fancy kind—Western, I think you call it. I like the old-fashioned country square dance, like they used to have at the local fire halls. They called those dances round and square dances."

"Who do you dance with?" Jay asked.

"I don't have anybody to dance with at present. I used to go to Woody's Campground to their square dances, but I don't go anymore."

"Why don't you go anymore?" he asked.

I handed him a cup of coffee. "I broke up with the guy I was seeing about two years ago. I'm really busy with my business, so I just don't go anymore. By the way, did you bring the pond estimate?" I asked.

"No, I just stopped by to tell you that I need more time to get it ready."

I heard myself invite him to come for dinner a few nights later, when he had the estimate finished. My oldest son was staying with me for a few months while his wife sold their home and they built a new one. He was starting a new job, and he would also be at this supper. I suddenly realized I would have to explain Jay's presence because delivering a job estimate and then staying for dinner would be unusual. I was creating a mess, but it was a done deal. Jay accepted the invitation without hesitation.

When the day came, I was in a frantic lather, cleaning the house and cooking scalloped potatoes with pork chops on top, home-canned green beans, a tossed salad, and a fresh rhubarb pie. I set the table for three and fought with myself about putting a candle in the middle, but I forced myself to refrain.

My son came home first and wanted to know who the third place setting was for and why I was so nervous. I tried to explain calmly that a guy was bringing an estimate to fix the leaky pond dike on another farm, and I had asked him to eat with us.

"And he is staying for dinner?" my son asked, with surprise showing all over his face.

"Yes, he is. His name is Jay. Please be nice. It's important."

"What's important, the estimate or the man?" my son asked. He had a smirk on his face and a twinkle in his eye.

"Both," I answered.

Supper went without a hitch, and Jay handed me a sealed envelope with the estimate inside. As he was leaving, he said, "There's a square dance at Woody's Campground on Saturday night. Would you like to go?"

"Yes," I answered without pause.

"I'll pick you up at seven thirty then."

Mirror had an opinion on that. "Woody's Campground is way off in the country and a long, lonely drive away. Are you sure you want to trust this man? You don't know him very well."

On Saturday I used the number on the estimate and called Jay. I told him that I was going to be a little late, so I would drive myself and meet him there.

Mirror continued, "Did you see how ragged he looks? Did you notice how skinny he is? I guess he looks healthy enough. His clothes were clean but patched. You need to think about this."

I thought about it and stressed over it. I decided not to go. Then I decided that I would go. Then I wasn't sure, and I asked my girlfriend what she thought. Finally, I just went. I drove and drove, and it was nearly dark when I arrived. I parked amid about a hundred vehicles and made my way to the table where the owner, old Barney, always sold the tickets for five dollars each.

I stepped right up. "Barney, do you allow single women to

come to this dance, and if I sit here alone long enough, will you square-dance with me once?"

Old Barney was a pleasant soul. He nodded and smiled and said, "I don't think you'll be alone for long, and I can't take your money because there is a friend of mine behind you who is ready to pay for your ticket. I know he'll dance your socks off."

I turned around, and there was Jay. He was spotlessly clean, with no patches on his clothes, and his hair was shiny white and fluffy as a cloud. I swear his eyes were injected with iridescent blue, and he was wearing cowboy boots that had just left a shoeshine boy.

"You know each other?" I asked.

"Yup, old friends. Been to a lot of country square dances around the area, Barney and me," Jay said. He held out his hand and led me straight to the dance floor. A five-piece country band was rhythmically, expertly rendering a lively two-step.

Jay's arm went straight around my waist, and he pulled me maddeningly close. My mind screamed in protest, but my body melted instinctively, intensely, against his, and my feet became an extension of his. Our rhythm melded, and he held my right arm rigid as he guided me around the floor. I tipped my head back so that our eyes met, and I became locked in the look. His lips were inches from mine, and his grip pulled me even closer against his body. I knew then that I had not been alone in feeling the amazing, magnetic physical attraction on the lonely corner outside my pickup truck on the night we talked about the pond dike for the first time.

The two-step became a simmering slow dance, and then the "Tennessee Waltz" began. He never paused or released me in between songs. A half hour later, I came up for air, to keep from drowning in the blue of his eyes, the grasp of his embrace, and the press of his hard body against mine. We were alone on the dance floor. The crowd was gathered around the edge and watching us. There was such a natural rhythm to his body and movements. My body had a mind of its own, seemingly separate from my rational thoughts. It was following his every lead and move. The dance felt beautiful, and the crowd clapped. Several folks came up to tell us that it was such a pleasure to see two people dance together so perfectly. There was then a polka and many square dances, and I had never had such fun in my life. Then the evening was over.

He walked me to my pickup truck, gave me a hug, and said good night. As I started to drive away, I looked in the rearview mirror and couldn't believe that there were no lights following me. He had asked me which way I was going home when I thanked him for buying my ticket. I had told him, and I was sure he would follow me. I had thanked him a second time for the lovely evening, and he had answered, "The pleasure was all mine, believe me." I had been certain he would follow me to be sure I got back to civilization. He was definitely a gentleman.

There were no lights behind me, and it was nearly one in the morning. The country roads were deserted. I wasn't comfortable. I began to relive the evening and felt certain that I'd been too aggressive with my dancing. I'd let my body have its own way. I'd been seductive. I was sure he was disgusted and would never be interested in me again. What in the world had I been thinking, and how could I have used such poor judgment at sixty-five years of age? Who was I kidding? After all, I was an old lady. Even though I weighed only 110 pounds, I had wrinkles. Oh God, I had messed up.

I watched the mirrors on my truck, and there were still no lights. Miles and miles of complete darkness stretched behind me. Dark road after dark road followed me in the rearview mirror.

Finally, I turned into my driveway, unlocked the door, and didn't even bother to turn on the lights or speak to Mirror. I went to bed with my clothes on because he had touched them and held me in them, and they smelled of his cigarettes. I hugged and embraced myself with the memory of that enchanted evening. Finally, sleep came, interspersed with dreams filled with blue eyes and strong arms and caressing hands.

When I awoke, the phone was ringing, and all I could remember was the rough, calloused, bent fingers on the strong hand that had held and guided me around the dance floor.

"Hello," I mumbled while I turned the clock around. I couldn't believe it was 6:00 a.m. "Hello," I said again.

There was a bit of silence, and then that deep, masculine, musical voice that had sung to me throughout the dancing said, "Where'd you go last night? I got blocked in the parking lot, and when I got out, you were gone. I tried to catch up with you, but you obviously didn't go home because when I went by your house, there weren't any lights on."

"I thought you didn't want to follow me when I didn't see your lights, and by the time I got home, I was pretty upset, so I didn't even turn the lights on. I just went straight to bed with my clothes on. I'm still dressed. I didn't sleep very well. Wow."

"Can I come for coffee?"

"Now?" I asked. I raised my head to look in the mirror. I was horrified at what I saw.

"I'm at the end of your driveway. Should I turn in?" he asked.

"Yes. Yes. Give me a minute. I need to comb my hair and brush my teeth and put on clean clothes and make coffee and let the dog out and straighten up the kitchen and put on some lipstick and—"

"No. No need. I don't care about all that. I'll make the coffee. Unlock the door, please."

212

And there he was, and I was in his arms, and he was kissing me and holding me. The sexual tension was unbearable, and we couldn't let go of each other.

Mirror was reflecting it all when I broke free of my involvement and emotion. "I need strong black coffee, and I need it now," I said, and I began to laugh.

Jay laughed too and said, "What's wrong with us? We're not fifteen. I haven't felt like this in ... ever. I'm seventy-five years old, for God's sake, and I'm shaking."

We had coffee every morning that week. When his friends and employees called his cell phone to ask why he was late at the job site, he would just say, "I told you what to do yesterday when I left. Just do it until I get there." And in answer to their inquiries about where he was, he would say, "I'm down by the lake, and Lake Erie's a big lake." Then he would hang up.

We went out for dinner on Friday and dancing again on Saturday night. I couldn't think straight, and my mind felt befuddled. He followed me home after the third week of dancing, and I invited him in for a drink of my homemade wine. We sat on the couch and watched late-night talk shows with his arm draped over my shoulder. It was so comforting to have someone to sit beside. His other hand found its way to my knee. First there was a caress, and then he kissed me lightly on the lips. I changed position so that I was facing him, and the TV ceased to exist. The only noise was a buzzing in my head. Feeling warm and contented changed instantly to scalding and drowning. My body was burning up, and my self-control was sinking to nonexistence.

I had forgotten to cover up Mirror. As you might expect, Mirror shouted, "What are you doing? What are you doing? Get a grip, girl. Does he have condoms? Are you really ready for this?"

I listened. My clothes were coming off way too fast. I grabbed his hands from under my shirt and at my belt buckle and said, "Don't take my jeans off." The words were muffled amid the kisses and heavy breathing.

As quickly as the action had started, it stopped. He dropped his hands, got up, walked to the door, and said, "See ya." He was gone, disappeared. The taillights of his truck went up my driveway and out of sight.

Mirror sighed. "You love guys with trucks. You just plain love guys. The combination of the two is too much for you to resist."

Mirror hung on the nail by the front door as always. The unsolicited judgments just kept pouring forth. I gave Mirror a mean, hard swat. I heard Mirror scrape the wall, but there was no crash. Just my heart crashed and burned. I cried. I sobbed. I turned off the lights, and I went to bed with my clothes on again. I just couldn't believe that he had quit loving me, quit adoring me with every stroke of his hard working hands, and walked away. Cold turkey—he had stopped cold turkey. There was no cooldown; he had just walked out the door.

Sunday went by, and there was no phone call and no visit. Monday, there was no coffee at six in the morning. There was only silence. I was cut off and cut to the bone.

I spent every bit of mental energy on self-recrimination. I reminded myself that I was sixty-five years old, and there were thousands, maybe millions, of women my age who would commit murder for the three weeks I had just enjoyed. I had been romanced, wined and dined, caressed, and kissed. What a fool I'd been. I was so old-fashioned and stupid. I had actually listened to Mirror. I had not had what promised to be incredible sex. How stupid could I possibly be? I wondered what any of the other thousands of lonely, single, sixty-five-year-old women would have done.

Mirror reflected my dour mood and sad countenance. "You did what you felt was right in your heart and moral conscience. Don't call him, girl. I don't know what the rules are for people your age. I don't know where they draw the lines or when they allow a relationship to turn physical, but he'll call you when he is ready. Why don't you go roller skating and get your mind on some music and exercise?" Mirror asked.

"Why don't you shut up, Mirror? You do make a point though. He walked away. He didn't stay to talk about my discomfort. You're right—why should I call him? If he wants anything other than sex, he knows where to find me. If sex is all he wants, then so be it; he'll have to find it somewhere else," I answered with resolve.

I put on my skates at the rink and poured all my energy into skating fast. Round and round the rink I flew, and with each lap I felt worse. I remembered the other million women who were doing without. Then I examined the question of just what else people at our age could want from one another. Was it long-term relationships that we craved? Was it wedding bands we desired? Or was it that we simply wanted to be wanted, loved, caressed, kissed, and valued as desirable human beings? Perhaps it was just companionship—someone to join us at the dinner table, someone to accompany us at social events, someone to keep us company in front of the fireplace while we watched television.

I concluded that what I wanted was someone to care for, as well as to care for me. I wanted—no, desperately needed—someone to sleep next to me in my bed, someone with whom I could share the day's happenings. I needed, craved, longed, and hungered for love. I needed to love another, and I needed to be loved by another, and of course, the ultimate expression of that love was the act of making love physically. I needed someone to care if I woke up in the mornings. All those things equated to love, even marriage. God forbid I even acknowledge the "m" word.

I skated like my life depended on it. I skated until I was soaked with sweat. I skated until my breath was coming in gasps and the muscles in my legs screamed with fatigue. Then, on my way home, I called him.

He must have recognized my number on his phone screen. "What took you so long, sweetheart?" he said. "I miss you. We need to talk. Can I come down for coffee in the morning?"

I wanted to scream. I wanted him now. I wanted him to rip off those jeans, throw me down, and make mad love to my aging body, and he wanted to come to my house and have coffee in the morning. I said, "Of course. See you then."

I went to bed lonely, worried, and perplexed and with my sweaty clothes on again.

The next morning, Jay showed up at 6:00 a.m. again. I was up, with coffee made and my hair combed. I said, "I'm so embarrassed about my behavior. I can't believe I came on to you in such a provocative way and then called a halt to the action." I stuttered. I stammered. I cried. I hung my head in shame.

He reached out for me, pulled me close against his chest, and started to laugh softly as he held me there. "Sweetheart, it's all right. I wouldn't do anything you didn't want me to do, but I was pretty worked up, and the only option was to walk away when you stopped me. I thought you wouldn't ever want to see me again. It's not my style to force myself on anyone. I've never had to do that, so I just waited, and I thought you would never call me. I'm so glad you did."

The tears ran down my face both from relief and from being terrified that he wouldn't want me. "Can we go to the dance on Saturday?" I asked.

"You gonna drive yourself, or are you going to ride with me?" he asked.

"Pick me up. I'll ride with you."

On Saturday we danced away another magical evening and then drove toward home in silence. We were both in our own quiet contemplation about the need and compelling physical attraction between us. Jay stopped at an all-night restaurant, and we ate hot fudge sundaes and drank black coffee until one thirty in the morning.

We were nearing the two fully furnished vacation homes that I rented to tourists when I remembered that one of them was empty due to a cancellation. The sheets were clean. The bathroom sparkled.

I said, "Would you like to see my vacation home? I could give you a tour."

"Where is it? You mean no one has rented it this weekend?" he asked.

"Nobody's there. I had a cancellation. It's right up here, about a mile ahead of us," I answered.

His hand was on my knee and rising rapidly. We were there in a flash. As we jumped out of the truck on his side, I had the key in my hand. The door got opened somehow amid the passion and groping, and we were inside. He pulled me into his arms, and the kiss was hot and overpowering with need.

I took his hand as clothes dropped off both our bodies and led him to the master suite, where there was a king-sized bed with a new pillowtop mattress. There was no need to say, "Don't take my jeans off," because they were back near the front door somewhere.

Jay smelled like soap and cigarettes and maleness. His body was a perfect fit with mine. He whispered, "I have wanted this for so long. I've dreamed of it, but this is better than all the dreams."

Nothing and no one else mattered; there was only Jay and me. Time, the world, family, friends, morals, work, pets, businesses, finances, food, hunger, meetings, appointments, children—nothing and no one else mattered at all. We were alone, our souls and bodies melded together as one. No words needed to be uttered between us, and we both knew that nothing could separate us again as long as we lived.

Chapter Forty-Seven: Blossoming Together

WE BECAME ACQUAINTED AND familiar with each other that beautiful summer. Jay started each morning by having coffee with me, and we shared each other's plans for the day at hand. He became familiar with my business and marveled at the physical work I was doing. He was determined to make my life easier. I helped him move his equipment from job site to job site, learned to operate several large pieces of equipment, and became proficient on a giant vibratory roller at one site where fill needed to be packed. I spent time helping Jay build the new ring road for the farm and craft market. The skid steer was my assignment, and I moved rocks and dirt and gravel for several weeks in the evenings.

We were compatible and stress-free.

Jay watched me struggle with a Sugar Shack display shed as I winched it up onto a trailer to transport it to a fairgrounds show where I was a vendor. He asked to take it to his farm as soon as I had it loaded. Two days later, he returned it with a roadworthy trailer permanently attached to the bottom. There was a tongue, which was detachable and made the shed fit a ten-foot show space, safety chains, and a full set of lights, all ready to hitch up to my truck. I no longer needed the winch. I didn't have to struggle. I didn't need any help. I just backed up to it and hooked it up, and away I went to all the venues on my schedule. I didn't have to wait for some man to help me. I was independent. I was so thankful.

Jay loved the gift bags and potholders I created in my sewing room. He would find me there and offer to help me select the fabrics and designs. I sometimes struggled with cutting pieces to consistent sizes. Jay arrived one afternoon with a personalized cutting table he'd built for my sewing room. It was installed next to my sewing machine.

That was not the end either. Soon I had a custom-made York rake–type attachment for my tractor so that I could maintain my nine hundred–foot–long gravel driveway. A large roller fitted with a hitch for my small tractor so that I could roll the lawns, an antique horse-drawn cultivator reengineered to cultivate my berries and gardens, and a custom-designed snowplow appeared over the summer months. Each came with his personal training and instructions on how to attach, maintain, and use the novel equipment. Jay brought to fruition large projects like an addition to the Sugar Shack kitchen and a bigger seating area for diners. The list was endless. Sometimes permits and architectural drawings or engineering stamps were necessary. Every time professional reviews and stamps were required by the building inspector, Jay's plans and work were acceptable.

It was the first time any man had taken better care of me than I had of him. I was, at last, loved and cherished unconditionally. Jay asked for nothing but my love in return, which I gave completely

Jay gave me the most valuable gift a woman could receive. He made me independent. Most of the men I had known had wanted me to depend on them. They had made sure I could not operate machinery or conduct business without them, which put them in control. Not Jay. He was always there to help if I needed it, but he helped me more by setting me free, making me independent and self-sufficient.

The holidays arrived. We had known each other about seven months. Jay had seen many ways to make my life easier. I could vend at fairs, festivals, and convention centers with no additional help. My business had grown, and a bigger customer base had developed. The fairs, festivals, and shows were a new way to advertise and provided additional options and opportunities. These venues were independent of any local political control, and that reduced my stress.

We had found a common interest in making homemade sauerkraut, fresh bread, strawberry freezer jam, pies, and beef and pork stews from animals that he raised on his farm and we butchered together. We sampled all the wines I'd fermented over the past few years and found that the red raspberry semisweet was our favorite. We made ten gallons for the long, cold winters.

Jay commented, "Sweetheart, I can't wait to enjoy a plate of fresh fruit, cheese, and crackers and a bottle of this wine while we warm ourselves another time with the wood we cut, split, carried, and stacked." Life was simple and good. We found great satisfaction in our self-sufficient, simple country lifestyle.

Jay accepted my invitation to a special dinner on Christmas Eve for just the two of us. I served a pork loin roast from a hog we'd butchered together. It was smothered in our homemade sauerkraut. I served several vegetable side dishes and salads made from produce we'd grown and preserved. We finished with homemade fruitcake. We held hands and sipped homemade wine, contented.

The dishes were done, and some leftovers were resting in to-go containers for his later enjoyment when Jay handed me a huge gift-wrapped box with a card on top. I began to open the gift, and Jay moved close to me on the couch. Eager anticipation lit up his face as I held up the heavy flannel pajamas. He wanted to know if the size was right. I went to check, and another box, a bit smaller, fell from inside the pajamas to the floor. I unwrapped that box to find some flowered long underwear wrapped around yet another gift box, which contained a winter hat to keep me warm while I plowed my long driveway with the custom-made snowplow. I commented that there would be no more paying for plowing—I was independent and could do it myself, as I preferred. I thanked him profusely for his thoughtful kindness and the equipment he had engineered just for me.

I lifted the hat to try it on, and a very tiny gift fell out. My heart nearly stopped beating. I thought I knew what might be in the tiny box. I was excited, and my hands shook as I untied the little bow and worked at the tape to free the wrapping paper.

Jay kept saying, "Open it." Now he was standing up, eager with anticipation. He was leaning forward, a huge grin on his face. Those gorgeous blue eyes were glued to mine as I struggled with the wrappings. I knew he was happy to be with me on Christmas Eve, but I hoped his excitement was about more than that.

Nothing about the next step in our friendship had ever been discussed, but the gift was the size of a ring box. I tore at the tape, and with each piece I removed, I wondered what I would do—if I could fake a liking for whatever was inside—if it wasn't a ring. I was startled by that feeling because it had never surfaced with this intensity before. I'd have to be an award-winning actress to avoid letting disappointment show if it wasn't a ring. Finally, the paper was off. The little cardboard box had a lid on it, and I held it for a long, long time. He moved closer, leaned in, and insisted I open it. I lifted the lid, and there was a little dome-topped velvet box inside.

I hesitated. My hands shook even worse than before. My breath was coming in ragged gasps, and I had difficulty opening the hinged top.

"Come on, get it open. Open the box," he said while his eyes sparkled with anticipation.

Finally, I lifted the lid and saw the most gorgeous, sparkly diamond ring. I hadn't seen one this lovely since looking at the one my dad had given my mother many decades before. It was not a huge diamond; the beauty was in the cut. It shot sparkles, colored sparkles, in every direction. I remembered that my mother had always said that the more a diamond ring sparkled, the more love came with it.

Jay took the ring out of the box and slipped it on my left ring finger as he looked unwaveringly into my eyes. The tears poured from my eyes. I couldn't speak. I was shaking all over with happiness, and the smile on my face was so big that salty tears were running right into my mouth. We hugged and kissed and laughed and danced in circles.

Winter passed, and spring brought sunshine, promise, and fishing in my farm pond. Jay noticed that weeds were becoming a problem and asked if I knew the depth of the pond, which was the water reservoir for my home and business. I did not know the current depth. He measured and declared that it had filled in considerably.

"I'd like to drain and deepen your pond for you," Jay said.

"The problem is, my excavator is under repair, and by the time it is fixed and I catch up with all the work that is waiting, it may be too late."

"I could try to rent an excavator. We could have it delivered to the edge of the pond," I suggested.

Water was a difficult commodity along the Lake Erie shoreline. Wells were not successful due to the shale in the area, and if there was any volume in a well, it was usually sulfur water. This water smelled like rotten eggs and usually had a lot of iron in it, but it was safe to drink if a person could get past the smell.

We had no public water supply. No water and sewer districts existed. Property owners had to obtain a private water supply. Ponds were the answer. Nearly every house had a pond and purification plant to ensure water safe for human consumption. The only difference at my farm was that I had a public restaurant and needed to provide a tested, certified, potable supply of water.

Jay assured me that he had built many public water-supply ponds. He knew the regulations, and soon my pond was fifteen feet deep and lined with blue clay, which is a great filtering agent, and the edge was lined with deep stone to further filter the runoff. He dug up the holding tank and replaced the old filter stone, sand, and clay. He cleaned and inspected the inside of the tank and replaced the pumping system as well.

A bonus of the huge project was that I had a chance to see how much skill and talent it took to operate the machinery. Spending a few hours each evening sitting in the operator's seat of the giant excavator, trying to learn the skills needed to operate that monstrous machine, was a challenge. It gave me great respect for the men and women who build our highways and scratch Mother Earth's back to rearrange our environment to suit our needs.

Life was sunshine and happiness, with enough challenges to keep it interesting. It was a perfect blend of love and labor at last.

Chapter Forty-Eight: Heartbreak

WE'D PARTIED AND PICNICKED, made bread and wine, watched sunrises and sunsets, attended my grandkids concerts and special events, celebrated birthdays and holidays, built his and my businesses bigger, picked berries in the woods, butchered our own cattle and hogs, and built ponds. Learning was constant and made me respect the talent, knowledge, and perseverance Jay exhibited every day. I could see why he was well respected and in demand for demolition projects, pond building, highway construction, and more.

Our lives were full of wonderful family members, workplace challenges, business deals, wine, dancing, and most of all, unconditional love. We each pursued our passions but shared the stories, events, puzzles, problems, challenges, and successes. We always helped each other. We shared everything at day's end.

The Sugar Shack pancake breakfast business was growing weekly. We had waiting lists for reservations and lines at the door. The weekly food supply deliveries grew and consumed more of my time. Cooler and freezer space were at capacity, and room for kitchen prep work was scarce. We needed to enlarge the kitchen. Jay volunteered to build on to the existing building and remedy the problem. We drew up plans, got permits, and brought in materials, and the project was in full swing when winter arrived.

One cold, snowy, blustery day in January, we needed rough lumber, and Jay and I ventured into Amish country. The truck was in four-wheel drive, visibility was limited, and we were bundled up in anticipation of loading the two-by-fours ourselves. Jay couldn't seem to stop coughing. I had the sniffles. We arrived, located the boards we needed, and paid for them. Only the wife of the sawmill operator was at home, and she was pregnant. She couldn't help us dig the materials out of a snowbank or put them into my truck. We managed to get the truck close to the lumber pile, next to the sawmill, and we were starting to shovel the snow out of the way when Jay began to wheeze. He doubled over and had severe difficulty inhaling. I suggested we just go home, but he wanted to sit in the warm cab for a bit and see if the problem would ease up. I slowly loaded the wood alone. He was sick; I feared pneumonia.

We finally made it back to the Sugar Shack, and I called our doctor. Jay was seen immediately. Jay's health had deteriorated rapidly. The doctor said he should have a chest x-ray. Antibiotics were prescribed for him. In addition, I doctored him with my dad's old remedy—a whiskey sling, made with hot water, lemon juice, butter, honey, and whiskey—kept him in bed with hot compresses on his chest. Nothing seemed to affect the infection in his chest.

By April, Jay could not walk, work, or function. He finally had the chest x-ray that revealed the worst. He had lung cancer.

Jay didn't go home to his farm at night anymore. He was too weak and sick to be alone. I started to grieve the day we received the terrible news that, even with treatment, he had six months to live at best.

My cousin came the same day the hospital equipment arrived. She volunteered to help me lift and care for him. She filled in at my gift shop and with customers. His family and friends visited whenever they could, regularly showing up to care for him and give me a bit of time off.

Jay told me many times during his final six months that he was fortunate to have time to plan for his exit. He was able to make amends with estranged friends and relatives and often directed me to invite them to visit him. This eased, for him, his passing. He was able to sell equipment and make arrangements for others to finish his contracts. He summoned his attorney and updated his will and issued a personal invitation to the funeral director for a visit at the Sugar Shack to have his last needs and wishes met.

He felt in control when each chore was completed and crossed off his list, as his last months, weeks, and days raced by. Planning and paying for his funeral and burial helped him accept the inevitable conclusion of his life. The process also helped to prepare me for his permanent absence. He engaged me in decisions, asked me to sit in on discussions, and always held my hand through those difficult meetings.

I knew, as did the funeral director and his attorney, exactly how he'd lived his life and how he wanted to exit it. He told them, and assured me, that I was loved and wanted. He insisted on involving me in his will.

The attorney asked Jay who he wanted as the executor of his last will and testament. Without any hesitation he said, "Gail, of course. She's the only one I would trust to take care of it the way I direct and to do that with kindness."

I interjected, "But Jay, I'm not your blood relative or your wife. You need to think about that."

"I want you. I've already thought about it, and that's the final word," he insisted.

"I'll never refuse you, Jay, but blood is thicker than water, so while the attorney is here, I want to lay down some conditions," I said. "First, you need an alternate. Second, I want it in writing that I waive any fees, payments, or inheritance."

The attorney raised his eyebrows and, with questions in his eyes, looked from Jay to me and then back again several times.

Jay said, "It's only fair for you to take a percentage for the work and time you will have to invest. C'mon, Gail, take the fee."

I was feeling very uncomfortable. This was family business. So I insisted. "I will not, don't need, and absolutely refuse to take any fee for anything I do for you. You've done so much for me. Furthermore, you have special family members, and everything should go to them."

"She has a point," the attorney said. "I handle lots of estates when they are settled, and relatives are brutal once the loved one is gone."

We found a relative willing to be the alternate and made that person aware of all the final arrangements and people in charge.

I never took the ring off my finger until after Jay died. He would take my hand while he was having his chemo treatments and tell the nurses and doctor, "If I can just live long enough, I'm going to marry this woman." As he said it, he would finger the ring and squeeze my hand.

I tried hard to present a positive attitude. I feared the outcome, and my grief crushed me every time I left his side.

The last night we spent together, when he weighed less

than one hundred pounds and struggled to breathe even with oxygen, he said to me, "Gail, this isn't fair."

I said, "No, many things are not, and this is one of the big ones that isn't fair. I'm so sorry, Jay. You don't deserve this, as hard as you've worked and as many good things as you have done for others, especially me."

With a rasping, ragged voice, struggling to get the words out, he said, "No, Gail, it's not about me. It's not fair to you. I'll be gone and at peace, but you'll have to struggle with the loss of our love and the loneliness. Be sure you find somebody to love. I'm not the only one. Please just lay down here beside me and hold me while this pill helps me get to sleep."

I did. His words were true. They broke my heart.

Hospice was in charge of moving him to his family home at the end. They were aware of all the final arrangements and the meeting with the funeral director of Jay's choice. There were no surprises or secrets at all.

Chapter Forty-Nine: Grief and Living

THE DAY JAY WAS taken to his farm, I ordered a dozen long-stemmed red roses and had them delivered to him early in the evening. He and I had discussed the fact that we didn't like the separation, but in view of his family's desire to provide his care and spend time with him, we had agreed to this move. I wanted him to have something from me to remind him that I wasn't far away, would visit daily, and loved him unconditionally. I sent him long-stemmed red roses.

Jay survived the move to his farm. He hung on as his family took shifts to care for him. I visited him the day after the move and wondered how he kept going. Suddenly, it became clear to me that he was hanging on because he was worried about me. I said, "I'm okay, Jay. I'll be all right. Don't worry about me. I love you, and I'll never forget you and me. I'm going to be okay."

"Kiss me once more," he pleaded as he tried to lean toward me. He was so weak, but the lingering kiss was strong enough to be remembered for eternity.

The final call came at eleven the next morning, just a few hours after our last kiss. One of the caregivers said in a matter-of-fact voice, "Jay is gone. He's dead. You'll hear from the undertaker."

A few hours later, the undertaker confirmed that information and offered to keep a portion of Jay's ashes out of the urn the family would receive and give them to me. He said, "You are one hell of a woman, and you were so good to my friend Jay. God bless you, Gail Black."

I declined the offer and said, "Don't divide Jay up. Let him rest in peace."

The funeral director said, "I'll be in touch and tell you how to locate the grave site."

Every time I left flowers at the grave, my tears soaked into the ground and watered the soil where the memory of Jay's soul would remain.

My wonderful cousin stayed on for a couple of weeks after Jay disappeared from my presence. She encouraged me to pick up my normal schedule, resume my interactions with my customers, return to roller skating, and try to put the broken pieces of myself back together. She was an angel.

My grief was nearly unbearable. It was incapacitating. My cousin had stood beside me at Jay's bedside that last night we were together. She reminded me now, "Gail, move on. I know this is final, and this grief is fresh, but the grief has been with you ever since Jay was diagnosed. At least you both had time to prepare for this, and I know that's not very comforting. Everyone grieves differently. There is no right or wrong, and I understand that your heart is broken. Still, Jay would not like to see you like this. Fill this time with exercise and stay busy. Go skating. Go for a walk in the woods. Hold your dog. Pray. Move on, like Jay told you to. He saw your broken heart and didn't like it. He gave you instructions. Follow them. Don't let this crushing grief destroy you."

I listened to her. Roller skating was something I'd done just before we met, and now it was fitting to go again just after our final goodbye.

The Sugar Shack workload continued. The workload was once again my sole responsibility and also my salvation from grief.

CHAPTER FIFTY: BUSINESS AND LIFE GO ON

DAYS, WEEKS, AND MONTHS moved slowly but became my past. I redecorated my bedroom and bathroom and installed some improvements. I participated in extra craft shows when opportunities presented themselves. Busy was good. Busy was a healing strategy. The Sugar Shack continued, and so did the growing, picking, processing, bottling, labeling, and selling of my fruit syrups. The pancake breakfasts thrived, and the vacation rental properties were fully booked. But time passed slowly, my chest ached, and I thought I had heart trouble because of that constant pain. Every day, I missed Jay. There were constant reminders when I enjoyed all the wonderful improvements he had brought to my life. Hard work and long hours helped me sleep.

Grief is an individual, personal journey, and there is no right or wrong way to get through it, just as my wise cousin said. I knew that my sorrow had started the day Jay's cancer diagnosis was declared. His death had really been a blessing for both of us because it had been excruciating to watch him suffer and decline. His pain was obvious, but we never heard a complaint, except that he voiced his concern for those of us who loved him. He recognized our pain. He worried about his family. His last wish was that one of them would continue to inhabit his family farmland. Thankfully, his grandchildren now romp and run through the meadows of his family lands. The sunshine and moonlight illuminate their lives, and I'm sure Jay's spirit watches over them most of the time.

I continue to conduct my business, including the licensing, fees, permits, taxes, and physical farm work necessary, to this day. But I will never forget. Jay's love will always be a special gift I was privileged to enjoy.

CHAPTER FIFTY-ONE: UNWORLDLY EVENTS

MIRROR TRIED TO COMFORT me. "You know, Gail, you keep finding pennies. You've been emptying them out of your pockets and dropping them in that pickle jar on the kitchen counter. Do you realize that they are messages from Jay?"

"Mirror, I think that is just an old wives' tale. I know you are trying to help me through the grief and loneliness, but finding them is just a coincidence. I'd love to believe it was more, but not a chance," I replied, feeling so sad.

I had to go to Walmart that evening, even though torrential rains were pouring down. I dressed for the downpour, drove to the store, and parked in the closest space I could find. As I got out of the car, I noticed a man in a poncho loading groceries into his trunk. It was difficult to see, with the rain coming down sideways in the wind. He made eye contact and said, "Oh my God. Gail, I am so glad to see you."

I was mildly irritated at having to stop. I was getting soaked even through my raincoat. I said, "Nice to see you too, Johnny." He was the owner of a store I frequented. He was always very helpful, and he lived in the same town as Jay. I always enjoyed seeing him and his wife, but they were not close friends.

He continued to ignore the deluge of water trying to drown us. "You'll never guess who had dinner with us tonight. He gave us a message for you. Let me get Zerena. She will tell you exactly what the message was."

I asked who that person might have been, and he said, "Jay."

"Oh, you mean Jay's grandson, the one who is named after him?"

"No, I mean your Jay," he said.

My heart began to pound as the grief poured down like the rain around us. I yelled over the pounding sound of the rain hitting cars nearby, "Oh, Johnny, didn't you know Jay died a few months ago?"

"I know. I know that. His spirit was at our table for dinner. Let me get my wife. She is a spiritualist, and she'll give you the full message," he yelled back nervously.

I froze with shock. I hadn't known they were spiritualists. Fresh grief rolled over me. Memories consumed me. I felt disbelief and kind of creepy standing there in the rain.

The passenger window descended at that exact moment. There was absolutely no way she could have heard our conversation over the pounding rain and wind. She said, "Gail, what a wonderful surprise. I have a message for you from Jay. He said to tell you that he isn't going to send any more pennies to you. He said to tell you that he would be sending you feathers from now on."

Pleasantries were exchanged, and I continued into the store. I couldn't shake the encounter. The grief I had been managing came crashing back and flooded my whole being. I couldn't remember what I had come to Walmart to buy. I hurried back through the storm and drove home empty-handed.

At home there was a folded paper tucked into the storm

door, and when I opened it, I found a drawing from my little granddaughter who was in kindergarten. It was a very fine, beautifully colored drawing of a feather. Usually, her artistic endeavors were displayed on her parents' refrigerator door. I felt chills, and they weren't from the rain.

Everywhere I went, I gathered feathers. They were usually white. The first white one was near some white gladiolas Jay had planted. The white bulb had continued to produce blooms for weeks after his passing, long after all the others were dead. Every day, I found more feathers. There were no more pennies. I found not a single one.

I refrained from telling my family. They knew I was having a difficult time with grief. One of my sons called me one morning the same week and said, "Mom, I've got the strangest thing happening. I'm finding all these feathers. They are of every size and color, and there's so many that I'm sticking them into the bark on the row of huge sugar maple trees in front of my house. It's the damnedest thing. I had to share it with you. Are there a lot of birds losing feathers right now?"

I told him about my experience. He didn't call me crazy. Instead, he said, "Jay and I had a real connection over maple syrup production."

We still find feathers in unusual places. Many things are not easy to understand.

Chapter Fifty-Two: Heavy Hand of the Health Department

A REGISTERED LETTER ARRIVED one summer day from the local health department. It declared that I was operating a restaurant with an unlicensed kitchen.

I thought the notice had been sent to me in error, but as I read the accompanying subpoena, I realized it was definitely meant for me. I was confused because my commercial kitchen had been inspected and licensed by a special state health agency officer. The license had been issued to me just three months before, and it was posted in my facility as required by law.

Of course, as is always the case in difficult, questionable situations, the registered letter arrived in late afternoon on Friday. All offices were closed. I had the whole weekend to stress about the situation.

On the same farm where I grew Concord and Niagara grapes, I had lost the fight and the right to have a pond and fish farming operation. The Sugar Shack gift shop, selling syrups from the fruit I grew, was prospering in spite of the loss of most of my roadside advertising signs. The gift shop was a different endeavor than a fish farm. It was now threatened by another government agency.

As the Sugar Shack had progressed according to a master plan that I had not devised and over which I had no control, other business ventures had surfaced, and major hurdles loomed.

It is a stretch to understand how blackberries, mink farming, retail sales, grapes, fish, a bait business, paper mills, a community farm and craft market, and billboard advertising could have any connection to each other and all become significant in my life. That is because my plan was not the Master's plan. God's plan continued to move along in spite of me, and the picture that emerged was like a jigsaw puzzle. I couldn't see the whole until all the pieces were in place. However, some of the pieces had fallen off the puzzle board, and as I retrieved them, the picture began taking clearer shape.

Mirror asked, "Are all those pieces on a collision course?"

"I think a lot of things in my life are on collision courses. I've read this registered letter twenty times since it arrived, and I am dreading this call to the local health department. I can only speculate that they've hired some new people who aren't trained yet, and therein we'll find the difficulty. They probably need to justify the cost of more employees. The growth of their department looks good in their proposed budget. I certainly don't want to end up in court fighting the health department."

I waited for someone to answer the phone at the health department as Mirror reflected my nervous discontent. I'd done due diligence. I'd been inspected by the state agency just three months before. The current, up-to-date state license was posted in a conspicuous place in my place of business as required by law.

The conversation was standard for government offices. The receptionist put me on hold, and then finally someone at the bottom of the pecking order told me that there was nothing she could do for me and attempted to end the call. After several more employees offered a variety of excuses and meaningless explanations, I finally got someone who had the authority to make decisions. The exchange was difficult but congenial, and compromise was reached when I threatened legal action.

"Mrs. Black, don't call your lawyer. We'll take care of the subpoena if you'll let us inspect and license your public water supply and your commercial kitchen," he said.

"It doesn't make sense. I still don't know why my state license for a 20-C kitchen is not acceptable to you. It would seem to me that the state license would supersede your license. It's a duplication of licensing. I already paid for a 20-C commercial kitchen license and was inspected by the state. The license is good for two years, and it is legally posted in my facility. I'm angry about having to pay another fee charged by you, having to go through another inspection by your department, and the time and inconvenience you are costing my business."

"Mrs. Black," the responsible official droned in a monotone, bored voice, "you've received a registered letter, and a court appearance is where you can voice your complaints. You're operating a public kitchen using a public water supply that is unlicensed as far as we're concerned. A few weeks ago, we took over the licensing of your facility from the state agency you named. You haven't complied by having us inspect your business. That's all there is to it. See you in court."

"Let me get this straight—you took over the licensing of my facility, but you did not send me a registered letter to let me know that?" I asked.

"It's not required by law."

"Sir, with all due respect, how was I supposed to know that you took over? When did that occur?" I asked.

"Earlier this summer. And let me remind you—ignorance of the law is no excuse. It's your responsibility to keep your food service business inspected," he asserted.

I was more than annoyed. "I'm not clairvoyant," I said. "In other words, you could send me a subpoena in a registered letter and threaten me with shutdown and more, but you couldn't notify me of a change in the licensing agency when that happened? How in the hell was I supposed to know about that change?"

"The state should have notified you," he said, passing the buck.

"You're telling me that the state should have called or sent a letter saying, 'By the way, someone else has taken control of the licensing for your 20-C kitchen, and you now have to call them and pay them a fee to inspect your business. What we charged you for your three-month-old license that is supposed to be good for two years is now no good. Sorry,'" I said in a singsong, mimicking voice.

"Mrs. Black, you're being unreasonable. It's your responsibility to know these things and comply with the changes. It's unfortunate that you can't accept the law, but as I said, you can appear in court," the official repeated.

"How do we fix this?" I asked, realizing, but not liking, that the only way to get along with this agency was to put them in control.

I was sure I could hear the change in his voice as he took control. He was still condescending when he continued, "It's as simple as letting us send our inspector to your business.

You get an updated water test. If your kitchen passes the inspection, you will receive a license from us, not the state."

"Send your inspector then. I'll get water samples to the lab and get the results sent to you. You win. I'll pay again for the duplication of licensing. Will we be okay then?" I asked.

The "in charge" man on the phone agreed, and the inspector showed up a few days later. She inspected every nook and cranny in my commercial kitchen, all the corners in my gift shop, and the labels on everything I sell, my own products as well as resale and consignment items. She could find no shortcomings. Then she walked past my new public bathrooms.

She stopped dead in her tracks and pointed at the top of the doors as if she had found a prize. She waved her clipboard and grinned broadly as she said, "That's it. That's it. You don't have automatic closers on your bathroom doors. I found something. I have to find something. You need to go and get them, but don't put them on. Just put them on the shelf because I have to find a violation, some deficiency, every time I inspect you."

I just looked at her. This was incredible. What a scam. I was about to make a nasty comment when she puffed herself up and said in an authoritative voice, "Now I need to see your water purification plant. I assume you do have one."

I was beyond arguing or making smart-ass comments. I just said, "Follow me."

The chlorination system was in my basement with the water pump. My personal supply of home-canned fruits and veggies was stored on shelves nearby.

She examined the water plant and asked, "Who installed this system and when? Who maintains it and checks the chlorine?"

I told her that it had been installed and was maintained by a well-renowned water business that also did a lot of government work. I pointed out that the company used locally purchased name-brand parts and local labor.

Then she turned her attention to my canned goods. "Well, well, I guess I need to inspect these shelves also," she declared.

"Over my dead body," I shouted at her, my patience completely gone. "Those jars are my personal food supply for my family, and you will not touch one single jar. They are none of your business, and your work is done here. Now out you go, up the stairs and out."

"Not so fast, Mrs. … what was your name again?" She was faking ignorance to make me feel unimportant. "I need to see your water supply. I have information that it is a surface water pond. I have to inspect that also."

"Up and out, and I'll show you the way. Follow me," I said as I tried to regain control of my temper.

At the pond's edge, she made notes on her clipboard. She shaded her eyes from the sun, gazed north and south, east and west, and looked very self-important.

I just waited. Jay had engineered the pond-deepening and cleaning project, and I was well aware that he also had worked with the local health department on septic and water projects, both private and public. I told myself I could afford to just be quiet and wait.

Finally, she sighed and said, "Well, it looks fair. However, there is only one man in this vicinity who is experienced and authorized to sign off on the construction of this pond. His first name is Jay. He has a lot of heavy equipment in his yard. He is located in a little town twenty miles east of here. He will have to provide a letter after he inspects this. I can't certify that it has the proper stone and clay filters to qualify as a public water supply."

I asked her again for the man's name and location because I could not believe what I was hearing. She repeated all the information, confirmed it on a card taped to her clipboard, and said I should get that inspection done immediately.

I was fighting a grin that was erupting on my face. I wished I could take a video of her when I spoke next, but I didn't have a camera with me. I kicked some stones around, cleared my throat, and savored the moment, and then finally, as she finished writing up my pond and was getting impatient to leave, I said, "You really need to check your information about that inspector."

"Mrs. Black," she said condescendingly, "I have the most current information available. Jay does not have a phone. I can assure you that he is at his place of business every afternoon to schedule these inspections. We've had this arrangement with him for years. Now I've told you how to contact him, and this inspection is over. I'll send you a report that includes your deficiencies. You'll need to address them and call us to inspect the changes you need to make."

"Ma'am, I hate to tell you this, but Jay built this pond. You see, he was my significant other and spent time here for several years, and he has changed his address. He now lives in the local cemetery. He died a year ago. You need to update your information."

Her mouth could have welcomed a bald eagle or a vulture, it opened so wide. The last I saw of her was her vehicle racing up my driveway.

The pond was not listed as a deficiency on my report; only the automatic door closers were there. They are still on the shelf.

The health department sent me a tablet of tear-off sheets with instructions to test the water for chlorine daily at every faucet on the farm and turn the sheets in at the end of each month. There were a total of sixteen faucets on my farm, and I calculated an hour a day for the testing and recording in addition to my already full work schedule At the end of the month, given my past experience with government agencies, I opted to take the reports personally to the local health department because I didn't dare depend on the US mail to get them there by the deadline. I also thought it was prudent to get a signed receipt each time. After all, they didn't even know their inspector had been dead for a year.

A few years later, the state inspector called me and said, "Mrs. Black, I used to inspect your facility in years past. It was always one of the cleanest maple and 20-C facilities in my jurisdiction. Would you like to have our state agency inspect you again?"

"You bet I would," I agreed enthusiastically.

We made an appointment, and when the inspection was finished, the inspector asked me to sit down because he had a story to tell me.

"Mrs. Black, your kitchen and maple operation pass with flying colors," he said. "There are no deficiencies except your public bathrooms, which need signs on them designating male and female. Now I want to say goodbye to you, as I am retiring. There is a law or a rule that you need to understand. The local authority took over inspection of your facility. That should never happen again unless you make drastic changes. I want you to know that the law reads and always has read that the state has jurisdiction over licensing 20-C kitchens and commercial food operations if more than fifty-one percent of the total production is consumed off-premises. The local authority has jurisdiction only if more than fifty-one percent of the total production is consumed on-premises. With your jam and jelly products and only one-day-a-week pancake restaurant, you should always be inspected by the state."

Mirror was listening. "Well, well, I guess that means you don't ever have to let the local money-grabbers in here again, doesn't it?"

CHAPTER FIFTY-THREE: BUSINESS GREAT, LONELINESS NOT SO MUCH

ROLLER-SKATING AT AN ADULT session thirty miles away was my only social outlet and relief from my workload. It was great exercise, and the music was upbeat and delightful. Most of the other skaters were friendly senior citizens. Five years had passed since I had wheels on my feet. Like riding a bike, I never forgot the skill. I still used my 1953 Chicago full-precision skates, and it was magic when I had them laced up and stepped out on the hardwood floor of the rink. The organ music made my feet dance and my body move to the rhythm. I knew I was past seventy years of age, but my feet and my body didn't care. I remembered the all skate, couples' skate, two-step skate, waltz, dance steps, and other announced skates in the program, and I found them exhilarating. A sport that I had enjoyed since I was a little girl, skating on the hardwood floors in my childhood home, was still giving me pleasure. The exercise and balance practice were healthy, and so was the social interaction. I noticed that I was attracting attention from old geezers I did not know or remember, and it made me uncomfortable. I felt like a fresh piece of meat thrown into a lion's cage at the zoo.

Mirror had asked me, with a smirk reflecting in the glass, if I could still fit in my sexy little skating skirts. The thought of exchanging my jeans for one of those brightly colored miniskirts with matching tights had given me pause. I now was so glad I had not given in to that sexy temptation on this initial comeback trip.

New faces and some fine skaters began circling the crowded rink. The beat of the organ music filled the air. The first couples' skate was announced. Men and women paired up to enjoy meeting new friends and to have stimulating conversations. The snack bar beckoned, and the aroma of coffee enticed me to the counter. The coffee promised a caffeine energy spike, and a perfect view waited at the empty booth at the end of the rink. The foot-tapping music began. Someone tapped me on the shoulder and held out his hand.

I was pleased to skate. The man had great rhythm, and he was steady on his feet and a really good skater. He asked me my name and where I was from and volunteered that he and three other gentlemen drove many miles twice a week just to skate at this particular rink. A short while later, he introduced me to his son and friends. I experienced a delightful evening. I drove the many miles home with a smile on my face and tired legs, but I looked forward to the next session of skating. I realized I was out of shape. Even that was an understatement, and the little skirts were several diets away.

The next afternoon, as I was closing up the Sugar Shack, a fancy sports car drove in. Two men stepped out. There stood my skating partner from the night before and his son. "We've been to an auction and were passing by and decided to look you up," the great skater volunteered. His son just grinned.

Gail L. Black

We visited a bit, and I was happy to see the nice man again, but there wasn't any spark or romantic interest.

The realization did surface that many women over seventy would love to have some attention from any man, spark or not. It didn't go unnoticed that this man was interested. His name was Manly, and that he was.

I continued to see and skate with Manly, and Mirror, of course, kept asking questions. "So you have a new love interest," Mirror observed.

"No, Mirror, I don't. The guy's name is Manly, and he is rather manly, but I just like to skate with him. He waltzes like a pro, and we two-step fast and with lots of energy. I love to skate fast, and so does he. It's so much fun." I was chattering on and on.

"But no romantic interest, you say?" Mirror kept asking.

"He asked me out for dinner. We'll see," I answered.

Weeks and months passed during which I skated twice a week and had a few occasional dates with Manly. I had coffee with him and his fellow skating buddies after each skating session, and there was a lot of leg bumping under the table, but not much else.

Mirror still wouldn't give up the inquisition. "I think you're hiding something. I don't think you're being honest about this guy. I don't understand the hesitation."

"Okay, Mirror. I'll level with you, and maybe it will clear up this ambivalent feeling I have. The second time I skated with Manly, he said he was having trouble with his left knee, and his right knee wasn't much better."

Mirror reflected a puzzled look and said, "Soooo?"

I continued, "He said the knee in the middle didn't have any issues though, and that knee's name was 'Russell the Love Muscle,' and I just can't get past that."

Mirror laughed uncontrollably and was still laughing when I picked up my skate bag and left for the evening.

It wasn't long before another new lady started skating, and sure enough, Manly (or Russell, whichever name he used) behaved like a lion sniffing out a fresh hunk of meat. I decided that perhaps it was time to research internet dating. My business demanded long hours of farm work. Many times it was difficult to find time or energy to roller-skate. Besides, I had already mined that diamond field and come up empty.

My new internet dating experience exposed me to a whole new class of men who didn't reflect class at all. However, I remembered my dad's advice: if at first you don't succeed, try, try again, and so forth.

Meeting men on the internet is, first of all, dangerous. But there is a thrill when you receive a flirt or a message. It made me feel desirable, proud of the creation of my profile, and successful in the selection of the photos I had included. With each flirt hope sprang forth. In my case, I had limited opportunities to meet men, and I was old. I was, however, not dead. I still craved male attention and fantasized about finding unconditional love while I picked berries, processed fruit, farmed my land, canned and froze the produce from my garden, and sat alone, naked in my hot tub. Fantasizing was my only option. At night as I tried to drift off to sleep, I remembered all the toads I'd kissed while I waited for one to turn into a prince. The internet dating sites were dangerous because they encouraged those fantasies. However, they did fill the long, lonely hours in the evenings.

In contacting and being contacted by dozens of men from across this great nation, I learned about their lives, hopes, and dreams. These interactions also presented new opportunities. My business, website, and mail-order business were of interest to them. It was a diamond mine in free advertising and increased my mail-order business. Such business opportunities were simply everywhere. All I had to do was take advantage of them.

Mirror reflected the intense keystrokes as I pounded out responses to gentlemen far and near. Mirror saw the look of hope as I applied makeup for meetings in coffee shops and restaurants. "You'd better let someone know who, where, and when you are meeting new guys," Mirror advised.

Knowing the risks, I was willing to take the chance that I might find that elusive unconditional love. Internet dating most often gave me false hope and then dashed that hope. Anticipated meetings and unsavory discoveries left me bereft, lonely, sad, and needing to start over. Each time I met a self-proclaimed athletically toned, single, nonsmoking, fun guy who listed endless likes and interests online, what I found in person was a potbellied, quadruple-chinned, inarticulate, huffing, puffing couch potato whose only athletic interest was Sunday football on television. I wondered if I was wasting my time. It was discouraging, but the advertising my business received kept it from being a total waste of effort. I concluded that nothing can completely prepare a woman or a man for the lack of truth in self-advertising on internet dating sites. I blundered forward anyway.

My first venture into that hopeful but twisted world was meeting a tall, thin guy from Vermont whose picture promised a good-looking, sexy guy. His profile was ideal and full of thoughtful ideas about how he would treat the woman of his dreams. We communicated on the dating site for several weeks and decided to exchange phone numbers.

After several weeks of conversation, we decided to meet. We each drove halfway to our destination and arrived at almost the same time. He was very well dressed, in businesslike fashion, and held out his hand for a handshake instead of a hug. That was a great beginning from my point of view. Then he said, "Before we have dinner and get to know each other, I need to ask you a personal question. What are your political leanings? Are you Democrat or Republican, conservative or liberal?"

Years ago, that was not as important as it seems to be now. Taken aback by the question, I answered.

He joked, "Oh, thank God. I just drove a lot of hours, and I'd have committed suicide if you'd answered differently." We were a match politically. He did not even allude to my religious or financial preferences. He didn't ask about my family either.

The dinner was delicious and friendly. He was polite and well mannered. I felt encouraged and surprised that this very first internet date was so acceptable. I liked him. There was general interest but no instant attraction or sex appeal.

Over dinner he shared personal stories about his journey through life. We enjoyed a hug before we each headed home, with promises to see each other again.

Soon an invitation arrived. Pink Martini was in concert near his home, and he invited me to visit and enjoy the show. My cousin lived about an hour from that city, and she was delighted when I asked to visit her and stay for a couple of days. My internet friend agreed to pick me up at her house.

When we arrived back at her home after the delightful and entertaining show, my cousin was waiting for us with chilled wine, a fire in her fireplace, cheese and crackers, and great conversation.

After just a couple of glasses of the intoxicating, smooth-as-silk wine, my new friend said, "Let me show you something." He swiveled his hips and slithered up and down on a pole lamp.

He proceeded to demonstrate his talents as a pole dancer with her art deco 1970s pole lamp.

An hour later, he said, "My name is Kit, and that dance was a ten, so now I am your kit-ten." He made a purring sound as he left.

On the drive home, I recalled how much I did not like cats. I was allergic to them. A kit-ten was not in my future. I couldn't wait to drive down my driveway to the sanctuary of the farm I call home. Work, isolation, never-ending repairs—*so what?* I thought. This mini vacation had been a great eye-opener. I was anxious to get home and go to work. The new experience had been a recharge and a reason to be thankful for my long hours and self-sustaining hard work.

First kittens and then canines—the next candidate I interviewed on the dating site was a dog lover and the proud owner of two big ones. I found his handsome face and his profile outlining a successful career and busy life fascinating. I sent the flirt this time. It was answered immediately, and soon we were talking on the phone. He had the most wonderful, soothing, masculine voice. All went well, and soon I was driving halfway across the state to meet him, but it wasn't meant to be. His dogs bounded out of his pickup truck and jumped on the doors to my vehicle, scratching the paint, and he laughed about it. They could do no wrong. The inside of his new pickup truck stank of wet dogs and poop. His profile glowed with descriptions of his dogs' tricks, but vehicle-scratching was not supposed to be one of them. I filled my gas tank at the station where we met and headed home, never to hear from the three of them again.

Internet dating would have to wait. It was show time. I loaded my products into my truck, hitched the display shed to the trailer, attached each safety chain, and checked the lights before heading out for the city to sell my syrups at a sport and travel show. The roads were bare, the winter weather was at bay, and it was time to start a series of shows to sell my products and advertise my agritourism business.

Three shows, three weekends, two hours per day of travel time, and interaction with potential customers for the farm would consume every ounce of strength I could muster. I always enjoyed great vending spaces, and traffic at these winter/early spring shows was brisk. People were tired of winter and ready to hear about my free tasting experience, farm tours, and Lake Erie shoreline walks that included wildflowers and birds. I was ready for some face time with people after the long winter of isolation, internet dating, and snowplowing on my farm. Meeting people of all makes and models was exhilarating. I couldn't wait to smile and reach out to them with my brochure as I offered free samples. I forgot the internet and its disappointments.

As I was locking the front door of my house, Mirror said, "Forget the internet—you always seem to mix business and pleasure against all odds. I can't wait for you to come home from this show and vent about the mixture. It's always a trip." Mirror knew what it was talking about.

A very handsome fellow vendor passed my booth space regularly on his way to the men's room. My location near that important facility was a bonus I had not anticipated. Soon, he returned my smiles, and each time he passed my booth, he brought me a coffee or donut and made small talk. The sport and travel show ended, and I was backing my truck up to the shed inside the convention center when that dude walked up and said, "I think you and I need to find a time to discuss the sale of my products at your gift shop. Could I bring some things to your shop for you to consider?"

I was quite surprised by the inquiry, but because I was always looking for new products to augment my syrup sales, I agreed to see him the following Wednesday, before I repacked my truck and headed to another city for the next show.

The handsome man's name was Danny, and he had a soft, deep, melodic, masculine voice, a weakness of mine. When he came to the shop, I stocked his framed wildlife pictures in a special display he provided and agreed to have lunch with him the following week. Mixing business with pleasure meant taking a chance, but it was promising and fulfilled my need for male companionship. Our lunch date followed my speaking engagement about entrepreneurship at a local high school in a neighboring city. After we ate, he took me for a drive along a nearby river and showed me his camp. It was spring cleanup time, and there were lots of other camp owners raking leaves and repairing winter damage on that spring day. He introduced me to his neighbors, and we sat in lawn chairs with them on that warm spring day, watching the river flow past.

He held my hand, and just before we parted to drive in opposite directions at the interstate entrance, he pulled me into an embrace and gave me a very warm kiss. Soon I agreed to a dinner date—no business, just for fun.

Danny was an expert turkey hunter, and spring turkey season was just around the corner. He offered to teach me how to use a turkey call. I was interested and excited.

Danny said, "I'll call you Sunday about a time and place to eat. Turkey season starts on Monday, so I'll call you on Sunday night. I think we should meet at a halfway location."

We agreed to a date the following Friday evening when we talked on Sunday night. I wished him luck for a fat turkey to put in his freezer on opening day. He said that depending on his success, he would call me again Monday or Tuesday with a time.

On Monday he called and said, "Hello, babe. I called to tell you that while I sit in my camouflage garb, I think of nothing but you. You have me distracted more than I can believe. I can't stop remembering your kiss. You're hot, babe. Should I reserve us a motel room? Are we still on for Friday night?"

Although I was attracted to him, that suggestion was crude, and I was done with crude.

"No, you should not plan on anything but dinner. The kiss was hot, and I enjoyed it too, but I'm certainly not ready for a motel room. Maybe we should just forget dinner on Friday." I knew him from shows, but I knew virtually nothing about his life except that he was retired from law enforcement. We laughed about kisses, hand-holding, and him sitting against a tree in the woods, where he said he'd gotten all hot and bothered by the kiss we'd shared.

"I'll call with a time for us to meet up before dinner," he said. Then he continued, "You know you have a heart-stopping effect on me, don't you, babe? I'll call you. Think about me, please," and he hung up the phone.

Mirror said, "That guy has got it bad for you. How do you feel about that? You can always call him tomorrow if you change your mind or he doesn't call you."

"I'm undecided. There's an attraction, but he's a retired cop. You know my history with law enforcement. I don't think I want to get involved. He's moving way too fast, and besides, he didn't give me his number, so I can't call him."

He didn't call me on Tuesday night. He didn't call me on Wednesday morning or afternoon or late afternoon. There were no calls on Thursday or Friday either, but I got ready to go to dinner with him and waited and waited. He didn't call.

There was no call over the weekend or the next week or the week after that.

Mirror asked, "What did you say to that Danny guy? He sure disappeared fast."

"Mirror, if you must know, he suggested that we go to a motel room after the dinner we were supposed to have. I said no. I guess all he wanted was a roll in the sheets. I'm disappointed because I thought there was a possibility of a friendship, but I guess not."

A month later, when a group of Sugar Shack visitors signed my guest book, I noticed that they were from Danny's home city. I said, "I only know one person from that city, a guy named Danny who is a retired law officer and a turkey hunter."

The words just came out of my mouth without thought, but the lady sucked in her breath and said to her husband, "Isn't Danny the name of the guy they found dead in the woods in his turkey hunting gear? Wasn't he just sitting up against a tree with his gun on his lap, dead from a heart attack?"

Her husband confirmed her recollection, and I blurted out, "I had a date with him for a Friday fish fry at the end of that first week of turkey hunting. He stood me up."

The woman's husband said, "No, he didn't, because he was dead on Tuesday, the second day of turkey season. It was my birthday, and he was a member of the same hunting club I belong to. I went for a drink with the guys, and that's all we talked about. He told his best buddy that he'd met a heart-stopping, dynamite woman, and he was looking forward to getting to know her. That must have been you. We still talk about the 'heart-stopping' description when we think of him. He had a massive heart attack and died instantly. He liked his women."

My heart was pounding, and I couldn't speak. The lady said,

"I still have the newspaper clipping. I cut it out for my husband, and I'll send it to you."

She was true to her word, and the article with Danny's picture at the top arrived in the mail a few days later. I took it out of the envelope with trembling hands and thoughts of what could have been. I was standing in front of Mirror, and I began to cry with disappointment.

The obituary said he was survived by children and also by a woman "with whom he made his home for thirty years."

Mirror was on it fast. "You see, sweetheart? The Master Planner was looking out for you. Aren't you relieved that you didn't go to dinner, fall head over heels in love, go to a motel, and all that crap? You might feel a little sad and cheated, but this guy was the one who owned the word 'cheat.' The woman who made a home for him for the last thirty years is the one who was cheated."

Chapter Fifty-Four: Endless Variety of Opportunities

Two of my girlfriends, who happened to be gay, came to my pancake restaurant for breakfast the next Sunday. The tables were all full, my gift shop was busy, and folk music filled the air. I was almost—almost—too busy to miss Jay. A few years had passed, but grief was still in my heart, and I guess I must have had a moment of sadness that showed in my face.

One of the girls came to my counter while waiting for her breakfast and said, "Gail, you're looking very pale and stressed. Sally and I are worried about you. We have been watching you, and we can see how tired you are. We'd like to help. If you will come to our house, we'll give you a full body massage. We have been thinking about your situation. You are such a hard worker, but you have no help since Jay died. You live so alone here on your farm. We know you've met some guys through a dating site, but we think you should try a woman. Please don't be offended. If we didn't feel your strong friendship and nonjudgmental attitude, we would never speak so honestly with you. Will you come for the massage? Please give our suggestion some thought."

I was speechless. I had been put on the spot in the middle of a busy morning, with God knows who listening. Possible responses whirled around in my head as I was interrupted time and again to seat customers, add up guest checks, and enter them in the sales program on my computer. I was cashing folks out and handling a dozen demands all at once.

First and foremost, I wasn't gay. I didn't care if that was my friends' sexual orientation. They'd always been my friends, and they were great businesswomen, successful and fun to be around. But I wasn't gay, and I couldn't imagine what would make them even consider such a suggestion.

Between figuring up two guest checks, I quietly said, "Thank you for your kindness. We've been friends for years, and I thought you knew that I really, really like men. We are different, and that doesn't make you guys or me less of a person or wrong or right—we are just different. I'll not judge you or try to change you, and I'd appreciate the same consideration from you."

They paid their bill with the usual friendly banter, but they never again came back to eat, to visit, or to offer solutions for my personal problems. I missed their friendship.

Chapter Fifty-Five: Endless Jerks

THE SHOWS WERE COMPLETED, the show shed was cleaned and stored, and I had moved on to different work. My girlfriends and I enjoyed dinner out occasionally. A customer stopped by to ask if I would be interested in meeting a friend who had recently returned from overseas employment. The customer thought we would be a perfect match. It was March, and snow still covered the ground, but winter was fading fast. Lonely was my middle name, so I agreed to speak with this blind-date opportunity on the phone. All work and no play made me kind of grumpy.

The man called. He was well-spoken, sophisticated, and worldly, and I felt like a country bumpkin because I could not relate to his foreign travel experience. He wanted to meet so I invited him to come to my shop and farm on a Saturday afternoon and offered to give him a farm tour. He asked if there was a nice restaurant where he could treat me to dinner, and I suggested a gorgeous private club on a local lake. I belonged, so I knew the food was good. When he asked for the name, I told him it was a hunting and fishing club. I suggested that he come to my farm, see my gift shop, and have a farm tour. I pointed out that then if we didn't like each other or the meeting was strained, there would be a window for backing out of dinner. He could go back home, no obligations or strings attached. I further suggested that after dinner we could go to a nearby American Legion, where a great local country band would be playing. He said he didn't dance, but he'd like to do that if we were somewhat compatible. He asked for the dress code. I said, "Casual would be fine."

The guy arrived in a sexy little black sports car, and I was impressed. I watched and anticipated his appearance. I thought he would be tall and handsome and well dressed, so I had taken extra care with my hair and makeup and my black slacks, sweater, and sparkly black and white jacket. Mirror said I looked great. I watched with horror from the window as he walked toward the porch. He was a nice-looking man, but he was wearing work shoes that I would put on my feet to shovel manure. His jeans were baggy, discolored, and torn. He wore a flannel shirt with a frayed collar and a jacket suitable for feeding the cows. On a scale of one to ten for casual, he was a minus fifty.

The gentleman offered to drive, but a late spring snowfall had started, and the stuff coming down was heavy and wet and sticking to the ground and pavement. I suggested that I drive my four-wheel-drive truck in view of the weather and my familiarity with the route.

After I finished giving him the tour, I got my leather jacket, and we climbed into the truck. My truck was new and had heated seats, and because it was cold and snowing outside, I showed him where the control was for his seat.

He patted the seat and said, "Nice plastic seats. I bet you can wipe 'em off if you spill on 'em."

I said, "They're not plastic. They're leather."

"When I left the country years ago to work in Germany and then in China, cars had plastic seats. I forgot to tell you, I brought three hundred slides of my years in Europe and China to show you. I brought the projector and the screen too."

I hadn't heard of slides in years. I was a country bumpkin, but I did know pictures were on DVDs now.

When we arrived at the club, I pulled my membership card out of my pocket to show the doorman, and my date said, "Oh my, you belong to a private club? This is nice, really nice. You have to show your card to get in?"

"I do," I said, and then no more conversation was required of me, as he talked on and on through dinner.

He talked at length about his foreign employment and told me how wealthy and important he was. Fellow diners stared at him. His voice was loud and abrasive. His unshaven face, torn vest, and ragged shirt cuffs and the path of dried dirt on the floor from his shoes attracted unwanted attention.

We moved on to the American Legion. The country band irritated his musical taste. It had started to snow, and after a couple of songs and no opportunity for me to dance, I suggested that we start the long trip to my home due to the blizzard conditions outside.

I had to put the truck in four-wheel drive because of the slush on the roads. The visibility was nearly zero, and the traffic on the two-lane road was heavy. I left plenty of room between my truck and the car ahead of us. My date never stopped for a breath and continued with the details of his wonderful sojourn in China.

I concentrated on the driving as he droned on and on. Then he announced that I should turn down the dash lights because they were too bright and hurt his eyes. I explained that it was a new truck, the driving was dicey, and I didn't know how to dim them. He suddenly unclasped his seat belt and announced, "That's fine. I'll just cover up the dash lights with my hands."

"Put that seatbelt back on, settle back in your seat, and stop talking please. I am concentrating on the bad road conditions, and I need it quiet," I demanded.

He was quiet for a few miles, and then, out of the blue, he said, "You need to know something."

I could see him in my peripheral vision, looking at me expectantly. I kept looking straight ahead, trying to see through the blowing snow and follow the taillights of the car in front of me, and said nothing.

He continued, "My little boy parts don't work anymore."

I almost wrecked the truck. He had gone from his glorious escapades in China to the most personal information I did not want to hear. "Look," I said without turning my head, "I'm having trouble seeing, the road is icy, traffic is heavy, and I don't give a damn. Just sit there and be quiet. I'll get you back to my house safely. I don't want to hear any more."

He quit talking for about five miles, and then he asked, "What about you? Do you still like sex?"

I was speechless. This guy was certifiable. I didn't answer. I just drove. I kept my eyes on the road, my hands on the wheel, and my mouth shut. However, my mind was working overtime. How was I going to get rid of him when we got to my house? I sure didn't want to see three hundred slides of his boring life outside the USA. Then I had an idea, and I didn't have to wait long to try it.

"Well, you didn't answer me," he said. "Do you still enjoy sex?"

I was ready. I exaggerated, "Oh yes, I like it morning, noon, and night and sometimes at coffee break too. I always have, and I always will."

It worked. Just then, I pulled to a stop in front of my house. He jumped out of my truck like the seat burned him. He raced across the parking lot, and the sports car was headed out my driveway before the headlights were even turned on.

I unlocked the door, and Mirror said, "Tell me, how was the date? Where is the clod in the barn clothes?"

I looked at my reflection in Mirror and started to laugh, and I could see that Mirror wasn't surprised. "He said his little boy parts don't work, and I sent him home to his mommy."

Spring sparkled by, and my girlfriends and I enjoyed concerts, fish fries, music, and dancing. At least my fruit syrup business and my farm kept me constantly busy. Reworking my business plans each year kept me focused most of the time on something other than my personal shortcomings and absent love life.

Those new plans saw the closing of some enterprises, the sale of others, and the prospect of success in storytelling in book form as I penned my first memoir, *Asses and Angels*.

A clean-cut, retired, successful man arrived, uninvited and unpursued, in my life. He invited me to accompany him on a trip to Europe and then suggested that I could finish my book writing at his home. Five years later, when I was comfortable in the relationship, and when the book was published and selling very well, he walked out of my life as suddenly as he had arrived. At seventy-five-years of age, that is a huge, traumatic event.

CHAPTER FIFTY-SIX: FIRE IN THE EYES

LONELINESS IS PART OF life, as are happiness, health, illness, work, finances, relationships, business, boredom, excitement, and a long list of experiences and emotions. We embrace them, extract good or evil from them, and hopefully learn and grow from them.

Mirror observed my pensive state of mind and honed in on my philosophical ramblings. "You're trying to make sense of things again, aren't you?"

"Mirror, I'm disappointed. What I thought was a great relationship, even though not necessarily love, didn't pan out. I guess it was just excitement, something new and different, and a relief from loneliness. Maybe it was the hope of unconditional love, but it was probably just lust on my part. A long dry spell in my sex life made me horny as hell," I replied.

"You never have been able to distinguish between lust and love. You keep letting your sex drive get in your way. You move too fast in that direction. You need to go visit an adult bookstore for some self-help advice or lessons or whatever, girl," Mirror jeered.

I was embarrassed and mad at Mirror's revelation about

my most private, delicate, personal thoughts. "You have some nerve to criticize me. You just hang there and reflect with hindsight. You don't know anything. Shut up."

"Are the facts and your track record too much for you?" Mirror relentlessly continued. "You keep meeting guys, looking for some elusive emotion, being disappointed, holding grudges, and believing that each one will lead to unconditional love. From my point of view, either the Master Planner will see that a happy relationship comes to you, or you can just keep trying to control the situation. Accept the things that happen, learn from them if there are lessons, and quit viewing every man as a possible answer to your loneliness. Only you can make yourself happy. You are the one who decides. Most of the fellas you've known have had their own agenda, as you should know. This last one certainly had his. It was a good run. You had some travel, saw a lot more of the world, met great people, and wrote your first memoir. Now it is time to get over it and move on. I'm sorry about the lecture, sweetheart, but you need to hear it."

I continued with the self-pity party. The last guy had absolutely been a jerk. I'd never before encountered a narcissist and I'd been slow to recognize the behavior. I slammed the front door as I went to pick wild black raspberries to make syrup to sell in the Sugar Shack. Mirror was right; I had learned another lesson, and it was expensive and heartbreaking.

At least I still had the Sugar Shack business, my health, and enough experience mixing work and romance to grudgingly admit it was time to go back to work.

Chapter Fifty-Seven: The Fog of Disappointment

I DO MY BEST thinking, deciphering, learning, and clearing my head when I am in the woods walking, observing nature, or even picking berries.

As I picked berries on this day, I asked myself why I had glorified this last man in my mind and my book. Why had I felt so disappointed at the end of the relationship? It was what it was. I had provided him with a woman on his arm, which included the appearance of someone idolizing him. He had provided a ring for my finger, which had given the appearance of a lasting relationship for me. Had there been love? Had there been hot sex? Had there been any promises of love forever more? Had there been long-range plans? No. The answer was simply no. There had been daily companionship, friendship, someone to turn the light off for me at night.

I decided that the end of the relationship was like the death of an old friend. We had grown comfortable, complacent, and ho-hum in our daily interactions.

It was a difficult struggle to adjust to single life again. Mirror looked stunned, pale, unhappy, and sick—bereft, like the grim reaper—and said nothing each morning. Mirror just reflected the unending river of tears dripping from my chin on those summer mornings after my companion of five years simply said goodbye and walked out. Failure was the overwhelming feeling I couldn't seem to shake.

I slunk across the backyard one morning, hanging my head like the failure Mirror thought I was. I disappeared into the brush along the edge of the trail. I moved along, nearly doubled over, as I sobbed in the silent woods. I had to grieve my loss before my store opened. I knew the show must go on, and my customers wouldn't like my depressed self-pity.

I made my way to the edge of the cliff and found my secret path leading to the bluff at the top of the rocks. The lake was calm and glistened in the warm sunshine. I fell to the ground, rolled onto my stomach, and sobbed loudly.

My beautiful cocker spaniel was in tune with my distress. She had followed me and now curled herself against my side, whimpering. We stayed like that for a while, and then I gathered her into my lap and cried some more. She submitted to the wet tears, seemed to understand my emotional pain, and lay still.

This land and this dog were my confidantes. They comforted me and healed me. The trees, the lake, the sun—all of nature—put my heartbreak and discomfort into perspective. I began to hear my ragged breath, my groans, and my sobs and realized that they were getting softer and farther apart each day as I made the trip to the lake's edge. I remembered to think about an important fact, that all things are relative. This was just a moment no longer than the twinkle of an eye in comparison to the beauty that surrounded me. I heard my voice, like it was someone else praying: "Thank you for all you have given me, even the five years with that bastard. Forgive me, but I am still upset, but thank you for keeping me safe and sane—well, maybe not sane, but able to move on. Help me. It seems that you, God, are my only unconditional love. Maybe that's the lesson I'm supposed to learn. Help me."

I was cried out. I felt peace. A smidgeon of forgiveness edged into my thoughts. My dog was ready to go.

Walking back to the house, I realized that life simply moved on, and there was no change or apparent dark cloud hanging over me. It was time to open my gift shop. Whatever fate befell me, the Sugar Shack business remained stable.

Romance was an escape from my work; my work was a healing tool when romance failed. Prayer seemed to open up my thoughts and calm my pain.

CHAPTER FIFTY-EIGHT: RELEASE, FORGIVE, MOVE ON

TWO DAYS PASSED, AND it was Memorial Day weekend, a busy time in my Sugar Shack gift shop. I wasn't sleeping or eating properly, and I said to Mirror, "You know, I can't imagine how I will get through this weekend. There are so many unanswered questions. I roll around in my bed, and the years with this guy just play over and over. If I drift off, I wake with a start because I am dreaming about all of it. I consciously know that I have a business to run, and I have to get past this, but I can't."

Mirror, no longer disgusted with me and wise as always, said, "Do what you always find helpful—write. Write the inconsiderate jerk a letter and get it off your chest. Tell him how you feel and what you're thinking and how much he hurt you. Then send it to him. In years to come, you'll find comfort in having written it. Maybe there'll be a hidden clue in the letters about why, or what you learned about it or contributed to the cause of it. Write the bastard a letter. You'll feel better."

Mirror was wise. I wrote more than one letter and documented all that I could remember about our years together, him and me. The process was cathartic, insightful, and a great release as it cleared my mind. Throughout that stressful summer I learned that Mirror was truly wise but not always right. Most of all, I realized that over time, as I wrote those letters, the disappointment, hurt, and grief diminished. Once in a while, I had better judgment than Mirror though. I did not mail the letters.

Noticing my continuing distress, Mirror offered more unwanted advice. "Do you remember, Miss Sad Eyes, the guy who offered to help with the grape farm work after your second husband, the chief of police, shot himself?"

I ignored Mirror, but to no avail, as Mirror's monologue continued. "That guy gave you the best advice possible. He said, 'Quit griping. Put your nose in front and your ass behind and get on down the road.'"

I considered Mirror's comments and decided I didn't like them. However, there was merit in the memory of that long-ago conversation. I crossed the yard to the old farmhouse I call home, and I prayed again. I asked God to help me through this loneliness. I said, "If I have to have another failed relationship, be alone, suffer the humiliation of being dumped, and then spend the rest of my life alone, please help me learn to like it. I don't like being alone, and I don't see any reason for it. Just let me understand why I keep ending up alone with no long-term relationship. Lord, know that I am thankful for all the great parts of my life, all the really important things in my life that are more than fine. Help me to not complain about the stupid things like this failed relationship."

I desperately needed to remember that the Master Planner would not let me down. There were so many things for which to be thankful, but I couldn't see out of the tunnel of my despair and loneliness. I could never have imagined the direction my life was taking.

My farm, work, gift shop, and customers were my therapy. They were a constant source of fulfillment as I picked the berries to fill the demand of my customers. and then welcomed them into my business to shop. My dog, the work, and my children and grandchildren were my map back to happiness.

I found reasons to laugh. I found great humor in the fact that my former friend had decided that I didn't need a parcel of land that I owned. He had installed a "For Sale by Owner" sign on it, including my phone number, just before he walked out. Thus, a constant parade of eligible suitors came by to inquire about that parcel of land. Business and personal problems intertwined in a surprising turn of events.

Time passed, and the former friend was not important enough to receive the letters I had written. In fact, by the end of my summer of distress, he was not important at all.

CHAPTER FIFTY-NINE: MORE LOSS

MY LITTLE COCKER SPANIEL, Iwannago, was a constant source of comfort. She was my companion. She listened attentively to every complaint and cuddled with me through all my tears. We went for long rides in my pickup truck. We walked the wooded trails on my farms. She greeted every customer, filling the void in my life in a way I never could have foreseen.

Iwannago kept me company as I picked fruit, created product, waited on customers, and ate my meals and even as I slept. The sharp pain of loss was buffered and eased by her presence.

The crisp coolness of fall stung my face one morning. Iwannago wasn't keeping up on our walk through the falling leaves by the edge of Lake Erie.

Mirror was jealous because I was talking to Iwannago in place of our long conversations of the past. Iwannago never criticized me. Iwannago cuddled with me by the fireplace and licked my hand, things Mirror couldn't do. Iwannago did not argue with my reasoning. That was my train of thought as I looked back to see her lying in the path. I called her. She looked up but made no effort to follow.

Finally, when I turned to retrace our steps home, she heaved herself to her feet and trudged along behind me. I had to slow down and keep encouraging her to follow me. I remembered that her appetite had been waning. She'd been sleeping a lot. Something was terribly wrong. She was drinking a lot of water and eating very little.

Mirror said, "You'd better take that little wimp to the vet. She's not acting like her perfect little self, Miss Smarty-Pants."

"I know, Mirror. I'll make an appointment. It is time for another round of shots and some flea medicine anyway."

I put the visit off for a while, and she seemed to get better. Then there was a rapid decline. I noticed that she did not drink from the pond as she used to when we passed by on our walks. She slept a lot, but she was eating normally. I reasoned that she was just getting old. After all, she was thirteen.

The day of her appointment came. That afternoon, before loading her in the truck for the trip to the vet, I took her for a walk. She walked to the edge of the sparkling pond water, took a couple of half-hearted laps, and lay down. I called to her, but she didn't get up. Finally, I picked her up, carried her to the porch, and held her. She was panting on that hot fall afternoon.

Iwannago was always in tune with my feelings and emotions, and I was worried. She looked up at my eyes as I held her in my lap. There was a pleading look about her as she relaxed on my lap and I stroked her head.

"Iwannago, I know you're very sick. I know you're old. I've seen a change in you in the last few weeks. I'm so thankful for the friend who painted your portrait. That charcoal picture is a treasure, and the lady captured your sparkling personality when she created it. I'm so worried about you now, because in the last couple of days I've noticed that your sparkle is gone.

You seem to be in pain. We're going to the vet now to find out how to make you better. I promise I won't let your pain hurt you, no matter what she finds wrong," I said.

Iwannago just licked her lips in a tiny doggy kiss way and cuddled closer as I carried her to the truck. The trip was short, and when we arrived, I carried her into the doctor's office.

The news was not good. The vet said, "Mrs. Black, I believe Iwannago has pancreatitis. You have some choices to make. There are treatments and operations to prolong her life if you wish. They aren't painless and come with no guarantees. Usually, this diagnosis is ugly, and the treatments are not successful in older dogs. The choice to treat her or not is yours. She's suffering. What's your wish?"

My eyes filled with tears. I had anticipated bad news even though she'd been sick only a short time. "Are you saying I should put her to sleep?"

"No, no. I will treat her if you want to try that route. I'm just being honest with you about the prognosis and her discomfort throughout the treatment. I'll do as you wish, but you have to decide."

Sobbing, I said, "I promised her that I wouldn't let her suffer. I want to take her home to say goodbye to her."

When the vet spoke again, I could see that this was difficult for her too. "I think you've decided to end her suffering, and I think that's a humane decision. I know how hard it is for you. We can set up a time, or you can take her home, say your goodbyes, and get her favorite blanket and toys, and we can do this in about an hour. The suffering for both of you will be shorter that way."

My best friend and constant companion cuddled against me on the way home. We sat on the living room floor, and my tears fell on her face. She never looked away, and I saw

277

understanding and connection in her eyes. I gathered her favorite things and then took her for one last long walk by the pond. Again, she tried to drink from the pond. When she couldn't get out of the edge of the water I carried her to the dock. I said to her, "Iwannago, I love you so much. You've given me your unconditional love for thirteen years. This past summer we've been inseparable, and you've given me extra love and strength. You may be a dog, but you understand so much. It has occurred to me that the word 'dog' is God spelled backward, and you've given me love similar to His unconditional love. I'm going to end this suffering for you. I will hold you and cradle you in my love as you leave this world and go to your reward. I just need to know where you would like to have your final resting place. Kanigo, your predecessor, is buried right outside my kitchen window, where I can think of her every time I look out that window. I wish I knew where you'd like to be. I'll miss you and remember our bond forever."

Iwannago eased free of my lap, wobbled straight to Kanigo's grave site, and lay down. It was unbelievable, surreal, and uncanny. I tried to call her back to my lap. She wouldn't get up, or maybe she couldn't get up. At any rate, I picked her up and took her for her final ride. It was all I could do to drive with the tears cascading down my face. My chest heaved with sobs as she lay close against my side.

Holding her while she went to her final sleep was one of the hardest things I've ever done. I kept reminding myself she was a dog, not a child. It didn't help. The loss and grief were overwhelming and incapacitating. I buried her before dark, right next to Kanigo, in the spot she chose. I vowed to never own another dog. The pain was excruciating.

It seemed that the loss of Iwannago was too much on top of

the newest relationship loss I had just experienced. Every day was empty and devoid of love and companionship.

Crisp fall days turned to snow that covered doggy graves. The dead flowers I had picked for those graves blew away in the wind, joining the fallen leaves and gusts of swirling snow on their trip to the waves of Lake Erie.

The house was quiet and dark as the days leading to winter shortened. I ate whatever I could find, cold, leftover, canned, or donated by a worried friend or family member.

Mirror finally had enough of my self-pity. "Get off your ass, girl. Start that computer of yours and search for puppies. Kanigo and Iwannago would not want you to waste your heart full of love. Find a new dog. After all, you were broken by the loss of Kanigo, and your daughter-in-law and granddaughter took you to a pet store. You had vowed to never have another pet then too, but Iwannago stole your heart the moment you saw her, and you brought her home that night."

A few days later, a woman from a nearby spiritualist enclave came by to purchase a gallon of maple syrup. She asked if I'd ever had a reading, and I told her no, but I'd always been curious. She suggested a trade—a reading for the maple syrup. I agreed, thinking that she just might bring me a message from my dad or Jay. I was feeling so lonely and sad. I was depressed, and she had no way of knowing who I was or whom I had lost permanently.

She did have messages that no one could have predicted or contrived. I was amazed and pleased and comforted. Then she said, "I have a message from a different spirit. It is not a human spirit. The message is from a small dog. She wants to thank you for not letting her suffer. She wants you to love again." The session was over. The spiritualist left with her maple syrup, and I've never forgotten the messages.

New experiences broadened my education and expanded my beliefs. Mayigo came to me just before Christmas. She has taken up the greeter's role at the Sugar Shack, where she continues to do a fine job every day.

Chapter Sixty: Answered Prayers, Maybe

Days, weeks, and months passed slowly, with lonely, agonizing self recrimination. I tried to stay busy enough and work hard enough on my farm and in my gift shop so that I could sleep. I was recovering from my damaged self-image and my companionship losses. I went to bed sad and woke up with tear-swollen eyes.

The loss of any love causes grief and grieving because it is the death of a dream, the end of a lifestyle, and an irreversible change over which there is no control.

Customers came and shopped. I picked berries, and I worked longer each day to take up the alone time. My girlfriends called every day, as girlfriends do, to make sure I was okay. I wrote more letters to the disappointing man who had let me down, moved out, and moved on. I stayed busy, which I believed was the best way to overcome problems of all kinds.

I remembered that I still had the twelve acres of land with a "For Sale by Owner" sign posted. People called my number, which was listed on the sign, walked on the land I wanted to sell, came by and picked up a map of the property, thought about it, and walked away. I didn't really care if I sold it or not. Not much mattered to me.

One afternoon I got a telephone inquiry from a man who wanted to walk the twelve acres. I offered to give him a map if he wanted to stop at the Sugar Shack, where I kept a stack of them. He said he'd think about it and be along if he had an interest after he walked around. I gave him directions to the shop.

A few hours later, the phone rang again, and the same man said, "I must have gotten the directions wrong because I'm not at the right place. Where are you? I'd like that map. I'm at the Caddy Shack golf course."

I said, "You went in the wrong direction. If you come here, I'll give you the map and tell you about the property." I gave him directions again. The problem was, when I reached for the maps, they were all gone.

On my way across the lawn to my office to make more copies for this prospective buyer, if and when he showed up, I prayed. I said, "Please, Lord, help me. I'm so broken and lonely that I can't handle it. If I have to be alone, please help me to like it. If you want me to have someone for company and companionship, or maybe unconditional love, then send somebody. I can't do this on my own. It just never works. I always make a mess of it. So, it's up to you. Your will be done."

A few minutes later, a pretty pickup truck with gold trim parked in front of my Sugar Shack. I was startled because the truck looked almost exactly like Jay's from years ago. It was five o'clock, the same time Jay had always come for supper before he got sick. I drew in a sharp breath, stiffened my spine, and started over toward the truck. The door opened, and a tall, thin, handsome, twinkly-eyed, smiling gray-haired man stepped out. The sight of him took my breath away. I couldn't even speak.

"Hello, ma'am. I'm the one that called about the map," he said.

"I just printed some new ones," I told him.

He stood by his truck, and as I approached, he asked, "What is this place? What do you have here?"

"I make fruit syrups, and this is a gift shop. Please come in and look around. I offer free syrup tastings on ice cream. I grow, pick, process, bottle, label, and sell them all right here."

He followed me into the shop, and I got him some ice cream and a spoon. After a few samples, he said, "My family would love these."

"Well, go get your wife and family; I'll give them samples. I offer a free farm tour too," I said, as I thought that she was one lucky lady to have this soft-spoken gentleman for a husband.

"I don't have a wife. She died three years ago," he said. He looked so sad that I thought he might cry. "Do you do all this by yourself, or does your husband help you? You must have a lot of employees," he commented, obviously trying to recover from the stab of his grief.

"I don't have a husband, but I did have a significant other who helped me a lot here in the shop, waiting on customers. A while ago he announced he was moving out and moving on." I couldn't help the tears that ran down my cheeks as I revealed this.

I saw sympathy and understanding flash in the handsome customer's eyes. "Please don't be upset. You know, sometimes things happen at the perfect time. I might like to take you out to dinner sometime this summer."

Out of my mouth came unexpected words. "How about

tonight? I know where there are fifty-cent wings and really good pizza."

He took three steps backward and was quiet for a minute, and I realized what I'd said. I was embarrassed. I was about to apologize when he said, "I'll go change my clothes and come right back. Is about six thirty okay?"

Chapter Sixty-One: Stay Tuned

THE HANDSOME GENTLEMAN RETURNED at six thirty on that summer evening. We dined, conversed, walked, and became acquainted. I learned that his life was full to overflowing. He was a southern gentleman. His family business brought him to my area each summer and had done so for decades. After our pizza and wings, we toured my farm, and he suggested that his friend who lived nearby would be a great blind date for me. He offered to introduce us.

"What exactly do you do when you are here all summer? What kind of family business travels north for just two and a half months?" I asked, trying to cover my disappointment at being pushed off onto his friend. The fact that he obviously was not interested in me personally and was giving my friendship away, before we even explored the eye twinkles, smiles, and possibilities of this connection, was disconcerting to say the least. I wondered if the match I was striking was just going to spark and go out. I had been sure I noticed a virtual match in his hand as well, with plenty of sparks flying from it. He was a big flirt and had created the impression that he was available but now wanted to pass me off to his widowed friend.

"We are food vendors at fairs and festivals," he said. "If you ever go to the county fairs, perhaps you have tasted my family's waffles or pizzas. I'm originally from this general area and a farm boy at heart, so I'm really interested in your grapes and equipment and procedures."

"You know, I wrote a book, my life's story, or part of it," I offered, "and a good bit of it is the story of this farm, how I bought it, the struggles I had as a female grape farmer, and a lot more."

"My daughters might be interested in the book, but I'm not much of a reader. Where do you sell it?" he asked.

"I sell it on the internet, on Amazon, but I sell most of the copies right here in my gift shop," I answered as we walked back from the vineyard, orchard, and lake trail.

He asked, "Do you happen to know a woman named Marge, known as the Jelly Lady? She's from the neighboring town to the west."

I was surprised that he knew my competitor in the homemade fruit product business. She was a friend of mine. "I do. She is in her nineties, I believe. She still makes and sells her jellies at fairs and wine festivals. She has been a friend and inspiration to me for years. She visits here once in a while. I love her and want to be like her when I grow up," I joked.

He smiled and said, "She comes to my waffle stand when I'm at the local festivals. She always has a jar of jelly in one hand and a dollar bill in the other to make up for the discrepancy between the price of her product and mine. I always say, 'Now, Marge, you put that dollar bill right back in your pocket. I'll take the jelly and a hug, and we'll call it even.' She's a great old lady. I've known her for most of the years we've been coming north for the summer."

"Would you like to see my setup for the fairs and festivals I do?" I asked.

As we rounded the corner of my barn, I said, "It's a trailer that my one true love, Jay, put together for me so that I could move from show to show without any help. I understand the loss of your wife, and I'm sorry. My friend died of lung cancer soon after he put my display shed on the trailer. It startled me when I saw you drive in because he drove a truck that was almost identical to yours. It even had a fuel tank in the bed behind the cab."

Just then, we rounded the corner and came to where my rustic, board-and-batten, farm stand–type shed was parked. My new friend said, "I have a picture of this in my phone. I don't believe it. You do a couple of the same fairs I do, don't you?"

"I guess so. I vend at the grape festivals, some local craft shows, and sport shows in about a seventy-five-mile radius."

As he searched the pictures in his phone, he said, "How much is your book? I do think I want a copy."

We reentered my gift shop as it was getting dark. I signed a copy of *Asses and Angels*, and he asked the price.

I had thoroughly enjoyed my evening and had forgotten all the pain of the last few weeks. Now I felt panicked that he was about to leave. What I really wanted was to hug him, but he had tried to fix me up with a friend of his.

I was putting the book in a bag with a brochure and a bookmark when he asked again, "What do I owe you?"

I heard myself say, in an unrehearsed way, surprising even my subconscious being, "Oh, I couldn't charge you. You paid for the pizza and wings, and you drove. The book is free to you."

"Oh no, I won't have it that way," he said, and he started to hand me more money than the cost of the book.

I still desperately wanted to hug this handsome, kind man.

"Okay then, I'll tell you what," I heard myself say. "I know you value your hugs at one dollar each because you told me the Jelly Lady's product cost a dollar less than yours, and you told her to put her dollar bill away and you would take a hug instead. So the book is ten dollars, and I'll take the price in hugs starting right now. That will be ten hugs, plus another one for the sales tax and packaging."

I held my breath and waited for him to turn and run out the door to his truck. Instead, he held out his arms and said with a twinkle in his eye and a big smile, "Well, come on around the counter, and I'll make a payment."

A moment later, I thought I had fallen into an abyss of safety and happiness. What a hug that was. It threw colored sparks all over the inside of the Sugar Shack gift shop. I handed him the bag with the book from the counter and said, "That's one dollar on your bill of eleven dollars, sir."

We walked across the lawn to his truck. It was nearly dark. Halfway there, I heard myself say, "You know, that hug was really good. I think I'd like another."

He turned and gave me another long, delightful embrace, complete with a kiss on my cheek, and said, "It's been a great evening. We'll have to do this again sometime this summer."

"I'd like that," I said. "How about Friday night for a fish fry, my treat? I'll take you to a rod and gun club where I belong."

"About the same time, six thirty?" he asked.

I felt like I was dancing among the stars and moon as they came alive in the night sky. I couldn't believe my ears when this fine southern gentleman, who had insisted on driving, opening the door, and helping me in and out of his pickup truck, who had held my elbow as we toured my farm, and who had given me the most intimate, warm hugs I could ever remember, said,

"You know, two hugs is not a third down on my bill. I think I need to give you one more before I leave."

We were standing by his truck, and he had the driver's door open as he put the book in the backseat. He turned and pulled me close and didn't let go, and I heard two little moaning sounds, one from each of us.

Just then, we were illuminated in the brightest light I could imagine. At first, I had the fleeting thought that it was lightning, that the hug had caught the universe on fire. I untangled myself and looked toward the back of his truck, and there was one of my sons, standing in the glow of his own truck's headlights.

"Are you okay, Mom? Is everything here all right?" he asked.

"Oh. Yes. It. Is." The southern gentleman's hugs were most enchanting.

Chapter Sixty-Two: Asses and Taxes

HOLIDAYS BECAME MEMORIES. GRANDCHILDREN matured, gave me great-grandchildren, and took them to homes far away. Others grew into their lives and found meaningful activities, and we all enjoyed the highs and endured the challenges of maturing young adults as life moved on. My life was filled with quiet, calm, unruffled days. Texts and phone calls came daily from my southern gentleman as our friendship thrived.

Winter passed, spring bloomed, and my phone rang. My gentleman friend from the south said, "Good afternoon. I'm back in the area for the summer. How about meeting me for dinner tonight?"

I was ecstatic. The gloom and loneliness of the long, cold, isolated, dark winter had finally passed. The winter chores of sewing potholders and gift bags, deep-cleaning the commercial kitchen and the gift shop, and shoveling snow and even the pleasant but lonely evenings of reading by the fire in the fireplace were memories. I parked at the designated restaurant and waited for him to arrive.

When dinner was over, I couldn't decide which had tasted better, his hello kiss or the food. We walked out to our trucks, and he released my elbow, stepped in front of me, and took me in his arms. The hug was miraculous, healing, calming, and followed by a lingering, smoldering, igniting kiss. Suddenly, we were bathed in bright flashing lights. Loud, rhythmic honking filled the quiet spring evening. We jumped apart, startled and embarrassed to be caught in such an intimate kiss in a public parking lot. It was the second time we had been caught in the headlights.

Something was tickling my tummy beside my hip bone. "Oh my God," I said. "That hug squeezed the panic button on my key fob." I tried to extract the thing from the pocket of my jeans, but it was stuck. The blowing horn and flashing lights continued unabated. The earsplitting, intrusive, attention-attracting spectacle seemed endless as I fought that tight pocket for the gadget.

"I've kissed a lot of women in my lifetime, but it has never caused such a commotion," he said, smiling.

When the noise finally stopped, and the crowd of curiosity seekers had dispersed, I said, "At least those people weren't my son, and they don't know us. That's twice in the headlights. Some folks see stars. We seem to have progressed from lights to flashing lights and a loud horn blowing." We were both doubled over with laughter.

A couple of winters passed as our friendship grew. Life was filled with enough happiness to make me forget the storms. As years passed, we learned the intricacies of each other's families, businesses, and lifestyles.

Mirror had been quiet for a long time. Now Mirror wanted to be active again. "You know, smarty-pants, it seems that either you have a successful romance, or you have a consuming business happening. You never can seem to have both at the same time. Why is that?"

"Mirror, where have you been? The Sugar Shack is thriving, and the Florida guy is very much in the picture. Both are compatible." Sometimes Mirror just seemed to disappear or be out of touch. "You never seem to be interested in my successes, only my difficulties," I said. "But it also appears that you are a prophet because you always share your opinions with me when there is trouble on the horizon in one or another area of my life."

I continued to bring Mirror up to speed. "While you've been comatose, absent, quiet, I have been really busy. In fact, I have been so busy that I actually forgot about you. Let me catch you up. I published my first book several years ago. I have enjoyed many speaking engagements about the book, both locally and in several out-of-state locations. Some of those audiences were very prestigious. I have moved on, met new people, and prioritized some important things in my life.

"I am still learning how to balance all my life events while delegating the not-so-enjoyable aspects of business to people who are more qualified to handle them than I am. You might notice, I have figured all that out without your help, Mirror."

Mirror reflected a doubtful, uncertain look. I continued, "I realized that the bookkeeping, accounting, and mundane chores like cleaning were consuming my time. I have learned to delegate those unpleasant chores to allow more time for fun. I hate bookkeeping. I hate math. I can create, organize, farm, produce and manufacture, run a gift shop, and write a book, but keeping track of figures is just not my thing. During one of my speaking tours, I found a qualified businessperson from a CPA's office. I hired that person to do what I don't like to do. The person's qualifications and experience were exceptional. You don't notice when things are going well. But now you're speaking up again, so of course, it is because you smell a rat, isn't it?"

Mirror returned my stare. Neither of us looked away. Mirror commented, "And so you have become a manager, not a doer of chores you don't like. Is that wise, smarty-pants?"

I had just returned from the mailbox at the end of my long driveway and had thrown the newspaper and mail on the kitchen table as I removed my wet raincoat. Because of the rain, I had not looked at the stack of envelopes, and now I began to sort through them, throwing away the junk mail as I went. To my surprise, there was a letter from the Internal Revenue Service. Now I was sure I knew why Mirror had become alert. It was the uncanny ability Mirror had to sense disaster.

I tore open the letter to find that I was being audited. Suddenly, I remembered that the expert I had hired had not filed the current year's taxes by the April 15 due date. When I inquired, the expert had told me not to worry—an extension had been filed because of the heavy workload in the firm's office. I was on the list, and my taxes would be filed soon. I wondered if the extension had triggered the audit. I was not yet aware that a lot of bad advice, misdirection, unapproved changes, poor tax decisions, and more were responsible for the audit.

When I contacted the expert, I was assured that there was no need to review my tax return, rehash decisions that had been made for me, or provide answers to the written questions from the auditor because my trusted representative was a professional.

Mirror yelled, "Yeah, right. Can't you see that the expert person you hired doesn't want you to go to the audit? Do you suppose that is because you will see that the 'expert' is responsible for your problem?"

"Just be quiet, Mirror. You are offering unwanted, intrusive advice again. Shut up."

I began to assemble the required list of documents. First, I had to gather receipts for expenses. I questioned that because I had given those to the accountant on a zip drive from my QuickBooks program. They had been in order and the information on the zip drive was basis for the tax return for the year being audited. I went to my records and found the individual paper receipts, sorted by month, and began the assembly process. I wasn't worried. I had never had a need to go over past returns or question the advice the expert gave to me.

Mirror asked, "Is that why you bought the new truck? Was it because this so-called expert told you more depreciation was needed? Is that why you bought the new tractor a couple of years after that, for more depreciation?"

I glared at Mirror. Mirror glared right back as I answered, "Mirror, I pay this professional to manage my tax liability, to advise me on spending so that I keep my taxes under control. I am not good at such management skills. I trust the accounting business team's knowledge and judgment."

Next, I needed a copy of my business plan. I found the original from twenty-plus years ago and also all the yearly updates. I checked that off the list. I wrote answers to all the questions that the auditor had submitted and added that to the pile, along with tax returns from the years before the expert began handling my accounting. Finally, it was all done, and I called my expert representative to suggest we meet and go over the answers. I asked to attend the audit in case more information was needed. I wanted to cooperate completely and get the whole thing over in one visit and as quickly as possible.

The expert representative said, "Gail, those things are not necessary. I am experienced with these audits. I see that the auditor assigned to your case is known to this office. We have another client we are representing with her. She's a bitch. She doesn't listen to reason, and your presence would only cloud the issues. You'd give her too much information and influence the audit in a negative direction. This is our job. It is what you've been paying us for. Let us do our job."

That made sense to me, so I delivered the package, including a list of the contents, to the CPA's office.

As I explained all this to Mirror afterward, Mirror exploded, saying, "That's not smart! How can you let someone else speak for you on such an important matter? You aren't dumb, even though I call you smarty-pants and make fun of you."

"I know, Mirror, but I'm ignorant about filing my taxes. That's why I hired a licensed professional. I don't even read my tax returns. They have my power of attorney and assured me that they would save me money and keep me out of jail. I told them that should be easy because I've never minded paying my fair share. It's what a person pays for the freedom we all enjoy. Taxes are part of the cost of that freedom. I used to ask the expert if I could go over my tax returns when they were completed and before they were filed. The expert always said there was no need for that, because that's why I pay the big bucks for their services. Mirror, CPA stands for Certified Public Accountant. It's a large, professional, licensed business. Stop worrying. I'm good. I'm safe."

Mirror continued, "Yeah, right. What's this expert charging you for appearing on your behalf?"

"When I signed on with this firm, I was told that if I ever got audited, it would be taken care of with my yearly fees."

About then, the phone rang, and it was my expert

representative, calling to remind me to send a check for fifty dollars an hour for the time spent checking and reviewing my package of materials for the audit, plus the time spent on travel to and from the auditor's office, time spent on phone calls to their office, and the actual time spent at the auditor's office, estimated to be two hours. The amount was four hundred dollars. I wondered how Mirror had gotten so smart.

I was upset but not in a position to argue at that time. I wrote the check. The representative was to call me with a report immediately following the audit.

Three business days and one weekend later, I received the call and was told that all was going as expected. I was being assessed thousands of dollars in back taxes plus fines, but not to worry, said the accountant—it was just the luck of the draw, a random audit.

The following week, I received a written report of the audit from the auditor, explaining the deficiencies. The report listed nine criteria for reclassifying a business from a for-profit business to a hobby business. It explained that the decision to reclassify my business was based on those nine criteria and included the answers my representative had given to those questions. It said the decision had been made by a panel of auditors and had taken place because of five years of losses on my tax returns. My trusted experts had never notified me of the losses; they had said that there was enough money in my escrow account to cover my expenses and that there was no need to go over the returns. That's why I had hired them. I trusted them.

I read the letter out loud. Mirror hissed and squawked and screamed, "It's your own fault! You trusted. You didn't do your homework. You got lazy. You abdicated your responsibility."

My expert told me that there was no opportunity for input

from me now. The questions had been answered on my behalf because of the power of attorney I had signed. The firm's employee had given no knowledgeable or truthful answers. My business plans had not been submitted. When the auditor asked about why I had needed a new tractor for my agritourism business, my representative had replied, "Oh, she loves to ride around in her tractor." Five years of losses were reported.

I called the accounting office, made an appointment, asked that my records be available, went there, fired them, and took all the records they said they had in their possession.

Now I had no recourse. I paid the assessed thousands of dollars. I got on the internet and began to search for a law firm or CPA firm that would do battle with the IRS. Each one I found had since stopped dealing with the IRS. I expanded my search from a one-hundred-mile radius to statewide and finally to nationally advertised firms that handled IRS disputes. I found one thousands of miles away. The location was unimportant, the company said, because the process was all done electronically. I checked the firm's references. There were many five-star reviews. I negotiated the price, got assurances of success, listened to their advice based on experience, and sent them a check. Their advice was that I must close my business because it had been reclassified as a hobby business, and I could no longer claim any depreciation and could claim only limited expenses. They pointed out that I showed five years of losses, and the IRS had calculated those losses at nearly two hundred thousand dollars.

Mirror roared, "Two hundred thousand dollars? How could you lose that much money and not question the CPA's office?"

"I don't know, Mirror. I never noticed it. The expert didn't tell me, and I didn't read my returns, and I didn't ask."

I noticed Mirror shaking, and the reflected tears blurred my vision. I had to close the business. There was no choice.

"Mirror, I'm eighty years old and still working twelve hours a day. I produce my product from scratch. I can't grow the fruit and care for the farm without a tractor. I can't vend at shows, fairs, and festivals in a hundred-mile radius without a reliable truck and gasoline to haul the sales shed and product. I'm truly thankful for the health and strength to continue my business each day, but I get tired, and it sure as hell doesn't feel like a hobby endeavor. I don't work this hard and long for the fun of it. It pays my bills and taxes. I get to continue living here in the house on the farm I call home. I've been here for fifty years. I've always worked hard to pay the expenses, and now, like other old folks, I may have to leave if I can't continue to farm."

Mirror was grim. "I remember when your friends went to the town officials a few years ago," Mirror recalled. "They had bought a raw piece of useless scrub brushland, cleared it, developed it themselves, and struggled to build a lovely home and grounds. They asked the assessor how they could reduce their tax liability, and her answer many years ago was 'Sell it and let somebody who can afford it live there. You can move to senior housing.'"

It seemed hopeless. The auditor had written in her report that the answers my representative provided to her questions, her own investigation of my website, the available tax returns in IRS records, and the panel's decision indicated that my business was a hobby. She had even somehow checked my bank account, education, and experience in retail and decided my future without ever personally speaking to me.

Mirror summed it all up, saying, "The auditor, the CPA firm, your expert representative—all of them fit the first category in the title of your book."

Weeks and months passed in a blur. I stopped picking and processing fruit. I couldn't sleep at night. I wondered how I would pay my taxes and bills. I steered my supposedly pleasure-oriented tractor, with the brush chopper running, right over the gooseberries, raspberries, and wild elderberries and a lot of the wild blackberry patches. I was distraught. I mowed them all down. It was difficult to wait on my customers, knowing that my new national accounting firm was working to close my business at the end of the year. My lifestyle was coming to an end through no intended action of my own. I calculated the thousands of dollars I would not have to spend on advertising, resale gift stock, fuel for my truck and tractor and equipment, and the rents for vending space where I would no longer be present.

Twenty-five years were over. The tourism business I had generated and the infusion of travelers into our economy were now ending. Giving tourists a reason to exit the interstate highway in our town was finished. I couldn't eat. I couldn't sleep. I lost weight.

Mirror also believed it was hopeless. But I was thankful that this problem was what it was and not a tragic accident or illness. I felt that there must be a reason, and I was sure the Master Planner would show it to me.

Festivals, fairs, and shows were scheduled for the months before I was to close. I had paid for space, inspections, and licenses and put aside money for expenses like food, gasoline, and lodging. I decided to keep those commitments and reduce my inventory at those venues. My family supported my decisions, recognized my distress, and offered help. My southern friend was supportive and encouraged me to keep exploring options. I thought about reinventing my gift shop and commercial kitchen into an antique store, bookstore, candy store, or combination of them all. I considered Airbnb, vacation rentals, and more.

A local wine festival was next on my list of venues, and I paced and prepared before attaching my mobile sales shed trailer to my pickup truck and hauling it to the festival.

The first day of the event was stressful as I realized that I no longer needed to hand out maps and brochures and invite potential new customers to my Sugar Shack, which was no longer going to be open for business. I fought tears and depression. The next day, my son and granddaughter took my place and continued to reduce my inventory with their fine sales abilities.

My granddaughter held out a spoon for a man passing by and said, "Come on over, sir, and taste our fruit syrups. We make them on our farm, and they are really good."

He stepped up, took the spoon, tasted, and bought three bottles. My son bagged his purchase, handed him a brochure with his change, and said, "Thank you for supporting local agriculture."

The gentleman replied, "I always support local agriculture. I am an accountant, and I represent mostly farm cooperatives and work with farm businesses involved in disputes with the IRS. I especially love to represent farm businesses that are being reclassified as hobbies instead of for-profit businesses."

My son said he felt disbelief and fought tears as he realized the man could help us. He reached out and shook the man's hand as he said, "Sir, let me tell you what is happening to us."

He told the accountant our sad story and present state of affairs, and the gentleman handed him a card and said, "Have your mom call me." Then he explained how reclassification is a problem in the business of horse breeding. If an auditor asks the owner if he rides the horses in his enterprise, and the owner says he does, the auditor judges that the enjoyable activity of riding the horses makes the business a hobby instead of a for-profit business.

Mirror had some thoughts as this story unfolded. Mirror said, "I guess that means the IRS does not think any business owner should enjoy any aspect of a business. I guess it means a business owner should always find his work unpleasant."

A week later, I called the gentleman/customer and set up an appointment. I then took my paperwork to his accounting office two states and many miles away.

My case is being investigated, disassembled, microscopically assessed, and handled with efficiency and honest interest. I am being shown where the tax filing errors were made, how to rectify them, and how the bad advice and deceptive representation affected the reclassification of my agritourism business. I am learning how to manage and interpret my business finances.

Summing up the matter, Mirror said, "You know, Miss Smarty-Pants, you took a shortcut. You tried to overlook and delegate responsibility for the tasks you dislike. Business is like life. There is good and evil, fun and failures, profit and losses, highs and lows, just as in life. You can't just ignore the parts you don't find enjoyable. You can't pass the tough stuff to someone else to handle. You have to pay attention to detail and oversee even the minute details and fine print."

"I know that now, Mirror. I am still learning. I didn't notice the huge losses because they were due to the way my depreciation was handled, to how accounts and expenses were treated, to the use of a personal instead of a farm schedule, and more. The more unpleasant or uninteresting a task is, the more important it is to become familiar with every part of it."

Mirror voiced another question. "Do you think that perhaps

this second book got stalled in the publishing process and your work schedule prohibited you from finishing it because the Master Planner wanted you to include your new insights in this book? Your business had not been reclassified when you sent this manuscript off to your publisher. Now the timing is right, and you have learned another lesson and have illuminated more asses and angels. Will the lessons ever end for you?"

"I'll keep learning until the Master Planner is ready to take me home. It isn't my choice," I answered.

Epilogue

TIME PASSES. THANKSGIVING IS nearly here again.

Today I will start my traditional baking for Turkey Day. That includes perusing my collection of family recipes dating back four generations. In my collection I also find snippets of memories, notes about the kitchens of my ancestors, stories that were told about their triumphs and hardships, and news clippings about the successes and continuance of my descendants.

In years past many family members and friends would gather around my dining room table to enjoy our traditional dinner and pie extravaganza, which included a dozen varieties of homemade pies. This year we will thank the Master Planner for each and every friend and family member. We will discuss our thankfulness, and we will appreciate the measure of work, food, health, and peace we each enjoy. We will find time to express our love of God, our appreciation of each other, and our hopes and plans for the future. It seems as though those times will continue forever, but we know it is but the twinkling of an eye.

Age happens. Time passes. Lives change. Children grow up.

Elders pass. The only thing in life that never changes is change itself. I am thankful this year for sons who stop by often, for their evolving families, and for the regular contact I enjoy with my growing number of descendants.

I am thankful for new folks and old friends who visit the Sugar Shack, and I am happy that it will continue until the Master Planner decides otherwise.

I have learned that hard as I try, I am first and always a sinner. I cannot live even one perfect day without mistakes, failures, or shortcomings, even though I try repeatedly.

I have learned that only by the grace of God Almighty, through His love, and the gift of His Son, Jesus Christ, can I hope for eternal life.

I have learned that the Master Planner is available whenever, wherever, and for whatever problems I might have. I have learned to let go of the control switch, ask for His guidance, and understand that His direction is always perfect.

Mine, not so much.